NATO's
AirWar
for KOSOVO

**A Strategic
and Operational
Assess~~ment~~**

Benjamin S. Lambeth

Prepared for the United States Air Force

Project AIR FORCE

RAND

The research reported here was sponsored by the United States Air Force under Contract F49642-01-C-0003. Further information may be obtained from the Strategic Planning Division, Directorate of Plans, Hq USAF.

Library of Congress Cataloging-in-Publication Data

Lambeth, Benjamin S.
    NATO's air war for Kosovo : a strategic and operational assessment / Benjamin S. Lambeth.
        p. cm.
    "MR-1365."
    Includes bibliographical references.
    ISBN 0-8330-3050-7
    1. Kosovo (Serbia)—History—Civil War, 1998—Aerial operations. 2. Operation Allied Force, 1999. I. Title.

    DR2087.5 .L36 2001
    949.7103—dc21

                                                            2001048221

Cover design by Peter Soriano

Published 2001 by RAND
1700 Main Street, P.O. Box 2138, Santa Monica, CA 90407-2138
1200 South Hayes Street, Arlington, VA 22202-5050
201 North Craig Street, Suite 102, Pittsburgh, PA 15213-1516
RAND URL: http://www.rand.org/
To order RAND documents or to obtain additional information, contact Distribution Services: Telephone: (310) 451-7002; Fax: (310) 451-6915; Email: order@rand.org

Map of Kosovo

On March 24, 1999, NATO embarked on a 78-day air war aimed at compelling the government of Yugoslavia and its elected president, Slobodan Milosevic, to halt and reverse the human rights abuses that were being committed by armed Serbs against the ethnic Albanian majority living in Yugoslavia's Serbian province of Kosovo. That effort, called Operation Allied Force, ended on June 9 after Milosevic finally acceded to NATO's demands and a withdrawal of Serb forces from Kosovo had begun. The air war was a first of that magnitude for NATO and represented the third largest strategic application of air power by the United States since World War II, exceeded only by the Vietnam War and Operation Desert Storm in scale and intensity.

With a view toward capturing the many useful insights to be extracted from that experience, the U.S. Air Force chief of staff, General Michael Ryan, asked Headquarters United States Air Forces in Europe (Hq USAFE) shortly after Allied Force ended to establish a studies and analysis office (USAFE/SA) to manage all USAF-sponsored assessments of the air war. The director of that office, Brigadier General John Corley, in turn asked RAND's Project AIR FORCE to contribute to the assessment effort across a wide spectrum of topics, ranging from individual platform and systems performance to command and control, operational support, strategy and planning, and other considerations bearing on the air war's effectiveness.

This book examines the conduct and results of Operation Allied Force at the strategic and operational levels. An earlier and less developed version appeared as a chapter in the author's previous book *The Transformation of American Air Power,* which was published by Cornell University Press in September 2000. The research documented herein was carried out in Project AIR FORCE's Strategy and Doctrine Program and was completed in August 2001. All photographs included in this study were provided by the U.S. Department of Defense. The book should be of interest to USAF officers and other members of the U.S. national security community concerned with strategy and force employment issues raised by NATO's air war for Kosovo and with the implications of that experience for force development, air power doctrine, and concepts of operations for joint and coalition warfare.

Other documents published in this series currently include the following:

MR-1279-AF, *Command and Control and Battle Management: Experiences from the Air War over Serbia*, James E. Schneider, Myron Hura, Gary McLeod (Government publication; not releasable to the general public)

MR-1326-AF, *Aircraft Weapon Employment in Operation Allied Force*, William Stanley, Carl Rhodes, Robert Uy, Sherrill Lingel (Government publication; not releasable to the general public)

MR-1351-AF, *The Conflict over Kosovo: Why Milosevic Decided to Settle When He Did*, Stephen Hosmer

MR-1391-AF, *European Contributions to Operation Allied Force: Implications for Transatlantic Cooperation*, John E. Peters, Stuart Johnson, Nora Bensahel, Timothy Liston, Traci Williams

DB-332-AF, *Aircraft Survivability in Operation Allied Force*, William Stanley, Sherrill Lingel, Carl Rhodes, Jody Jacobs, Robert Uy (Government publication; not releasable to the general public)

Topics examined in series documents nearing completion include:

- Supporting Expeditionary Aerospace Forces: Lessons from the Air War Over Serbia

- Lessons Learned from Operation Allied Force Tanker Operations

Project AIR FORCE

Project AIR FORCE, a division of RAND, is the Air Force's federally funded research and development center (FFRDC) for studies and analysis. It provides the USAF with independent analyses of policy alternatives affecting the deployment, employment, combat readiness, and support of current and future air and space forces. Research is performed in four programs: Aerospace Force Development; Manpower, Readiness, and Training; Resource Management; and Strategy and Doctrine.

CONTENTS

FIGURES

Between March 24 and June 9, 1999, NATO, led by the United States, conducted an air war against Yugoslavia in an effort to halt and reverse the human-rights abuses that were being committed against the citizens of its Kosovo province by Yugoslavia's president, Slobodan Milosevic. That 78-day air war, called Operation Allied Force, represented the third time during the 1990s in which air power proved pivotal in determining the outcome of a regional conflict. Yet notwithstanding its ultimate success, what began as a hopeful gambit for producing Milosevic's quick compliance soon devolved, for a time at least, into a seemingly ineffectual bombing experiment with no clear end in sight. Not only was the operation's execution hampered by uncooperative weather and a surprisingly resilient opponent, it was further afflicted by persistent hesitancy on the part of U.S. and NATO political leaders and sharp differences of opinion within the most senior U.S. military command element over the most effective way of applying allied air power against Serb assets. Moreover, the plan ultimately adopted ruled out any backstopping by allied ground troops because of concerns over the potential for a land invasion to generate unacceptable casualties and the consequent low likelihood of mustering the needed congressional and allied support for such an option. All planning further assumed that NATO's most crucial vulnerable area was its continued cohesion. Therefore, any target or attack tactic deemed even remotely likely to undermine that cohesion, such as the loss of friendly aircrews, excessive collateral damage, or anything else that might weaken domestic support, was to be most carefully considered, if not avoided altogether. All of that, however unavoidable some aspects of it may have been, made

NATO's air war for Kosovo a step backward in efficiency when compared to the Desert Storm air campaign.

WHY MILOSEVIC GAVE UP WHEN HE DID

We may never know for sure what mix of pressures and inducements
ultimately led Milosevic to admit defeat. Yet why he gave in and why
he did so when he did are by far the most important questions about
the operation's experience, since the answers, insofar as they are
knowable, may help illuminate the coercive dynamic that ultimately
swung the air war's outcome.

One can, of course, insist that air power alone was the cause of Milosevic's capitulation in the tautological sense that Allied Force was an
air-only operation and that in its absence, there would have been no
reason for believing that he would have acceded to NATO's demands. Yet as crucial as the 78-day bombing effort was in bringing
Milosevic to heel, one should be wary of any intimation that NATO's
use of air power produced a successful result for the alliance without
any significant contribution by other factors. For example, beyond
the obvious damage that was being caused by NATO's air attacks and
the equally obvious fact that NATO could have continued bombing
both indefinitely and with virtual impunity, another likely factor behind Milosevic's capitulation was the fact that the sheer depravity of
Serbian conduct in Kosovo had stripped the Yugoslavian leader of
any remaining vestige of international support, including, in the end,
from his principal backers in Moscow.

On top of that was the sense of walls closing in that Milosevic must
have had when he was indicted as a war criminal by a UN tribunal
only a week before his loss of Moscow's support. Yet a third factor
may have been the mounting pressure from Milosevic's cronies
among the Yugoslav civilian oligarchy, prompted by the continued
bombing of military-related industries, utilities, and other infrastructure targets in and around Belgrade in which they had an economic
stake and whose destruction increasingly threatened to bankrupt
them.

Finally, one must take into account what Milosevic no doubt perceived, rightly or wrongly, to have been the possibility of an eventual

NATO ground invasion. Whatever NATO's declared stance on the ground-war issue may have been, its actions as the bombing progressed spoke louder than its words. By the end of May, it had become clear that the alliance was beginning to come to grips with the necessity for a ground intervention of some sort if the bombing did not produce the desired result soon. Milosevic knew that and fully appreciated what it meant for his political fortunes.

Some, however, have made more of that fact than the evidence warrants. In the early wake of the successful conclusion of Allied Force, revisionist claims began emanating from some quarters suggesting that the air effort had been totally ineffective and that, in the end, it had been Milosevic's fear of a NATO ground invasion that had induced him to capitulate. Those claims defy believability because any NATO ground invasion, however probable it may have been in the end, would have taken months, at a minimum, to prepare for and successfully mount.

In contrast, Milosevic was living with the daily reality of an increasingly brutal air war that was showing no sign of abating. Although the effort to find and attack dispersed and hidden enemy forces in Kosovo was consuming the preponderance of ground-attack sorties while accomplishing little by way of tangible results on the ground, more and more infrastructure targets were also being approved and struck every day. Accordingly, there is no basis for concluding that the mere possibility of an eventual land invasion somehow overshadowed the continuing reality of NATO's air attacks as the preeminent consideration accounting for Milosevic's decision to capitulate. The bombing ultimately persuaded Milosevic that NATO not only would not relent, but also was determined to prevail and had both the technical and political wherewithal to do so. By the same token, given the incapacity of Serb air defenses to shoot down significant numbers of allied aircraft, the bombing further convinced him that his own defeat was inevitable sooner or later.

FRICTION AND OPERATIONAL PROBLEMS

Although NATO's use of air power in Allied Force must, in the end, be adjudged a success, some troubling questions arose well before the operation's favorable outcome over a number of disconcerting problems that were encountered along the way. Among those arousing the greatest concern were the following:

- Assessed deficiencies in the suppression of enemy air defenses (SEAD).

- Locating, identifying, and engaging dispersed and hidden enemy light infantry forces in Kosovo.

- Inadvertent civilian casualties.

In contrast to the far more satisfying SEAD experience in Desert Storm, the effort to neutralize Serb air defenses did not go nearly as well as hoped. The Serbs kept most of their surface-to-air missiles (SAMs) in standby mode with their radars not emitting, prompting concern that they were attempting to draw NATO aircraft down to lower altitudes where they could be more easily engaged. The understandable reluctance of enemy SAM operators to emit and thus render themselves cooperative targets made them much harder to find and attack, forcing allied aircrews to remain constantly alert to the radar-guided SAM threat. By the same token, the enemy's heavy man-portable air defense system (MANPADS) and antiaircraft artillery (AAA) threat forced allied aircrews to bomb from above 15,000 ft, for the most part, to remain outside their lethal envelopes. Moreover, because of the mountainous terrain of Kosovo, the moving target indicator and synthetic aperture radar aboard the E-8 Joint STARS could not detect targets at oblique look angles, although the sensors carried by the higher-flying U-2 often compensated for this shortfall. On the plus side, although enemy SAM operators aggressively attempted to engage allied aircraft throughout the air war, superior allied SEAD operations forced them to employ emission control and mobility tactics to enhance their survivability, which significantly decreased their effectiveness. In the end, only two NATO aircraft were brought down by enemy fire, thanks to allied reliance on electronic jamming, the use of towed decoys, and countertactics to negate enemy surface-to-air defenses. However, NATO never fully succeeded in neutralizing the enemy's radar-guided SAM threat, even though no areas of enemy territory were denied.

Still another disappointment centered on what turned out to be NATO's almost completely ineffective efforts to engage mobile enemy troops operating in Kosovo. That disappointment underscored the limits of conducting air strikes against dispersed enemy forces hiding in favorable terrain in the absence of a supporting allied ground threat. Had Serb commanders any reason to fear a NATO ground invasion, they would have had little alternative but to position their tanks to cut off roads and other avenues of attack, thus making their forces more easily targetable by NATO air power. Instead, having dispersed and hidden their tanks and armored personnel carriers, Serb army and paramilitary units were free to go in with just a few troops in a single vehicle to terrorize a village in connection with their ethnic cleansing campaign.

Senior civilian defense officials and U.S. Air Force leaders freely conceded after the Serbian withdrawal that the problems encountered by the largely failed effort against fielded enemy forces reflected real challenges for the effective application of air power posed by such impediments as trees, mountains, poor weather, and an enemy ground force that is permitted the luxury of dispersing and hiding rather than concentrating to maneuver to accomplish its mission. Yet while it was essential for NATO to try its best to keep Serb forces pinned down and incapable of operating at will, the majority of the sorties devoted to finding and attacking enemy troops in Kosovo entailed an inefficient and ineffective use of munitions and other valuable assets. That said, the targeting of enemy ground forces operating within Kosovo was an inescapable political necessity, considering that those forces were responsible for committing the ethnic cleansing acts that NATO had vowed to stop. Failure to target those forces would almost certainly have caused the bombing effort to lose credibility in the eyes of the NATO civilian leadership.

Pressures to avoid civilian casualties and unintended damage to nonmilitary structures were greater in Allied Force than in any previous combat operation involving U.S. forces. Nevertheless, there were recurrent instances throughout the air war of unintended damage caused either by errant NATO munitions or by mistakes in targeting, including a dozen highly publicized incidents in which civilians were accidentally killed. One such bombing error resulted in part from constraints imposed by the requirement that NATO aircrews remain above 15,000 ft to avoid the most lethal enemy threats, making visual discrimination between military and civilian traffic more than routinely difficult. Another contributing factor was the occasional tendency of allied aircrews to maneuver their aircraft in such a way as to put clouds within the targeting pod's field of view between the aircraft and the target, thus blocking the laser beam illuminating the target and depriving the weapon of guidance. Moreover, Serb forces often used civilians as human shields in an effort to deter NATO from attacking military vehicles. The extraordinary media attention given to these events bore ample witness to what can happen when zero noncombatant casualties becomes not only a goal of strategy but also the international expectation. Thanks to unrealistic efforts to treat the normal friction of war as avoidable human error, every occurrence of unintended collateral damage became overinflated as front-page news and treated as a blemish on air power's presumed ability to be consistently precise.

LAPSES IN STRATEGY AND IMPLEMENTATION

NATO's leaders also had little to congratulate themselves about when it came to the way in which the air war was planned and carried out. There was a dominant sense among participants and observers alike that the desultory onset of Allied Force and its later slowness to register effects reflected some fundamental failures of allied leadership and strategy choice. In contrast to the relatively seamless performance by the coalition in Desert Storm, what unfolded during NATO's air war for Kosovo was a highly dissatisfying application of air power, which showed not only the predictable fits and starts of trying to prosecute an air operation through an alliance of 19 members bound by a unanimity rule, but also some failures even within the operation's U.S. component to make the most of what air power had to offer within the limits of the effort's political constraints.

To begin with, the conduct of the air war as an allied effort came at the cost of a flawed strategy that was further hobbled by the manifold inefficiencies that were part and parcel of conducting combat operations by consensus. In addition to the natural friction created by NATO's approach to target approval, the initial reluctance of its political leaders to countenance a more aggressive air campaign in terms of target numbers and force size failed completely to capitalize on air power's potential for taking down entire systems of enemy capability simultaneously. Further compounding the inefficiency of this multistage and circuitous process, two parallel but separate mechanisms for mission planning and air tasking were used. Any U.S.-specific systems involving special sensitivities, such as the B-2, F-117, and cruise missiles, were allocated by U.S. European Command (USEUCOM) rather than by NATO, and the Combined Air Operations Center (CAOC) maintained separate targeting teams for USEUCOM and NATO strike planning.

Because NATO had initially hoped that the operation would last only a few days, it failed to establish a smoothly running mechanism for target development and review until late April. Once NATO's going-in assumption proved hollow, a frenetic rush ensued to come up with additional target nominations that could be more quickly and easily approved by NATO's political authorities. Even then, there was little by way of a consistently applied strategy behind the target development process. Most of the attack planning done throughout the air war was not driven by desired effects, but rather entailed simply parceling out sortie and munitions allocations by target category as individual targets were approved, without much consideration given to how a target's neutralization might contribute toward advancing the overall objectives of the air war.

It was not only the alliance-induced friction that helped make for an inefficient bombing effort. As Allied Force unfolded, it became increasingly clear that even the U.S. military component was divided in a high-level struggle over the most appropriate targeting strategy—reminiscent of the feuding that had occurred nine years earlier between the Army's corps commanders and the joint force air component commander (JFACC), then–Lieutenant General Charles Horner, over the ownership and control of air operations in Desert Storm. Once the initial hope that Milosevic would fold within a few days after the bombing started proved groundless, NATO was forced into a scramble to develop an alternative strategy. The immediate result was an internecine battle between the Supreme Allied Commander in Europe, U.S. Army General Wesley Clark, and his air component commander, USAF Lieutenant General Michael Short, over where the air attacks should be primarily directed. Short maintained that the most effective use of allied air power would be to pay little heed to dispersed Serbian forces in Kosovo and to concentrate instead on infrastructure targets in and around Belgrade, including key electrical power plants and government ministries. However, Clark insisted, as was his command prerogative, upon concentrating on elusive enemy ground troops in Kosovo, and this targeting emphasis prevailed throughout most of the air war.

Despite the success of Allied Force in the end, one misjudgment of near-blunder proportions came close to saddling the United States and NATO with a costly and embarrassing failure. The worst call by NATO's leaders was their assumption that what had worked for Bosnia would work for Kosovo and their resultant failure to appreciate the special importance of Kosovo to the Serbs and its criticality to Milosevic's survival in power. Fortunately for the allies, their faulty assessment was not a show-stopper—although it could have been if Milosevic had refrained from launching his ethnic cleansing campaign and instead merely hunkered down to wait out the bombing in a win-or-lose contest of wills with NATO. Had he done so, he could have threatened the long-term viability of the alliance. Fortunately for the success of Allied Force, by opting instead to accelerate his ethnic cleansing of Kosovo, he helped unite Western opinion behind NATO and left NATO with no choice but to dig in for the long haul, not only to secure an outcome that would allow for the repatriation of nearly a million displaced Kosovars, but also to ensure its continued credibility as an alliance.

NATO'S AIR WAR IN PERSPECTIVE

Operation Allied Force was the most intense and sustained military operation to have been conducted in Europe since the end of World War II. It represented the first extended use of military force by NATO, as well as the first major combat operation conducted for humanitarian objectives against a state committing atrocities within its own borders. It was the longest U.S. combat operation to have taken place since the war in Vietnam. At a price tag of more than $3 billion, it was also a notably expensive one. Yet in part because of that investment, it turned out to have been an unprecedented exercise in the discriminate use of force on a large scale. In all, out of some 28,000 high-explosive munitions expended over the operation's 78-day course, no more than 500 noncombatants died as a direct result of errant attacks.

After the bombing ended, the predominant tendency among most outside observers was to characterize that effort as a watershed achievement for air power. Yet with all due respect for the un-matched professionalism of the aircrews who actually carried out the air war, it is hard to accept that characterization as the proper con-clusion to be drawn from Allied Force. To be sure, there is much to be said of a positive nature about NATO's air war for Kosovo. To be-gin with, it did indeed represent the first time in which air power co-erced an enemy leader to yield with no friendly land combat action whatsoever. This does not mean that air power can now "win wars alone" or that the air-only strategy ultimately adopted by NATO's leaders was the wisest choice available to them. Yet the fact that air power prevailed on its own despite the multiple drawbacks of a re-luctant administration, a divided Congress, an indifferent public, a potentially fractious alliance, a determined opponent, and—not least—the absence of a credible NATO strategy surely testified that the air instrument has come a long way in recent years in its *relative* combat leverage compared to that of other force elements in joint warfare.

The two most important accomplishments of the air war occurred at the strategic level and had to do with the performance of the alliance as a combat collective. First, despite the suggestion of some critics to the contrary, NATO clearly prevailed over Milosevic. Although NATO's air strikes were unable to halt Milosevic's ethnic cleansing campaign before it had been essentially completed, they did succeed in completely reversing its effects in the early aftermath of the cease-fire by forcing Milosevic to accept NATO's demands. Second, NATO showed that it could operate successfully under pressure as an al-liance, even in the face of constant hesitancy and reluctance on the part of many of the member states' political leaders. For all the air effort's fits and starts and the manifold frustrations they caused, the alliance earned justified credit for having done remarkably well in a uniquely challenging situation. In seeing Allied Force to a successful conclusion, NATO did something that it had been neither created nor configured to do.

Despite these accomplishments, there were enough disappoint-ments to suggest that instead of basking in the glow of air power's successful performance, air warfare professionals should give careful thought to the hard work that still needs to be done if air power's fullest potential in joint warfare is to be realized. As with the opera-tion's successes, the biggest failings of Allied Force occurred in the realm of strategy and execution. First, despite its successful outcome and through no fault of allied airmen, the bombing effort was a suboptimal application of air power. The incremental plan chosen by NATO's leaders risked squandering much of the capital that had been built up in air power's account ever since its success in Desert Storm nearly a decade before. Almost without question, the first month of underachievement in the air war convinced Milosevic that he could ride out the NATO attacks. Indeed, the way Operation Allied Force commenced violated two of the most enduring axioms of military practice: the importance of achieving surprise and the criticality of keeping the enemy unclear as to one's intentions. The acceptance by NATO's leaders of a strategy that ruled out a ground threat from the very start and envisaged only gradually escalating air strikes to inflict pain was a guaranteed recipe for downstream trouble, even though it was the only strategy that, at the time, seemed politically workable.

Although the manner in which the air war was conducted fell short of the ideal use of air power, it suggested that gradualism may be here to stay if U.S. leaders ever again intend to fight with coalition partners for marginal or amorphous interests. Insofar as gradualism promises to be the wave of the future, it suggests that airmen will need to discipline their natural inclination to bridle whenever politicians moderate the application of a doctrinally pure campaign strategy and to recognize and accept instead that political considerations, after all, determine—or should determine—the way in which campaigns and wars are fought. This does not mean that military leaders should surrender to political pressures without first making their best case for using force in the most effective and cost-minimizing way. It does, however, stand as an important reminder that war is ultimately about politics and that civilian control of the military is an inherent part of the democratic tradition. Although air warfare professionals, like all other warfighters, are duty-bound to try to persuade their civilian superiors of the merits of their recommendations, they also have a duty to live with the hands they are dealt and to bend every effort to make the most of them in an imperfect world. It follows that civilian leaders at the highest levels have an equal obligation to try to stack the deck in such a way that the military has the best possible hand to play and the fullest possible freedom to play it to the best of its ability. This means expending the energy and political capital needed to develop and enforce a strategy that maximizes the probability of military success. That was not done by the vast majority of the topmost civilian leaders on either side of the Atlantic in Allied Force.

On the plus side, the operation's successful outcome—despite its many frustrations—suggests that U.S. air power may now have become capable enough to underwrite a strategy of incremental escalation irrespective of that strategy's inherent inefficiencies. What made the gradualism of Allied Force more bearable than that of the earlier war in Vietnam was that NATO's advantages in stealth, precision standoff attack, and electronic warfare meant that it could fight a one-sided war against Milosevic with near-impunity and achieve its desired result, even if not in the most ideal way. That was not an option when U.S. air power was a less developed tool than it is today.

One of the most important realizations to emerge from Allied Force had to do with the opportunity costs incurred by NATO's anemic start of its air attacks without an accompanying ground threat. They included the following:

- A failure to exploit air power's inherent shock potential and to instill in Milosevic an early fear of worse consequences yet to come.

- The encouragement the initial lack of a NATO ground threat gave enemy troops to disperse and hide while they had time.

- The virtual carte blanche that lack gave Milosevic for accelerated atrocities in Kosovo.

- The relinquishment of the power of the initiative to the enemy.

These problems identified by the Allied Force experience suggest an important corrective to the unending argument between airmen and land combatants over the relative combat merits of air power versus "boots on the ground." Although Allied Force reconfirmed that friendly ground forces no longer need to be inexorably committed to combat early, it also reconfirmed that air power in many cases cannot perform to its fullest potential without the presence of a credible ground component in the overall allied strategy.

ON THE USES AND ABUSES OF AIR POWER

Viewed in hindsight, the most remarkable thing about Operation Allied Force is not that it defeated Milosevic in the end, but rather that air power prevailed despite a NATO leadership that was unwilling to take major risks and an alliance that held together only with often paralyzing drag. Lesson One from both Vietnam and Desert Storm should have been that one must not commit air power in "penny packets," as the British say, to play less-than-determined games with the risk calculus of the other side. Although it can be surgically precise when precision is called for, air power is, at bottom, a blunt instrument designed to break things and kill people in pursuit of clear and militarily achievable objectives.

To admit that gradualism may be the wave of the future for any U.S. involvement in coalition warfare is hardly to accept that it is any more justifiable from a military point of view for that reason alone. Quite to the contrary, the incrementalism of NATO's air war for Kosovo, right up to its very end, involved a potential price that went far beyond the loss of valuable aircraft and other expendables for questionable gain. It risked frittering away the hard-earned reputation for effectiveness that U.S. air power had finally earned for itself in Desert Storm after more than three years of unqualified misuse over North Vietnam a generation earlier.

As the Gulf War experience showed, and as both Deliberate Force and Allied Force ultimately reaffirmed, U.S. air power as it has evolved since the mid-1970s can do remarkable things when employed with determination in support of a campaign whose intent is not in doubt. Yet to conjure up the specter of "air strikes"—NATO or otherwise—in an effort to project an appearance of "doing something" without a prior weighing of intended effects or likely consequences is to run the risk of getting bogged down in an operation with no plausible theory of success. After years of false promises by its most outspoken prophets, air power has become an unprecedentedly capable instrument of force employment in joint warfare. Even in the best of circumstances, however, it can never be more effective than the strategy it is intended to support.

ACKNOWLEDGMENTS

This study has benefited from insights gained from conversations with numerous participants in Operation Allied Force, including Admiral James Ellis, Jr., USN, commander in chief, Allied Forces Southern Europe and Joint Task Force commander, Operation Noble Anvil; General John Jumper, USAF, former commander, United States Air Forces in Europe and now U.S. Air Force chief of staff; Lieutenant General Michael Short, USAF (Ret.), former commander, Allied Air Forces Southern Europe and Joint Force Air Component Commander, Operational Noble Anvil; Vice Admiral Daniel Murphy, Jr., USN, commander, 6th Fleet; Captain Dave Maxwell, USN, director of operations, and Captain Tony Cothron, USN, director of intelligence, 6th Fleet; Lieutenant General Charles Wald, USAF, former deputy director, J-5, Joint Staff and now commander, 9th Air Force; Major General (select) Dan Leaf, former commander, 31st Air Expeditionary Wing at Aviano Air Base, Italy, and now director of operational requirements, Hq USAF; Air Chief Marshal Sir John Day, RAF, the UK Ministry of Defense's director of operations during Allied Force and now commander in chief, RAF Strike Command; Air Vice Marshal Andrew Vallance, RAF, former chief of staff, NATO Reaction Force (Air); Major General P. J. M. Godderij, deputy commander in chief, Royal Netherlands Air Force; Captain C. J. Heatley, USN (Ret.), former commander, Joint Warfare Analysis Center; Colonel Jeff Eberhart, commander, and Lieutenant Colonel Ray Dissinger, deputy commander, 31st Operations Group, Aviano Air Base, Italy; and Lieutenant Colonel Steve Schraeder, commander, 510th Fighter Squadron at Aviano.

I am also indebted to Major General Eitan Ben-Eliahu, then–commanding officer of the Israeli Air Force (IAF), who invited me to brief the highlights of an earlier version of this book and to receive feedback from the entire senior IAF leadership at a special roundtable session convened during his weekly staff meeting at IAF headquarters in Tel Aviv in October 1999. In addition, I acknowledge Thomas Henriksen, associate director of the Hoover Institution at Stanford University, who organized a seminar for me at Hoover in April 2000, attended by Hoover's military fellows and former Secretary of Defense William Perry, to critique an earlier draft of this study; Major General Gary Dylewski, then-commander, and Colonel Bob Bivins, then–director of operations, Air Force Space Warfare Center, for having briefed me on the contribution of space systems to Operation Allied Force; General Patrick Gamble, commander, and Lieutenant General (select) Thomas Waskow, director of air and space operations, Pacific Air Forces, for sharing their insights into the Allied Force experience; Major Marshall Denney, USMC, Tactics Division, Marine Aviation Weapons and Tactics Squadron 1, for describing some of the highlights of EA-6B operations; Major General Leroy Barnidge, former commander, 509th Bomb Wing and later vice commander, 9th Air Force, for his observations on B-2 employment during Allied Force; and Loren Timm of Lockheed Martin Corporation for providing me with useful material on F-16 operations.

Most important in this respect, I thank General Gregory Martin, commander, United States Air Forces in Europe, for having put the extensive USAFE Air War Over Serbia (AWOS) data collection at my complete disposal, and Lieutenant Colonel Richard Sargent, director, operations studies and analysis, Hq USAFE, and Edward Ballanco, Hq USAFE, for carefully vetting the penultimate draft of this study and helping me to make the most of the unclassified documentation that General Martin made available to me. I also thank Captain John Wilbourne, 492nd Fighter Squadron, RAF Lakenheath, England, for his special effort to put me in touch with both individuals and resources at Lakenheath with a direct connection to 48th Fighter Wing operations during Allied Force.

Beyond this direct research support, I am grateful to Brigadier General Dan Darnell, commander, 31st Fighter Wing, for having provided me an opportunity to fly on a Block 40 F-16CG laser-guided bomb delivery training mission out of Aviano to sample at first hand the challenge of 100-percent target identification from medium altitude, as well as other operational problems associated with Allied Force; Lieutenant General Wald for having arranged a Block 50 F-16CJ SEAD mission orientation for me with the 20th Fighter Wing at Shaw AFB, South Carolina; General Martin, USAFE's commander, for having allowed me to fly on an F-15E Kosovo-type strike training mission into the Scottish highlands with the 48th Fighter Wing, RAF Lakenheath, England; and Lieutenant General Fred McCorkle, USMC, deputy commandant for aviation, Hq United States Marine Corps, for his support in enabling me to get a first-hand exposure to Marine F/A-18D operations during two ground-support training sorties with Marine All-Weather Fighter/Attack Squadron 332 at MCAS Beaufort, South Carolina. This hands-on familiarization with some of the principal mission employment practices used in Operation Allied Force was uniquely helpful in informing my characterization of those practices in this assessment.

Finally, for their helpful comments on all or parts of an earlier draft, I acknowledge General W. L. Creech, USAF (Ret.); General Jumper; Air Chief Marshal Day; Lieutenant General Short; Lieutenant General Bruce Carlson, USAF, director, J-8, Joint Staff; Lieutenant General Ronald Keys, commander, 16th Air Force; Lieutenant General John Dallager, former DCS/Operations, SHAPE, and now superintendent, U.S. Air Force Academy; Air Vice Marshal Tony Mason, RAF (Ret.); Lieutenant General (select) Lance Smith, commander, and Colonel Steve Carey, Lieutenant Colonel Russ Barnes, and Major Richard Leatherman, Hq Air Force Doctrine Center; Major General David Deptula, director, USAF Quadrennial Defense Review; Major General (select) Leaf; Brigadier General Robert Bishop, deputy director of operations, Hq United States Air Force; Brigadier General Darnell, Colonel Eberhart, and Lieutenant Colonel Dissinger of the 31st Fighter Wing at Aviano; Colonel Charles Westenhoff, USAF, director, Joint SEAD Joint Test Force; Colonel Wesley Jarmulowicz, USMC, formerly assigned to AFSOUTH J-5 and now commander, Marine Aircraft Group 31; Colonel Robert Owen, USAF, Hq Air Mobility Command; Professor David Mets, School of Advanced Airpower Studies, Air University; Robert Haffa and Barry Watts, Northrop Grumman Analysis Center; Mark Butler and Daniel Harrington, Hq USAFE; Bob Johnston and Major Mike Pietrucha, Hq USAF; and my RAND colleagues Nora Bensahel, Tom Hamilton, Ted Harshberger,

Steve Hosmer, Dave Kassing, Rob Mullins, Bruce Nardulli, David Ochmanek, Bruce Pirnie, Carl Rhodes, John Stillion, and Alan Vick. I am additionally indebted to Emily Rogers for her deft assistance with composition and formatting and to Miriam Polon for her invariably sure editing. My special thanks go to Ivo Daalder of the Brookings Institution and Alan Gropman of the Industrial College of the Armed Forces for their careful and constructive reviews of the final product.

ACRONYMS

AAA	Antiaircraft Artillery
AB	Air Base
ABCCC	Airborne Command and Control Center
ACC	Air Combat Command
ACTORD	Activation Order
AEF	Air Expeditionary Force
AEW	Airborne Early Warning
AFB	Air Force Base
AFSOUTH	Allied Forces Southern Europe
AFV	Armored Fighting Vehicle
AGM	Air-to-Ground Missile
AMRAAM	Advanced Medium-Range Air-to-Air Missile
AOR	Area of Responsibility
APC	Armored Personnel Carrier
ATACMS	Army Tactical Missile System
ATC	Air Traffic Control
ATO	Air Tasking Order
AWACS	Airborne Warning and Control System
AWOS	Air War Over Serbia

BDA	Battle Damage Assessment
BDI	Battle Damage Indications
C2	Command and Control
CALCM	Conventional Air-Launched Cruise Missile
CAOC	Combined Air Operations Center
CAS	Close Air Support
CBS	Columbia Broadcasting System
CBU	Cluster Bomb Unit
CIA	Central Intelligence Agency
CINC	Commander in Chief
CINCCENT	CINC U.S. Central Command
CINCEUR	CINC U.S. European Command
CINCPAC	CINC U.S. Pacific Command
CINCSOUTH	CINC Allied Forces Southern Europe
CNN	Cable News Network
CNO	Chief of Naval Operations
COMAIRCENT	Commander Allied Air Forces Central Europe
COMAIRSOUTH	Commander Allied Air Forces Southern Europe
COMUSAFE	Commander United States Air Forces in Europe
CONOPLAN	Concept of Operations Plan
CSAR	Combat Search and Rescue
DEAD	Destruction of Enemy Air Defenses
DMPI	Desired Mean Point of Impact
DMSP	Defense Meteorological Support Program
DSCS	Defense Satellite Communications System

DSP	Defense Support Program
ECM	Electronic Countermeasures
ECR	Electronic Combat Role
ELINT	Electronic Intelligence
EO	Electro-Optical
EW	Early Warning
EW	Electronic Warfare
FAC	Forward Air Controller
FLIR	Forward-Looking Infrared
FY	Fiscal Year
GAT	Guidance, Apportionment, and Targeting
GATS	GPS-Aided Targeting System
GBU	Guided Bomb Unit
GPS	Global Positioning System
HARM	High-Speed Antiradiation Missile
HMS	Her Majesty's Ship
HTS	HARM Targeting System
HUD	Head-Up Display
IADS	Integrated Air Defense System
ID	Identification
IFF	Identification Friend or Foe
IFOR	NATO Implementation Force in Bosnia and Herzegovina
IMF	International Monetary Fund
INS	Inertial Navigation System
IR	Infrared
ISR	Intelligence, Surveillance, and Reconnaissance

JAC	Joint Analysis Center
JCS	Joint Chiefs of Staff
JDAM	Joint Direct Attack Munition
JFACC	Joint Force Air Component Commander
JTF	Joint Task Force
JTIDS	Joint Tactical Information Distribution System
JWAC	Joint Warfare Analysis Center
KEZ	Kosovo Engagement Zone
KFOR	Kosovo Force
KLA	Kosovo Liberation Army
LANTIRN	Low-Altitude Navigation and Targeting Infrared for Night
LD/HD	Low Density/High Demand
LGB	Laser-Guided Bomb
LOC	Line of Communication
MANPADS	Man-Portable Air Defense System
MEU	Marine Expeditionary Unit
MFD	Multifunction Display
MLRS	Multiple-Launch Rocket System
MSTS	Multisource Tactical System
MTI	Moving Target Indicator
MTW	Major Theater War
MUP	Serbian Interior Ministry Police
NAC	North Atlantic Council
NATO	North Atlantic Treaty Organization
NCA	National Command Authorities
NIMA	National Imagery and Mapping Agency

NPIC	National Photographic Interpretation Center
NRO	National Reconnaissance Office
OCA	Offensive Counterair
ORI	Operational Readiness Inspection
OSCE	Organization for Security and Cooperation in Europe
PACAF	Pacific Air Forces
PGM	Precision-Guided Munition
POL	Petroleum, Oil, and Lubricants
POW	Prisoner of War
RAF	Royal Air Force
RCS	Radar Cross-Section
RNLAF	Royal Netherlands Air Force
ROE	Rules of Engagement
RWR	Radar Warning Receiver
SACEUR	Supreme Allied Commander Europe
SAM	Surface-to-Air Missile
SAR	Synthetic Aperture Radar
SAS	Special Air Service
SEAD	Suppression of Enemy Air Defenses
SFOR	NATO Stabilization Force in Bosnia and Herzegovina
SHAPE	Supreme Headquarters Allied Powers Europe
SIGINT	Signals Intelligence
STARS	Surveillance Target Attack Radar System
TACAN	Tactical Air Navigation
TARPS	Tactical Air Reconnaissance Pod System

TF	Task Force
TIP	Tactical Integrated Planning
TLAM	Tomahawk Land-Attack Missile
TOT	Time on Target
UAV	Unmanned Aerial Vehicle
UCAV	Unmanned Combat Air Vehicle
UHF	Ultra-High Frequency
UN	United Nations
USA	United States Army
USAF	United States Air Force
USAFE	United States Air Forces in Europe
USAFE/SA	United States Air Forces in Europe, Studies and Analysis Office
USAREUR	United States Army in Europe
USEUCOM	United States European Command
USMC	United States Marine Corps
USN	United States Navy
USS	United States Ship
VJ	Yugoslav Army
VTC	Video Teleconference

Chapter One

INTRODUCTION

Between March 24 and June 9, 1999, NATO, led by the United States, conducted an air war against Yugoslavia in an effort to halt and reverse the continuing human-rights abuses that were being committed against the citizens of its Kosovo province (see the Frontispiece, Map of Kosovo) by Yugoslavia's elected president, Slobodan Milosevic. As it turned out, that 78-day effort, called Operation Allied Force, represented the third time in a row during the 1990s, after Operations Desert Storm and Deliberate Force, in which air power proved pivotal in determining the outcome of a regional conflict. Yet notwithstanding its ultimate success, what began as a hopeful gambit for producing quick compliance on Milosevic's part soon devolved, for a time at least, into a seemingly ineffectual bombing experiment with no clear end in sight. Not only was the operation's execution hampered by uncooperative weather and a surprisingly resilient opponent, it was further afflicted by persistent hesitancy on the part of U.S. and NATO decisionmakers that was prompted by fears of inadvertently killing civilians and losing friendly aircrews, as well as by sharp differences of opinion within the most senior U.S. command element over the best way of applying allied air power against Serb assets to achieve the desired effects. All of that and more, however unavoidable some aspects of it may have been, made NATO's air war for Kosovo a substantial step backward in efficiency when compared to Desert Storm.

This book assesses Operation Allied Force from a strategic and operational perspective, with a view toward spotlighting what was most gratifying about the application of allied air power throughout the effort, as well as identifying and exploring aspects of air power's performance that indicated continued deficiencies in need of attention. The analysis is based entirely on openly accessible information, enriched at various points by inputs gleaned from interviews with selected Allied Force participants at both the command and execution levels. Although the U.S. government has yet to release many of the more recondite statistics associated with the air war's prosecution at the operational and tactical levels, more than enough confirmed information on the broader essentials has now been made public by the Department of Defense and by leading NATO officials to permit a confident reconstruction of what happened during Operation Allied Force. As in the case of the Persian Gulf War a decade ago, the principal distinguishing features of NATO's air war for Kosovo are no longer in dispute. What remains in contention are their meaning and implications.

As more details about the background and conduct of the Kosovo air war have become available, the debate over Allied Force and over the appropriate "lessons" to be drawn from it has tended to fragment into what one observer called "a series of mini-arguments about details and facts and figures," perhaps most notoriously with respect to how many enemy tanks were destroyed by allied air attacks and whether U.S. and NATO officials conspired to cover up the surprisingly poor performance of the air effort in that respect.[1] In contrast, this study seeks to maintain a steady lock on the larger picture. Although it freely ventures into operational and technical detail wherever appropriate, including on the tank issue and on related questions concerning how various items of equipment worked, it focuses more on such broader questions as what U.S. and allied air power accomplished by way of achieving their goals and what the operation's experience revealed about the state of air power's continuing evolution as an instrument of joint and combined warfare.

Toward that end, the book first describes the air war's strategic and operational highlights in chronological order. It then considers the various factors that interacted to induce Milosevic to capitulate when he did. After that, it explores air power's principal accomplishments, as well as the many problems that worked to render Allied Force a

---

[1]Christopher Cviic, "A Victory All the Same," *Survival*, Summer 2000, p. 174.

less than uniformly satisfactory performance by allied air power.[2]
The final chapter reviews Operation Allied Force in political and
strategic context and reflects on the most policy-pertinent conclusions to be drawn from the experience. Because of the study's predominant focus on matters pertaining to planning and execution, it
does not consider, other than by way of brief stage-setting, the politics and diplomacy that immediately preceded the air war, let alone
the deeper historical roots of the crisis.

---

[2]In the latter respect, this assessment consciously seeks to avoid the common
syndrome of so-called lessons-learned efforts whereby "losers tend to study what went
wrong while winners study what went right." Princeton University political scientist
Bernard Lewis, an adviser to the USAF's Gulf War Air Power Survey conducted in
1991–1992, called this cautionary reminder to the attention of the survey team as that
effort was getting under way. Quoted in Gian P. Gentile, *How Effective Is Strategic
Bombing? Lessons Learned from World War II to Kosovo*, New York, New York
University Press, 2001, p. 182.

Chapter Two

PRELUDE TO COMBAT

Operation Allied Force, largely prompted by humanitarian concerns, was a response by the United States and NATO to the steadily mounting Serb atrocities that were being committed against the ethnic Albanians who made up the vast majority of Kosovo's population. At bottom, the crisis was rooted in a centuries-long history of Balkan strife.[1] Its more immediate origins could be traced back to a decade before, when the disintegration of the Yugoslav

---

[1]For informed insight into the origins of the ancestral hatreds that animated the atrocities committed against the Kosovar Albanians by Serbia, one can do no better than the epic novel by Ivo Andric, *The Bridge on the Drina*, Chicago, University of Chicago Press, 1977. Written in Serbo-Croatian in 1945, this tour de force won the 1961 Nobel prize for literature. It speaks about Balkan conflicts from the earliest clashes between the Bosnian Turks and Serb Christians in the early 15th century to the coming of the First World War. In a passage hauntingly reminiscent of more recent Balkan horrors, Andric described how ethnic rivals as far back as the 17th century "were as if drunk with bitterness, from desire for vengeance, and longed to punish and kill whomsoever they could, since they could not punish or kill those whom they wished" (pp. 86–87). Of a later generation looking at the redrawn map of Bosnia after the Balkan war of 1912, Andric likewise wrote that they "saw nothing in those curving lines, but they knew and understood everything, for their geography was in their blood and they felt biologically their picture of the world" (p. 229). A balanced synopsis of this history that places it in the context of the 20th-century developments that led up to the 1999 Kosovo crisis is presented in William W. Hagen, "The Balkans' Lethal Nationalisms," *Foreign Affairs*, July/August 1999, pp. 52–64. For more on this background, see Ivo H. Daalder and Michael E. O'Hanlon, *Winning Ugly: NATO's War to Save Kosovo*, Washington, D.C., Brookings Institution, 2000, pp. 1–100. See also Michael Ignatieff, *Virtual War: Kosovo and Beyond*, New York, Metropolitan Books, 2000, especially pp. 11–65; Misha Glenny, *The Balkans: Nationalism, War and the Great Powers, 1809–1999*, New York, Penguin Books, 2000; and Tim Judah, *Kosovo: War and Revenge*, New Haven, Connecticut, Yale University Press, 2000.

Federation began during the waning years of the cold war.[2] Under the iron rule of Yugoslavia's independent communist leader, Marshal Josip Broz Tito, Kosovo had remained an autonomous and self-governing province of Serbia for nearly 40 years, and members of its largely ethnic Albanian populace were able to live a reasonable approximation of normal lives. Once communist rule began to unravel in the late 1980s after Tito's death, however, the Serb minority in Kosovo reacted forcefully against what they perceived to be willful discrimination against them by the Kosovar Albanian authorities.

After winning an election in 1989 in which he played heavily on Serb feelings of mistreatment, Milosevic decreed an end to Kosovo's autonomy, imposed Serb rule, and unleashed a resurgence of ethnic violence throughout the former Yugoslav Federation that, by 1995, had caused more than a quarter of a million innocent citizens to lose their lives in a renewed Balkan civil war. That, in turn, gave rise to a group of Kosovar Albanian nationalists who espoused the use of violence in pursuit of Kosovar independence, ultimately spawning a militant émigré group called the Kosovo Liberation Army (KLA, or UCK in Albanian, for *Ushtria Clirimtare e Kosoves*), whose members began waging a partisan war against the Serb army and police units that controlled the increasingly conflicted province.

In February 1998, in an escalating wave of reprisals against the rearguard actions of this nascent band of ethnic Albanian guerrillas, a unit of the Yugoslav interior ministry police, or MUP (for *Ministerstvo Unuprasnij Poslava*), counterattacked in force against the KLA in the Drenica region of Kosovo, wantonly killing some 80 Kosovar Albanian civilians in the process. In response, U.S. special envoy Richard Holbrooke was sent to Belgrade by the Clinton administration to beseech Milosevic to desist from further acts of violence against Kosovar civilians. Milosevic refused. Later, in early fall of 1998, some 30,000 Kosovar civilians were forced to flee their homes in the wake of resurgent Serb pillaging and terrorizing of the Kosovo countryside. That renewed violence prompted the passage on September 23, 1998, of UN Security Council Resolution 1199 warning of an "impending humanitarian catastrophe" and calling for an im-

---

[2]Today, Serbia and Montenegro (the latter is semiautonomous) are all that remain of the former Yugoslavia.

mediate halt to the escalating strife in Kosovo. The following month, the Clinton administration again dispatched Holbrooke to Belgrade in a bid to persuade Milosevic to agree to negotiations on Kosovar autonomy and to accept a presence in Kosovo of unarmed international monitors from the Organization for Security and Cooperation in Europe (OSCE) to verify Serb compliance with Resolution 1199.

In the end, Milosevic assented to negotiations and agreed to permit an OSCE verification mission to enter Kosovo after the endorsement by the North Atlantic Council (NAC), the political arm of NATO, of an Activation Order (ACTORD) laying the groundwork for NATO air attacks against Serb military targets as an inducement. The mission, headed by U.S. diplomat William Walker, aimed at ensuring that the KLA's partisans remained in the mountains and that the Yugoslav army, or VJ (for *Vojska Jugoslavskaya*), remained in its garrisons. Air surveillance for this OSCE presence was to be provided by NATO, and a NATO extraction force began forming in Macedonia to withdraw the OSCE observers under armed protection in case events turned sour enough to endanger their safety.

Before long, however, the OSCE monitors found themselves watching helplessly as the Serb killing of Kosovar Albanians continued at a slow but steady rate. In response, NATO declared that it would take "all steps," including air strikes if necessary, to compel Serb compliance in bringing about a settlement in Kosovo. Meantime, as Holbrooke continued shuttling between Belgrade and Washington, Kosovo remained all but absent from the Clinton administration's list of priorities. Among other preoccupations closer to home, final preparations for the president's impeachment trial in the House of Representatives had entered full swing by December 1998, and tensions with Iraq were about to escalate into the launching of Operation Desert Fox that same month, a four-day mini-air operation waged by U.S. and British forces in what turned out to have been an almost entirely symbolic and ineffectual response to Saddam Hussein's earlier summary decision to refuse further cooperation with UN arms inspectors.

The trigger event that finally spurred the Clinton administration into action with respect to Kosovo occurred on January 15, 1999, when

MUP and Serb paramilitary troops in hot pursuit of KLA fighters entered the village of Racak and proceeded to slaughter 45 hapless ethnic Albanian civilians. Ambassador Walker personally traveled to Racak the next day to view the carnage, calling it a crime against humanity and all but blaming Milosevic by name for having ordered it. Two days later, the Yugoslav government, in response, declared Walker persona non grata and issued an expulsion order, which Walker ignored.[3] The Racak massacre signaled the beginning of the end to any further active role for the OSCE monitors, who were now increasingly at physical risk themselves and who were ultimately withdrawn less than a week before the commencement of Operation Allied Force. It turned out to be a serious miscalculation on Belgrade's part. What Milosevic may have thought was "just another village" proved to be one too many as far as the United States and NATO were concerned.[4] The event marked the beginning of the final countdown toward NATO's ultimate decision to proceed with Allied Force. On January 30, the NAC approved the launching of NATO air attacks against Serbia if the Serb leaders continued to refuse negotiations with their Kosovar counterparts.

On February 6, the Contact Group (made up of representatives from France, Germany, Great Britain, Russia, and the United States), prodded by Secretary of State Madeleine Albright, summoned Serb and KLA representatives to the Rambouillet chateau on the outskirts of Paris for a last-chance round of talks aimed at producing an overarching settlement for Kosovo. Those talks ended without agreement on February 23. Further talks began in Paris on March 15. During the latter negotiations, Albright delivered an ultimatum to the Serbs and Kosovars alike that, as an incentive, offered to contribute 28,000 NATO peacekeepers, including 4,000 U.S. troops, to police any negotiated settlement. Three days later, the KLA signed a peace accord aimed at giving Kosovo broad autonomy within Serbia. The day after, however, Serbia refused to sign, insisting that it would not even consider the idea of foreign troops on Kosovo soil. More ominously yet, on the very same day that this second round of talks began, Milo-

---

[3]The expulsion order was later rescinded by Milosevic.

[4]On this point, NATO's Secretary General, Javier Solana, remarked that a Serb diplomat had been heard to cite a rule of thumb to the effect that "a village a day would keep NATO away."

sevic ordered a major escalation of the buildup of VJ forces both within and immediately adjacent to Kosovo that had begun the previous month, in a clear sign that a major move against the KLA and against ethnic Albanian civilians was imminent.

By all indications, Milosevic did not enter the Rambouillet process with any intent to negotiate seriously. On the contrary, in all likelihood he saw it as presenting a perfectly timed opportunity to position himself to launch Operation Horseshoe (*Potkova*), as his incipient ethnic cleansing campaign was code-named. By that point, he most likely fully anticipated that NATO would eventually bomb him, much as U.S. and British forces did in a token manner against Iraq two months previously in Desert Fox. Probably key to Milosevic's strategy was an underlying belief that he could take at least as much measured pain from a symbolic NATO air operation as Saddam Hussein had endured from Desert Fox. That belief most likely hinged on an associated conviction that NATO's limited tolerance for bombing would run out in short order and that he would then have Kosovo all to himself, with no further outside meddling by NATO, OSCE, or any other foreign peace-enforcement entities, and with no Kosovar Albanians. As if to bear that out, not only did Belgrade reject NATO's peace proposal outright, it simultaneously launched a new campaign of burning and pillaging by some 40,000 VJ troops in the central Drenica region of Kosovo, using tanks, heavy artillery, and mortar fire against dozens of villages. In the process, VJ and MUP forces destroyed three of seven known regional headquarters of the KLA and forced thousands of ethnic Albanian civilians to flee. In the wake of that renewed assault, the UN High Commissioner for Refugees reported 240,000 internally displaced persons in Kosovo, including 60,000 rendered homeless in just the preceding three weeks.

The refugee crisis quickly assumed all the earmarks of a humanitarian disaster. President Clinton ordered Holbrooke back to Belgrade on March 22 in an eleventh-hour bid to persuade Milosevic to desist from further ravaging of Kosovo or else face NATO bombing attacks. Holbrooke was instructed to warn Milosevic that NATO was preparing air and missile strikes that would destroy much of Yugoslavia's military infrastructure. Milosevic was further warned that the targets of those attacks would be not just in Kosovo but in Serbia as well.[5] Holbrooke made no attempt to bargain and stressed to Milosevic that he was in Belgrade solely to deliver a message. At the end of a four-hour meeting, he was rebuffed.

At that point, with the gauntlet thrown down by Holbrooke, U.S. officials presented NATO's ambassadors with a final proposed bombing plan against Serbia, the declared goals of which were a verifiable halt to ethnic cleansing and atrocities on the ground in Kosovo; a withdrawal of all but a token number of VJ, MUP, and paramilitary troops from Kosovo; the deployment of an international peacekeeping force in Kosovo; the return of refugees and their unhindered access to aid; and the laying of groundwork for a future settlement in Kosovo along the lines of the Rambouillet terms of reference.[6] Commenting on the threatened campaign, the Supreme Allied Commander in Europe (SACEUR), U.S. Army General Wesley Clark, warned that "if required, we will strike in a swift and severe fashion." General Klaus Naumann, the chairman of NATO's Military Committee, added that Milosevic was "severely mistaken" if he believed that NATO would engage merely in pinprick attacks and then await his response.[7]

Earlier, when the allies had empowered NATO Secretary General Javier Solana to authorize air strikes on January 30, the declared intent was to conduct limited raids over 48 hours and then pause to encourage Milosevic to reconsider. The plan this time was for a wider range of targets to be hit and for a longer operation aimed at causing considerable infrastructure damage. In an eleventh-hour bid to marshal public support for the impending air effort, President Clinton made an appeal, in a televised speech at a labor union lun-

---

[5]In his exchange with Milosevic, Holbrooke said: "You understand our position?" Milosevic: "Yes." Holbrooke: "Is it absolutely clear what will happen when we leave, given your position?" Milosevic: "Yes, you will bomb us. You are a big and powerful nation. You can bomb us if you wish." Bruce W. Nelan, "Into the Fire," *Time*, April 5, 1999, p. 35. Later, Holbrooke added that Milosevic was "tricky, evasive, smart, and dangerous," further noting that his mood in the final confrontation was "calm, almost fatalistic, unyielding." "'He Was Calm, Unyielding,'" *Newsweek*, April 5, 1999, p. 37.

[6]Jane Perlez, "Holbrooke to Meet Milosevic in Final Peace Effort," *New York Times*, March 22, 1999.

[7]R. Jeffrey Smith, "Belgrade Rebuffs Final U.S. Warning," *Washington Post*, March 23, 1999.

cheon on the day before the bombing commenced, beseeching the American people to support his actions in coming to grips with NATO's looming Kosovo predicament.[8]

To be sure, planning for an air operation of some sort against Serbia had begun as early as June 1998. Initial plans were for an option called Operation Nimble Lion, which would have pitted a substantial number of U.S. and allied aircraft against some 250 targets throughout the former Yugoslavia.[9] This option was developed wholly within U.S. channels by the 32nd Air Operations Group at Ramstein Air Base, Germany, at the behest of USAF General John Jumper in his capacity as commander, United States Air Forces in Europe (USAFE), in response to a directive from Clark in his capacity as commander in chief, U.S. European Command (USEUCOM). A separate plan called Concept of Operations Plan (CONOPLAN) 10601 was later developed by NATO and approved by the NAC. Although there was some overlap between these two plans, the thrust of each was different. Nimble Lion would have hit the Serbs hard at the beginning, whereas 10601 entailed a gradual, incremental, and phased approach. The latter ultimately became the basis for Operation Allied Force.

Two closely related U.S. joint task force (JTF) planning efforts called Operations Flexible Anvil (commanded by U.S. Navy Vice Admiral Daniel Murphy, commander of the 6th Fleet) and Sky Anvil (commanded by USAF Lieutenant General Michael Short, commander of the 16th Air Force at Aviano Air Base, Italy) followed in the summer of 1998.[10] Those efforts were terminated when Milosevic initially agreed to a cease-fire after his October 5–13 talks with

---

[8]Charles Babington and Helen Dewar, "President Pleads for Support," *Washington Post*, March 24, 1999.

[9]Telephone conversation with Lieutenant General Michael Short, USAF (Ret.), August 22, 2001.

[10]Flexible Anvil was a U.S.-only option that envisaged only ship-launched Tomahawk and conventional air-launched cruise missile attacks over a 48- to 72-hour period, roughly along the lines of Operation Desert Fox conducted against Iraq the following December. Sky Anvil envisaged follow-on air strikes in a transition to a NATO operation (or an operation involving a more truncated coalition of the willing). General Short believed that it was counterproductive to fragment these closely connected options into two separate plans, but he and Admiral Murphy were well acquainted and kept each other informed. Conversation with Vice Admiral Daniel J. Murphy, USN, commander, 6th Fleet, aboard the USS *LaSalle*, Gaeta, Italy, June 8, 2000.

Holbrooke.[11] In all, General Jumper later reported that by the onset of Allied Force, no fewer than 40 air campaign options had been generated and fine-tuned.[12] Those options were said to have included some that were at least implicitly critical of the proposed use of NATO air power without a supporting ground threat to encourage enemy troops to assemble and maneuver so they might be more easily targeted and attacked from the air.

In the end, however, the plan ultimately agreed to by NATO expressly ruled out any backstopping by ground forces for two avowed reasons. The first had to do with identified logistic difficulties, the anticipated challenge of the terrain, and poor access and basing opportunities. The second, and far more pivotal, reason entailed the Clinton administration's concern over lack of congressional support for such an option and the presumed unwillingness on the part of the American people and the NATO allies to accept combat casualties, reinforced by a near-certainty that the allies would not buy into a ground option. All planning, moreover, took for granted that NATO's most vulnerable area (or "center of gravity") was its continued cohesion as an alliance. In light of that, any target or attack tactic deemed even remotely likely to undermine that cohesion, such as the loss of friendly aircrews, excessive noncombatant casualties, excess collateral damage to civilian structures, or anything else that might undermine domestic political support or cause a withdrawal of public backing for the bombing effort, was to be most carefully considered—if not avoided altogether.

---

[11]Lieutenant Colonel L. T. Wight, USAF, "What a Tangled Web We Wove: An After-Action Assessment of Operation Allied Force's Command and Control Structure and Processes," unpublished paper, p. 1.

[12]General John Jumper, USAF, testimony to the Military Readiness Subcommittee, House Armed Services Committee, Washington, D.C., October 26, 1999. The most fully developed of these iterations, called Operation Allied Talon, was a true phased air campaign plan rooted in effects-based targeting and aimed at achieving concrete military objectives. Despite the best efforts of the JTF Noble Anvil leadership (Admiral James Ellis, General Jumper, and General Short) to sell this plan to SACEUR, General Clark never adopted it. Instead, he elected to cut and paste different elements of the different plans that he thought were most appropriate and labeled the resultant product Operation Allied Force. Comments on an earlier draft by Hq USAFE/SA, April 6, 2001. General Jumper himself later confirmed that Allied Talon was a nonstarter. Conversation with General John P. Jumper, USAF, Hq Air Combat Command, Langley AFB, Virginia, May 15, 2001.

NATO's final plan was conceived from the start as a coercive operation only, with the implied goal of inflicting merely enough pain to
persuade Milosevic to capitulate. Its first phase, against only 51 approved integrated air defense system (IADS) targets and 40 approved
punishment targets out of 169 in NATO's Master Target File, entailed
attacks against a combination of enemy air defenses and fixed army
installations that aimed at softening up Yugoslavia's IADS and
demonstrating NATO's ability to conduct precise air attacks with a
minimum of unintended damage. The second phase envisaged attacks against military targets mainly, though not exclusively, below
the 44th parallel, which bisected Yugoslavia well south of Belgrade
(see Figure 2.1). Only in the third phase, if need be, would the

Figure 2.1—Allied Force Area of Operations

bombing go in earnest after military facilities north of the 44th parallel and against targets in Belgrade itself.[13] NATO had approved this three-phase plan in principle the preceding October as a part of its ACTORD and had handed the keys for Phase I to Solana on January 30. Approval by the NAC of Phases II and III, however, would come only after the air effort began.

For his part, General Clark had called for punitive air strikes against Yugoslavia as early as January 1999, in response to the Serb massacre of 45 Kosovar Albanians near the town of Racak just days before. Persistent pressures from within NATO to explore a diplomatic solution, however, outweighed that recommendation for the early use of force. The resulting delay gave Milosevic time to bolster his forces, disperse important military assets, hunker down for an eventual bombing campaign, and lay the final groundwork for the ethnic cleansing of Kosovo. Owing to that delay, NATO lost any element of surprise that may otherwise have been available.[14]

In the end, Operation Allied Force came just 10 days short of NATO's 50th anniversary. The Clinton administration did not seek a UN Security Council resolution approving the air attack plan, since it knew that Russia and China had both vowed to veto any proposal calling for air strikes.[15] NATO's going-in expectation was that the bombing would be over very quickly. Indeed, so confident were its

---

[13]Charles Babington and William Drozdiak, "Belgrade Faces the 11th Hour, Again," *Washington Post*, March 22, 1999. For more first-hand comment on the intra-NATO politics that preceded Allied Force, see General Wesley K. Clark, *Waging Modern War: Bosnia, Kosovo, and the Future of Combat*, New York, Public Affairs, 2001, especially pp. 121–189.

[14]William Drozdiak, "Politics Hampered Warfare, Clark Says," *Washington Post*, July 20, 1999.

[15]This should not be taken to suggest that NATO's air war against Serbia was a unilateral action undertaken without regard for the UN whatsoever. On the contrary, in March 1998 the Security Council had expressly recognized in Resolution 1160 that the Serb government's repression of the ethnic Albanian population in Kosovo constituted a threat to international peace and security, a view later repeated in Resolution 1199 six months before the start of Allied Force, which called for action aimed at heading off "the impending humanitarian catastrophe" in Kosovo. As an IISS comment later noted, NATO's air war for Kosovo thus constituted "a highly significant precedent," in that it established "more firmly in international law the right to intervene on humanitarian grounds, even without an express mandate from the Security Council." *Strategic Survey 1999/2000*, London, England, The International Institute for Strategic Studies, 2000, p. 26.

principals that merely a token bombing effort would suffice to persuade Milosevic to yield that the initial attack was openly announced in advance, with U.S. officials conceding up front that it would take a day or more to program all of the TLAMs to hit some 60 planned aim points.[16] Only at the last minute did NATO's political leaders give Secretary General Solana authority for what one NATO official called a "much more diverse target list, a more intensive pace of operations, and an expanded geographical zone."[17] Once under way, the slowly escalating air effort put the United States into two simultaneous regional conflicts (the other being Operations Northern and Southern Watch against Iraq) for the first time since World War II. It also made for a uniquely demanding test for American air power and became the most serious foreign policy crisis of the Clinton presidency.

---

[16]Jane Perlez, "U.S. Option: Air Attacks May Prove Unpalatable," *New York Times*, March 23, 1999.

[17]Steven Erlanger, "U.S. Issues Appeal to Serbs to Halt Attack in Kosovo," *New York Times,* March 23, 1999.

Chapter Three

THE AIR WAR UNFOLDS

The operational setting of Yugoslavia contrasted sharply with the one presented to coalition planners by Iraq in 1991. Defined by a series of interwoven valleys partly surrounded by mountains and protected by low cloud cover and fog, Serbia and Kosovo made up an arena smaller than the state of Kentucky (39,000 square miles), with Kosovo itself no larger than the Los Angeles metropolitan area. Its topography and weather—compounded by an enemy IADS that was guaranteed to make offensive operations both difficult and dangerous—promised to provide a unique challenge for NATO air power.

Yugoslavia's air defenses were dominated by surface-to-air missile (SAM) batteries equipped with thousands of Soviet-made SAMs, including three SA-2 battalions; 16 SA-3 battalions, each with numerous launchers directed by LOW BLOW fire-control radars; and five SA-6 regiments fielding five batteries each, for a total of 25 SA-6 batteries directed by STRAIGHT FLUSH radars. These radar-guided SAMs were supplemented by around 100 vehicle-mounted SA-9 and several SA-13 infrared SAMs, along with a profusion of man-portable infrared SAMs, some 1,850 antiaircraft artillery (AAA) pieces, and numerous stockpiled reserve weapons and buried communications lines. Backing up these defenses, the Yugoslav air force consisted of 238 combat aircraft, including 15 MiG-29 and 64 MiG-21 fighter-interceptors.[1] Although the Yugoslav IADS employed equipment and technologies that dated as far back as the 1960s, albeit presum-

---

[1]"AWOS [Air War Over Serbia] Fact Sheet," Hq USAFE/SA, December 17, 1999. See also *The Military Balance, 1998/99*, London, International Institute for Strategic Studies, 1998, p. 100.

ably with selected upgrades, its operators knew U.S. tactics well and had practiced air defense drills and honed their operational techniques for more than four decades. They also had the benefit of more equipment and better training than did the Bosnian Serbs in 1995. Finally, they enjoyed the advantage of being protected both by mountainous terrain and by the cover of inclement weather when the air war began.

In addition, Serbia's SA-2s, SA-3s, and SA-6s were served by more than 100 acquisition and tracking radars, all of which were internetted by underground land lines and fiber optic cables. They were further backstopped by a robust civilian and military visual observer network that included covert Serb observers who monitored NATO aircraft as they took off from their bases in Europe.[2] In anticipation of a possible air offensive, Yugoslav defense specialists had met the month before in Baghdad with their Iraqi counterparts. Indeed, such Yugoslav-Iraqi collaboration had long preceded the Kosovo crisis. Baghdad had purchased some Yugoslav IADS equipment late during the cold war before the onset of Desert Storm. Iraq also very likely shared intelligence with Belgrade on U.S. suppression of enemy air defenses (SEAD) tactics, as well as its own experience and recommendations, in subsequent years.[3] According to General Salko Begic, the air commander for the Muslim-Croat federation in Bosnia and a former service academy classmate of the Serb generals who were running Yugoslavia's air defenses when the air attacks began, the intended tactic to be used against attacking NATO aircraft was to create a killing zone below 10,000 ft by means of AAA, SA-7 infrared SAMs, and Swedish Bofors man-portable air defenses.[4]

---

[2]Discussions with former East European strategic and tactical SAM operators on IADS visual observer employment doctrine, as reported to the author by Hq USAFE/IN, May 18, 2001.

[3]John Diamond, "Yugoslavia, Iraq Talked Air Defense Strategy," *Philadelphia Inquirer*, March 30, 1999.

[4]Michael R. Gordon, "NATO to Hit Serbs from 2 More Sides," *New York Times*, May 11, 1999. This last system featured the Bofors 40mm gun tied to the Giraffe radar-based low-altitude air defense system (LAADS). It was the only radar-cued (as opposed to radar-directed) AAA weapon fielded in the war zone and possibly the most potent low-altitude AAA threat because of its local Giraffe-based LAADS command and control system. Peter Rackham, ed., *Jane's C4I Systems, 1994–95*, London, Jane's Information Group, 1994, p. 107.

In commenting on this layered and redundant air defense net, USAF chief of staff General Michael Ryan, who earlier had commanded Operation Deliberate Force over Bosnia in 1995, frankly conceded in congressional testimony before the start of the operation that "these guys are very good" and that friendly aircraft and aircrew losses were "a distinct possibility."[5] Ryan added that Yugoslavia's IADS made for a "very substantive air defense capability" and that the Serbs maintained a "very professional army and air defense corps." Because of the assessed robustness of the Yugoslav IADS, Pentagon planners were said to have estimated before opening night that NATO could lose as many as 10 aircraft in the initial wave of strikes.[6]

INITIAL ATTACKS AND THEIR EFFECTS

Operation Allied Force began against Yugoslavia on the night of March 24, within minutes of President Clinton's announcement that air attacks were under way. The initial concept of operations envisaged night raids against so-called enabling targets, such as enemy air defense assets, in order to create a more permissive operating environment for subsequent attacks against other classes of targets. In announcing the commencement of attacks, the president declared that the operation had three goals: "To demonstrate the seriousness of NATO's opposition to aggression," to deter Milosevic from "continuing and escalating his attacks on helpless civilians," and, if need be, "to damage Serbia's capacity to wage war against Kosovo by seriously diminishing its military capabilities." At the same time, he pointedly stressed: "I don't intend to put our troops in Kosovo to fight a war."[7] To those opening words, the chairman of the Joint Chiefs of Staff, U.S. Army General Henry H. Shelton, added that NATO would engage "the full range of his military capabilities" if

---

[5]Paul Richter, "U.S. Pilots Face Perilous Task, Pentagon Says," *Los Angeles Times*, March 20, 1999. In testimony to the Senate Armed Services Committee on the eve of the war, Ryan added: "I ran the air campaign in Bosnia, and this defensive array is much more substantive . . . two or three times more so. It is deep and redundant. Those guys [in Bosnia] were good, but these guys are better. There is a very real possibility we will lose aircraft trying to take it on." David Atkinson, "Stealth Could Play Key Role in Kosovo, Despite Bad Weather," *Defense Daily*, March 23, 1999, p. 1.

[6]Bruce W. Nelan, "Into the Fire," *Time*, April 5, 1999, p. 31.

[7]Francis X. Clines, "NATO Opens Broad Barrage Against Serbs as Clinton Denounces 'Brutal Repression,'" *New York Times*, March 25, 1999.

Milosevic did not desist from his offensive in Kosovo.[8] As noted earlier, it was accepted as a given by the Clinton administration that Milosevic would settle quickly. As Secretary of State Albright clearly attested to this expectation in a television interview on the evening that the air attacks began: "I don't see this as a long-term operation."[9]

The air war commenced with 250 committed U.S. aircraft, including 120 land-based fighters, 7 B-52s, 6 B-2s, 10 reconnaissance aircraft, 10 combat search and rescue (CSAR) aircraft, 3 airborne command and control center (ABCCC) aircraft, and around 40 tankers.[10] As for NATO's additional 18 members, 13 contributed aircraft for use in the operation, with 11 allies (Britain, France, Germany, Italy, Belgium, Canada, Denmark, the Netherlands, Norway, Spain, and Turkey) eventually participating in offensive and defensive air combat operations of all types. The first wave of attacks on the night of March 24 consisted of cruise missile launches only, featuring TLAMs fired by four U.S. surface ships (including USS *Gonzales* and USS *Philippine Sea*), two U.S. fast-attack submarines (USS *Albuquerque* and USS *Miami*), and a British attack submarine (HMS *Splendid*) operating in the Adriatic Sea. This initial wave further included AGM-86C CALCMs launched against hardened enemy structures by six B-52s flying outside Yugoslav airspace. The latter were the first shots fired in the operation.[11] The initial target hits occurred shortly

---

[8]Paul Richter, "Time Is Not on the Side of U.S., Allies," *Los Angeles Times,* March 25, 1999.

[9]John T. Correll, "Assumptions Fall in Kosovo," *Air Force Magazine*, June 1999, p. 4.

[10]This study has taken special care to characterize Operation Allied Force as an "air war" or an "air effort," rather than as a full-fledged "air campaign." Although that effort continues to be widely portrayed as the latter, formal Air Force doctrine defines an air campaign as "a connected series of operations conducted by air forces to achieve joint force objectives within a given time and area." *Air Force Basic Doctrine*, Maxwell AFB, Alabama, Hq Air Force Doctrine Center, AFDD-1, September 1997, p. 78. By that standard, NATO's air war for Kosovo did not attain to the level of a campaign, as did the earlier Operations Desert Storm and Deliberate Force. Rather, it was a continuously evolving coercive operation featuring piecemeal attacks against unsystematically approved targets, not an integrated effort aimed from the outset at achieving predetermined and identifiable operational effects.

[11]The effectiveness of these initial standoff attacks was not impressive. During the first two weeks, no B-52 succeeded in launching all eight of its CALCMs. In one instance, six out of eight were said to have failed. Also, the two times that B-52s later fired the AGM-142 Have Nap cruise missile, both launches were reportedly opera-

after 8 p.m. local time in the vicinity of Kosovo's capital city of Pristina, shutting down the electrical power grid and plunging the city into darkness. The main commercial and military airfield at nearby Batajnica was also hit. In all, 55 U.S. cruise missiles were expended the first night.

These cruise-missile attacks were followed by fixed-wing air strikes that continued throughout the night, primarily against air defense targets such as SAM batteries and radar and military communications sites.[12] Allied aircraft operated out of Italy, Spain, France, Germany, the United Kingdom, and the Adriatic Sea.[13] Their targets included a radar site at Podgorica, the capital city of Montenegro. In addition, NATO aircrews hit airfields in Serbia, Kosovo, and Montenegro, as well as electrical power generating facilities, weapons-producing factories, military and police barracks, and command and control nodes, including some aim points located north of Belgrade. Among specific targets attacked were the VJ's Kosovoski Junaci barracks near Pristina in Kosovo, the Golobovci airport in Montenegro, munitions stores at Danilovgrad, and other military targets at Radovac, Sipcanik, and Ulcini.[14] Allied pilots were instructed to take no chances with enemy infrared SAMs and AAA and to honor an alti-

---

tional failures. See John D. Morrocco, David Fulghum, and Robert Wall, "Weather, Weapons Dearth Slow NATO Strikes," *Aviation Week and Space Technology*, April 5, 1999, p. 26, and William M. Arkin, "Kosovo Report Short on Weapons Performance Details," *Defense Daily*, February 10, 2000, p. 2.

[12]An important qualification is warranted here. Although the opening-night approved aim points largely entailed fixed IADS targets, the limited attacks conducted against them were not part of a phased campaign plan in which rolling back the enemy IADS was a priority. There was no strategic emphasis on IADS takedown in these attacks. Comments on an earlier draft by Hq USAFE/IN, May 18, 2001.

[13]Italian bases used included Aviano, Gioio del Colle, Villafranca, Amendola, Cervia, Gazzanise, Ghedi, Piacenza, Istrana, Falconara, Practica di Mare, Brindisi, and Sigonella. German bases used were Royal Air Force (RAF) Bruggen, Rhein Main Air Base (AB), Spangdahlem AB, and Ramstein AB. Bases made available by the United Kingdom were RAF Fairford, RAF Lakenheath, and RAF Mildenhall. Spain provided Moron AB, and France provided Istres. For a complete list of all participating allied air assets, their units, and their bases, as well as a tabulation of the Yugoslav IADS and air order of battle as of April 20, see Benoit Colin and Rene J. Francillon, "L'OTAN en Guerre!" *Air Fan*, May 1999, pp. 12–19. See also John E. Peters, Stuart Johnson, Nora Bensahel, Timothy Liston, and Traci Williams, *European Contributions to Operation Allied Force: Implications for Transatlantic Cooperation*, Santa Monica, California, RAND, MR-1391-AF, 2001.

[14]Robert Hewson, "Operation Allied Force: The First 30 Days," *World Air Power Journal*, Fall 1999, p. 16.

tude floor (or "hard deck") of 15,000 ft to remain above their killing envelopes.

Targets attacked the first night were reviewed with special care at the White House by President Clinton, Secretary of Defense William Cohen, and General Shelton. Some proposed targets were removed from the list by dissenting NATO leaders out of concern for causing collateral damage because of their close proximity to civilian buildings. In other borderline cases in which targets were reluctantly approved, the recommended bomb size was reduced to minimize or preclude collateral damage. One of every five laser-guided bombs dropped by an F-117 the first night was a 500-lb GBU-12 instead of a 2,000-lb GBU-27. That meant less likelihood of the bomb's causing inadvertent collateral damage, but also a lower probability of destroying the intended target. The rules of engagement were uncompromisingly restrictive, with pilots instructed to return home with their weapons unless their assigned target could be positively identified.[15]

In all, some 400 sorties were flown the first night, including 120 strike missions against 40 targets consisting of five airfields, five army garrisons, communications centers, and storage depots, in addition to IADS facilities. Only a few SA-3 and SA-6 SAMs were launched against attacking NATO aircraft the first night. All the same, Pentagon officials anticipated the day after that at least a dozen NATO aircraft losses could be incurred should the operation continue beyond just a few days.[16] Contrary to early Western press reports, Serb IADS operators never intentionally husbanded their SAMs. Instead, after experiencing allied SEAD operations for the first time, they adapted their tactics to balance lethality with survivability, with the result that they were always present and aggressive—even as they showed greater firing discipline than the Iraqis did during Desert Storm.[17]

---

[15]Nelan, "Into the Fire," p. 32.

[16]Steven Lee Myers, "Early Attacks Focus on Web of Air Defense," *New York Times,* March 25, 1999.

[17]Comments on an earlier draft by Hq USAFE/IN, May 18, 2001.

Numerous enemy fighters, including at least a dozen MiG-29s, sought to engage attacking NATO aircraft the first night.[18] One MiG-29 was reported to have fired an R-73 (NATO code-named AA-10 Alamo) radar-guided missile toward an ingressing NATO fighter in an ineffectual attempt to get off a counteroffensive shot. Two MiG-29s were downed by USAF F-15s and one by a Dutch F-16. In addition, a MiG-21 was believed to have crashed during an attempt to land. Only rarely did Serb fighters rise to challenge NATO aircraft after that. The following day, General Clark declared that the bombardment would "systematically and progressively attack, disrupt, degrade, devastate," and "ultimately . . . destroy" Milosevic's army if he failed to accept the American-drafted peace plan. Clark further declared that the air effort would be "just as long and difficult as President Milosevic requires it to be."[19]

Attacks carried out by NATO aircrews the second night were described as "significantly heavier" than those the first night. Targets included the VJ barracks at Urosevac and Prizren in Kosovo; the military airfields at Nis in southern Serbia and Golubovci near Podgorica, Montenegro; and other Serb military facilities near Trstenik and Danilovgrad.[20] That night, fewer than 10 SAMs were fired, none of which succeeded in scoring a hit. The third afternoon, a USAF F-15C downed two more MiG-29s, which evidently had lost contact with their ground controller and inadvertently strayed into Bosnian airspace. Although their intended NATO targets were never positively determined, it was the subsequent conclusion of the allied air commander, Lieutenant General Short, that the Serb pilots had simply lost any semblance of air situation awareness and, as a result, set themselves up as easy prey for the F-15.[21]

---

[18]This suggested that the Serb IADS may have been unable to deconflict its SAMs and fighters operating in the same airspace because of identification and discrimination problems.

[19]Barton Gellman, "Key Sites Pounded for 2nd Day," *Washington Post*, March 26, 1999. See also John D. Morrocco and Robert Wall, "NATO Vows Air Strikes Will Go the Distance," *Aviation Week and Space Technology*, March 29, 1999, p. 34.

[20]Hewson, "Operation Allied Force," p. 17.

[21]Telephone conversation with Lieutenant General Michael Short, USAF (Ret.), August 16, 2001.

Third-night attacks included targets in Mali Mokri Lug, Ayala, Voz-dovac, and, for the first time, nearer to the immediate outskirts of Belgrade. That night, 40 percent of the targets attacked were in Kosovo, as opposed to only 20 percent the first two nights.[22] These attacks, however, just like the ones that took place the preceding two nights, caused no serious inconvenience for the Serbs. On the con-trary, the gradually mounting intensity of the air war merely allowed the Serbs to adjust to a new level of pain, while pressing ahead with what they had planned all along: to redouble their effort to run as many ethnic Albanian civilians as possible out of Kosovo and thus be able to take an unobstructed shot at the KLA once and for all.

This escalated ethnic cleansing should not have come as a complete surprise to NATO. Weeks earlier, the director of the Central Intelli-gence Agency (CIA), George Tenet, had predicted that VJ and MUP forces *might* respond to a NATO bombing campaign with precisely such a strategy. Similarly, U.S. military leaders had argued behind closed doors that air power alone would not suffice to force Milosevic to back away from such a move.[23] The CIA had reportedly learned as early as fall 1998 that Belgrade was planning a move with tanks and artillery, called Operation Horseshoe, to drive ethnic Albanians over the southern and western borders of Kosovo as soon as the snow melted in the spring. The KLA would thus be stripped of a sur-rounding civilian population and exposed to direct attack.[24] The Serb incentive for such a move was not difficult to fathom, consider-ing that the heavily radicalized KLA, which represented the aspira-tions of most Kosovar Albanians, was (and remains) committed to the establishment of an independent Kosovo—and a Greater Albania over the longer term.[25]

In any event, Milosevic's unleashing of large-scale atrocities in Kosovo and his truculent defiance of NATO denied the alliance the quick settlement it had counted on and left both NATO and the

---

[22]Hewson, "Operation Allied Force," p. 18.

[23]John F. Harris, "Clinton Saw No Alternative to Airstrikes," *Washington Post,* April 1, 1999.

[24]Johanna McGeary, "The Road to Hell," *Time,* April 12, 1999, p. 42.

[25]For an informed treatment of the KLA and its origins, goals, and prospects by *The New York Times'* Balkans bureau chief from 1995 to 1998, see Chris Hedges, "Kosovo's Next Masters?" *Foreign Affairs,* May/June 1999, pp. 24–42.

Clinton administration with no alternative but to continue pressing the air attacks until NATO unambiguously prevailed. Because NATO's leaders on both sides of the Atlantic had banked on a quick win, no preparations had been undertaken to anticipate what the consequences might be should Milosevic raise the stakes by accelerating his ethnic cleansing plans. Lest there be any doubt on that score, General Naumann admitted a month into the bombing that from the air war's very start, "there was the hope in the political camp that this could be over very quickly" and that as a result, no one at any level had prepared for Milosevic's ethnic cleansing push.[26] As a result, what had begun as a coercive NATO ploy aimed at producing Milosevic's quick compliance quickly devolved into an open-ended test of wills between the world's most powerful military alliance and the wily and resilient Yugoslav dictator.

THE AIR WAR BOGS DOWN

Once it became clear by the fourth day that the air offensive was not having its hoped-for effect on Milosevic, Clark received authorization from the NAC to proceed to Phase II, which entailed ramped-up attacks against a broader spectrum of fixed targets in Serbia and against dispersed and hidden VJ forces in Kosovo. Attacks during the preceding three nights had focused mainly on IADS targets. Phase II strikes shifted the emphasis from SEAD to interdiction, with predominant stress on cutting off VJ and MUP lines of communication and attacking their choke points, storage and marshaling areas, and any tank concentrations that could be found. Immediately before Phase II began, NATO ambassadors had argued for more than eight hours, well past midnight, over whether to expand the target list. General Naumann insisted at that session that it was time to start "attacking both ends of the snake by hitting the head and cutting off the tail."[27] His use of that bellicose-sounding metaphor reportedly infuriated

---

[26]Carla Anne Robbins, Thomas E. Ricks, and Neil King, Jr., "Milosevic's Resolve Spawned Unity, Wider Bombing List in NATO Alliance," *Wall Street Journal*, April 27, 1999. Unlike nearly all other NATO principals, General Naumann cautioned even before the air war began that although the intent was to be quick, Operation Allied Force could well turn out to be "long and protracted." Paul Richter and John-Thor Dahlburg, "NATO Broadens Its Battle Strategy," *Los Angeles Times*, March 24, 1999.

[27]William Drozdiak, "NATO Leaders Struggle to Find a Winning Strategy," *Washington Post*, April 1, 1999.

the Greek and Italian representatives, who had been calling for an Easter bombing pause in the hope that it might lead to negotiations.[28]

NATO went into this second phase earlier than anticipated because of escalating Serb atrocities on the ground. Up to that point, the air attacks had had no sought-after effect on Serb behavior whatsoever. On the contrary, Serbia's offensive against the Kosovar Albanians intensified, with Serb troops burning villages, arresting dissidents, and executing supposed KLA supporters. The Serbs continued unopposed in their countercampaign of ethnic cleansing, ultimately forcing most of the 1.8 million ethnic Albanians in Kosovo from their homes.[29]

By the start of the second week, Clinton administration officials acknowledged that Operation Allied Force had failed to meet its declared goal of halting Serbian violence against the ethnic Albanians.[30] Echoing that judgment, Clark added that NATO was confronting "an intelligent and capable adversary who is attempting to offset all our strategies."[31] It was becoming increasingly clear that at least one element of Milosevic's strategy entailed playing for time. Yet although the humanitarian crime of ethnic cleansing gave the Serbs an immediate tactical advantage, it also came at the long-term cost of virtually forcing NATO to stay the course. The bombing effort thus evolved into a race between those Serb forces trying to drive the ethnic Albanians out of Kosovo and NATO forces trying to hinder that effort—or, failing that, to punish Milosevic badly enough to make him quit.

---

[28]The latter rumblings prompted concern in U.S. and NATO military circles that once any such pause might be agreed to, it would be that much more difficult to resume the bombing after the pause had expired. In the end, no pause in the bombing occurred at any time during Allied Force, other than those occasioned by bad weather.

[29]After careful examination, the provision of airlift relief missions for the Kosovar refugees was ruled out by U.S. and NATO planners because they were deemed excessively dangerous in the face of threats from enemy ground fire and because of concern that any delivered supplies would end up in the wrong hands.

[30]Bradley Graham and William Drozdiak, "Allied Action Fails to Stop Serb Brutality," *Washington Post*, March 31, 1999.

[31]Craig R. Whitney, "On 7th Day, Serb Resilience Gives NATO Leaders Pause," *New York Times*, March 31, 1999.

Five B-1Bs were added to the U.S. Air Force's bomber contingent at the start of the second week. In preparing them for combat, what normally would have taken months of effort to program the aircraft's mission computers was compressed into fewer than 100 hours during a single week as Air Force officers and contractors updated the computers with the latest intelligence on enemy radar and SAM threats. One aircraft with the latest updated software installed, the Block D upgrade of the Defensive System Upgrade Program, passed a critical flight test at the 53rd Wing at Eglin AFB, Florida, and two B-1s were committed to action over Yugoslavia two days later. These aircraft, which, alongside the B-52s, operated out of RAF Fairford in England, employed the Raytheon ALE-50 towed decoy to good effect for the first time in combat.[32] They were still test-configured aircraft flown by test crews. The B-1s, all test-configured with Block D upgrades, typically flew two-ship missions against military area targets, such as barracks and marshaling yards.

While the Serb pillaging of Kosovo was unfolding on the ground, NATO air attacks continued to be hampered by bad weather, enemy dispersal tactics, and air defenses that were proving to be far more robust than expected. In the absence of a credible NATO ground threat, which the United States and NATO had ruled out from the start, VJ forces were able to survive the air attacks simply by spreading out and concealing their tanks and other vehicles. More than half of the nightly strike sorties returned without any weapons expended owing to adverse weather in the target area. Only four days out of the first nine featured weather offering visibility conditions suitable for employing laser-guided bombs (LGBs). By the end of Day 9, only 15 percent of the 2,700 sorties flown had actually been bombing missions. In all, it took NATO 12 days to complete the same number of

---

[32]Of 10 known Serb SAMs that reportedly guided on B-1s during the course of the air war, all were believed to have been successfully diverted to the decoys. See David Hughes, "A Pilot's Best Friend," *Aviation Week and Space Technology*, May 31, 1999, p. 25. The commander of USAFE, General John Jumper, later explained the Serb IADS tactic employed: Radars in Montenegro would acquire and track the B-1s as they flew in from over the Adriatic Sea, arced around Macedonia, and proceeded north into Kosovo. Those acquisition radars would then hand off their targets to SA-6s, whose radars came up in full target-track mode and fired the missiles, which headed straight for the ALE-50 and took it out, just as the system was designed to work. "Jumper on Air Power," *Air Force Magazine*, July 2000, p. 43.

strike sorties that had been conducted during the first 12 hours of Desert Storm.

To all intents and purposes, the difference between Phase II and Phase I was indistinguishable as far as the intensity of NATO's air attacks was concerned. The commencement of Phase II was characterized as more of an evolution than a sharp change of direction. On that point, NATO's spokesman at the time, RAF Air Commodore David Wilby, said that the operation was "just beginning to transition" from IADS targets to fielded VJ and MUP forces.[33] By the start of the second week, merely 1,700 sorties had been flown, only 425 of which consisted of strike sorties against a scant 100 approved targets.[34] Up to that point, air operations had averaged only 50 strike sorties a night, in sharp contrast to Desert Storm, in which the daily attack sortie rate was closer to 1000. The operational goal of Allied Force was still officially described as merely seeking to "degrade" Serbia's military capability. In one of the first hints of growing concern that the air effort was not going well, a senior U.S. general spoke of at least "several weeks" of needed attacks to beat down VJ and MUP forces to the breaking point.[35] Similarly, by the start of the second week, an administration official declared that the goal of the bombing was to "break the will" of the Belgrade leadership, implying an open-ended air employment strategy.[36] Earlier, administration spokesmen had indicated that they believed that just a few days of bombing would do the trick.

NATO soon discovered that it was dealing with a cunning opponent who was quite accomplished at hiding. As a result, it conceded that it was being forced to "starve rather than shoot them out."[37] Even with clear skies at the beginning of the third week, NATO pilots were having little success at interdicting those VJ and MUP troops and

---

[33]Bradley Graham, "Bombing Spreads," *Washington Post*, March 29, 1999.

[34]The USAF flew 84 percent of those sorties, the NATO allies 10 percent, and the U.S. Navy 6 percent.

[35]Graham, "Bombing Spreads."

[36]Craig R. Whitney, "NATO Had Signs Its Strategy Would Fail Kosovars," *New York Times*, April 1, 1999.

[37]William Drozdiak and Bradley Graham, "NATO Frustration Grows as Mission Falls Short," *Washington Post*, April 8, 1999.

paramilitary thugs in Kosovo who were carrying out the executions, village burnings, and forced emigration of Kosovar Albanians, to say nothing of finding and attacking their tanks and artillery. Since attacking dispersed VJ troops directly was proving to be too difficult, attacks against fielded forces concentrated instead on second-order effects by going after bases, supplies, and petroleum, oil, and lubricants (POL).

On Day 6, Clark sought NATO approval to increase the pressure on Milosevic by attacking the defense and interior ministry headquarters in Belgrade. That request was disapproved by NATO's political leaders, on the declared ground that such strikes were still "premature."[38] The list of approved targets increased by about 20 percent at the end of the first week. Yet Clark still did not receive the full authority from NATO that he had sought. NATO Secretary General Javier Solana, in particular, expressed misgivings about a larger target set, saying that he was not persuaded that the time had come yet to intensify the operation so dramatically. As a result, Clark was forced to improvise changes to an original plan that had called for slow-motion escalation, punctuated by pauses, disturbingly comparable to the flawed strategy employed during Operation Rolling Thunder over North Vietnam a generation earlier.

Phase III, which entailed escalated attacks against military leadership, command and control centers, weapons depots, fuel supplies, and other targets in and around Belgrade, commenced de facto on Day 9 with strikes against infrastructure targets in Serbia. These included the Petrovaradin bridge on the Danube at Novi Sad; a bridge on the Magura-Belacevac railway; the main water supply to Novi Sad; and targets near Pec, Zatric, Decane, Dragodan, Vranjevac, Bajin Basta, and the Pristina airport.[39] No targets in or near Belgrade, however, were attacked. At this point, Allied Force was still generating no more than 50 ground-attack sorties a day.[40] There was mounting unease over the fact that attacks against empty barracks

---

[38]Thomas W. Lippman and Dana Priest, "NATO Builds Firepower for 24-Hour Attacks," *Washington Post*, March 30, 1999.

[39]The NAC did not formally approve strikes on Phase III targets per se, although it did assent to target classes within Phase III.

[40]Hewson, "Operation Allied Force," p. 22.

and other military facilities were having no effect on Serb behavior now that VJ and MUP forces were well dispersed. It soon became evident that Milosevic had hunkered down in a calculated state of siege. Evidently sensing that he had accomplished many of his goals on the ground and believing that he could now succeed in dividing NATO, he declared a unilateral cease-fire on April 6. The United States and NATO, however, rejected that transparent ploy and pressed ahead with their attacks.

U.S. naval aviation, unavailable for the initial phase of Operation Allied Force, joined the fray when the aircraft carrier USS *Theodore Roosevelt* arrived on station in the Ionian Sea south of Italy two weeks afterward, on April 6. The air wing assigned to the *Theodore Roosevelt* flew complete and self-sustaining strike packages, including F-14Ds and F/A-18s for surface-attack operations, EA-6Bs for the suppression of enemy air defenses, F-14s in the role of airborne forward air controllers, and E-2Cs performing as ABCCC platforms. These packages typically flew missions only against dispersed and hidden enemy forces in Kosovo, although on one occasion, on April 15, they struck a hardened aircraft bunker at the Serbian air base at Podgorica in Montenegro in the first of several allied efforts to neutralize a suspected air threat against the U.S. Army's Task Force Hawk deployed in Albania (see below).[41]   The E-2C, normally operated as an airborne early warning (AEW) platform to screen the carrier battle group from enemy air threats, was used in Allied Force to provide an interface between the CAOC and naval air assets

---

[41]Conversation with Vice Admiral Daniel J. Murphy, USN, commander, 6th Fleet, aboard USS *LaSalle*, Gaeta, Italy, June 8, 2000. See also Vice Admiral Daniel J. Murphy, USN, "The Navy in the Balkans," *Air Force Magazine*, December 1999, p. 49. According to a later account by General Jumper, the strike against the Podgorica airfield was the most concentrated effort placed on any target throughout the entire course of Allied Force. To satisfy SACEUR's objective, General Short needed to neutralize the airfield's sortie generation capacity completely. At the time the target was selected, only 50 percent of the aim points required to meet that objective had been identified. It took 48 hours to accomplish the additional target analysis and to free up additional required NATO assets to carry out this strike. Since the *Theodore Roosevelt* had just arrived in the theater, it had not been tasked in the April 15 Air Tasking Order and accordingly had assets that were immediately available. As a result, F-14 and F/A-18 aircraft struck the hardened aircraft bunker (the highest-value critical element) and used CAOC (Combined Air Operations Center) assets to assist in targeting and weaponeering. Other NATO assets struck the remaining critical elements 48 hours later and met SACEUR's objectives. Conversation with General John P. Jumper, USAF, Hq Air Combat Command, Langley AFB, Virginia, May 15, 2001.

operating in the theater, including both strikers and intelligence collectors.[42]

It was hard during the first few weeks for outside observers to assess and validate the Pentagon's and NATO's claims of making progress because U.S. and NATO officials had so deliberately refrained from disclosing any significant details about the operation. Instead, administration and NATO sources limited themselves to vague generalizations about the air war's effects, using such hedged terms as "degrading," "disrupting," and "debilitating" rather than the more unambiguous "destroying." On this studiously close-mouthed policy, the Defense Department's spokesman, Kenneth Bacon, declared that a precedent was being intentionally set, since both Secretary Cohen and General Shelton had seen a need to "change the culture of the Pentagon and make people more alert to the dangers that can flow from being too generous—or you could say profligate or lax— with operational details."[43]

In one of the first tentative strikes against enemy infrastructure, the main telecommunications building in Pristina, the capital city of Kosovo, was taken out by two GBU-20 LGBs dropped by an F-15E on April 6. Yet the air effort as a whole remained but a faint shadow of Operation Desert Storm, with only 28 targets throughout all of Yugoslavia attacked out of 439 sorties in a 24-hour period during the operation's third week.[44] As for the hoped-for "strategic" portion of the air war against the Serb heartland, Clark was still being refused permission by NATO's political leaders to attack the state-controlled television network throughout Yugoslavia. On April 12, attacks were

---

[42]See Commander Wayne D. Sharer, USN, "The Navy's War over Kosovo," *Proceedings*, U.S. Naval Institute, October 1999, pp. 26–29; and Robert Wall, "E-2Cs Become Battle Managers with Reduced AEW Role," *Aviation Week and Space Technology*, May 10, 1999, p. 38.

[43]Jason DeParle, "Allies' Progress Remains Unclear as Few Details Are Made Public," *New York Times*, April 5, 1999.

[44]In fairness to that effort, however, and given the many constraints that affected it— in contrast to the far fewer constraints that affected Desert Storm—weather, mainly an irritant during the Gulf War, was a significant factor during Operation Allied Force. Bad weather, combined with the higher population density of Serbia, the concern for collateral damage, and the increased surface-to-air threat, could easily have contributed to a lower relative intensity of strike operations. I thank Major Richard Leatherman, Hq Air Force Doctrine Center, for having called this possibility to my attention.

conducted against an oil refinery at Pancevo and other infrastructure targets, with the Pentagon announcing that all of Yugoslavia's oil refineries had been destroyed but that some stored fuel remained available. Also on April 12, the 20th day of the air attacks, NATO missions into the newly designated Kosovo Engagement Zone (KEZ) commenced with attempted attacks against VJ and MUP tanks, artillery, wheeled vehicles, and other assets fielded in Kosovo, in response to Belgrade's escalated ethnic cleansing of the embattled province.

By the third week, NATO's strategic goals had shifted from seeking to erode Milosevic's ability to force an exodus of Kosovar Albanian civilians to enforcing a withdrawal of Serb forces from Kosovo and a return of the refugees home. That shift in strategy was forced by Milosevic's early seizure of the initiative and his achievement of a near–fait accompli on the ethnic cleansing front. Up to that point, President Clinton had merely insisted that the operation's goal was to ensure that Milosevic's military capability would be "seriously diminished."[45]

As Operation Allied Force continued to bog down entering its third week, the influential London *Economist* pointedly observed that it was not "just NATO whose credibility is at risk. At home, the Defense Department's post-Gulf-war prestige is also in the balance, along with the doctrines of high-tech dominance that the Gulf war encouraged people to believe. America's faith in air power, formed by the precision bombing of Iraqi targets, has already been tested by Mr. Hussein's durability. If the current bombing fails to unseat Mr. Milosevic, the air power doctrine could collapse."[46] Numerous factors accounted for why the operation's early performance had proven so disappointing. They included adverse weather, difficult terrain, a wily and determined opponent, poor strategy choices by the Clinton administration and NATO's political leaders, and, perhaps most of all, the burdens of having to coordinate an air operation with 18 often highly independent-minded allies.

---

[45]John M. Broder, "Clinton Says Milosevic Hurts Claim to Kosovo," *New York Times*, March 31, 1999.

[46]"Hope for the Best, and a Spot of Golf," *The Economist*, April 3, 1999, p. 9.

By the end of the third week, in large measure out of frustration over the operation's continued inability to get at the dug-in and elusive VJ positions in Kosovo, Clark requested a deployment of 300 more aircraft to support the effort. That request, which would increase the total number of committed U.S. and allied aircraft to nearly 1,000, entailed more than twice the number of allied aircraft (430) on hand when the operation began on March 24—and almost half of what the allied coalition had had available for Desert Storm. For the United States, it represented a 60 percent increase over the 500 U.S. aircraft already deployed (see Figure 3.1 for the ultimate proportions of U.S. and allied aircraft provided to support Allied Force). Among other things, it prompted understandable concern about where to base

RAND *MR1365-3.1*

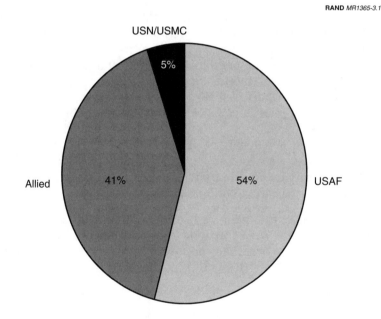

SOURCE: AWOS Fact Sheet.

Figure 3.1—U.S. and Allied Aircraft Contributions

them, with NATO looking to France, Germany, Hungary, Turkey, and the Czech Republic for possible options.[47]

The call for 300 additional aircraft followed on the heels of an earlier request by Clark for 82 more aircraft, which had been promptly approved by the Pentagon. This time, Pentagon officials expressed surprise at the size of Clark's request and openly questioned whether it would be approved in its entirety.[48] The principal concern was that it would draw precious assets, notably such low-density/high-demand aircraft as the E-3 airborne warning and control system (AWACS) and EA-6B Prowler, away from Iraq and Korea. The service chiefs reportedly complained that Clark's requested quantities represented a clear case of overkill and that USEUCOM was not making the most of the forces already at its disposal.

In addition, Clark asked for the USS *Enterprise* and its 70-aircraft air wing, which would necessitate extending the carrier's cruise length and thereby breaking a firm Navy rule of not keeping aircrews and sailors at sea for any longer than six months at a single stretch. The request was opposed by the chief of naval operations, Admiral Jay Johnson, and Secretary of the Navy Richard Danzig. In the end, the *Enterprise* was made available by the Navy for diversion to the Adriatic as requested, but its air wing was never tasked by the CAOC, and it never participated in Allied Force. Once the additional aircraft were approved, NATO asked Hungary to make bases available and Turkey to help absorb those aircraft. Figure 3.2 shows how the in-theater buildup of aircraft ultimately played itself out.

As a part of his requested force increment, Clark also asked for a deployment of Army AH-64 Apache attack helicopters. Although the other aircraft were eventually approved by Secretary Cohen and the Joint Chiefs of Staff (JCS), this particular request was initially

---

[47]Steven Lee Myers, "Pentagon Said to Be Adding 300 Planes to Fight Serbs," *New York Times*, April 13, 1999.

[48]One former senior U.S. officer commented that Clark had presented "a wish list that would choke a horse." Elaine M. Grossman, "Clark's Firepower Request for Kosovo Prompts Anxiety Among Chiefs," *Inside the Pentagon*, April 15, 1999.

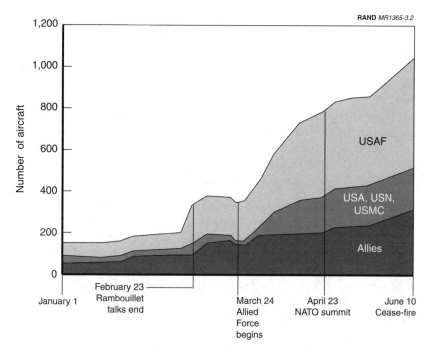

SOURCE: Hq USAFE/SA.

Figure 3.2—In-Theater Aircraft Buildup

disapproved, on the avowed premise that since attack helicopters are typically associated with land combat, the introduction of Apaches might be misperceived by some allies as a precursor to a ground operation. A more serious concern almost surely was that the Apaches might not survive were they to be committed to combat in the still-lethal Serb SAM and AAA environment.

In the end, despite Army and JCS reluctance, Clark prevailed in his request for the Apaches and announced that 24 would be deployed to Albania from their home base at Illesheim, Germany. Pentagon spokesmen went out of their way to stress that the Apaches were intended solely as an extension of the air effort and not as an implied prelude to future ground operations.[49] To support the major aircraft buildup requested by Clark, the Pentagon asked President Clinton to authorize a call-up of 33,000 U.S. reservists and National Guard members—in the largest single reserve-force activation since Desert Shield in 1990–1991, when 265,000 Guard and reserve personnel had been mobilized for possible combat or combat-support duty in the Gulf. As the bombing entered its 27th day, Clinton asked Congress for $5.458 billion in emergency funding to continue financing the air effort, with $3.6 billion to cover air operations from March 24 to the end of FY99, $698 million for additional cruise missiles and precision-guided munitions (PGMs), and $335 million for refugee relief.

Meanwhile, Operation Allied Force remained as stalled as ever, with no sign of tangible progress. Clark had wanted to go after command bunkers and other vital targets in Serbia from the very start of the operation, but it took more than a month for NATO's political leaders to approve an attack on Milosevic's villa at Dobanovci. The Dutch government steadfastly refused to grant approval to bomb his presidential palace because the latter was known to contain a painting by Rembrandt.[50] NATO's ambassadors would not even approve strikes against occupied VJ barracks out of expressed concern over causing too many casualties among helpless enemy conscripts.[51]

By the end of the first month, as many as 80 percent of the strikes conducted had been revisits to fixed targets that had been attacked at least once previously. This was due in part to rapid enemy regeneration and reconstitution efforts, but mainly to the limited number of targets that had been approved by NATO's civilian leaders, the often maddeningly slow target generation and approval process, and

---

[49]Bradley Graham and Dana Priest, "Allies to Begin Flying Refugees Abroad," *Washington Post*, April 5, 1999. In his subsequent memoirs, Clark frankly excoriated what he called "the reluctant Army mind-set in Washington" on this issue and dismissed other critics of his requested AH-64 commitment as "the voices of conventional air power" coming from "commanders who had no experience with the Apaches." General Wesley K. Clark, *Waging Modern War: Bosnia, Kosovo, and the Future of Combat*, New York, Public Affairs, 2001, pp. 230, 278.

[50]To which General Naumann countered in resigned exasperation: "It isn't a good Rembrandt." Robbins, Ricks, and King, Jr., "Milosevic's Resolve Spawned More Unity in Alliance and a Wider Target List."

[51]Michael Ignatieff, "The Virtual Commander: How NATO Invented a New Kind of War," *The New Yorker*, August 2, 1999, p. 32.

SACEUR's desire to keep the bombs falling on Serbia notwithstanding those constraints. The Serbs repeatedly demonstrated an ability to perform workarounds and rebuild their damaged communications facilities, with some IADS installations being brought back on line less than 24 hours of having been attacked.[52] Furthermore, among all the Air Tasking Order (ATO) releases of combat aircraft against preassigned targets, some failed to get airborne because of weather cancellations or maintenance-related aborts, and others either returned home without having expended their ordnance because of rules-of-engagement constraints or having failed to hit their assigned aim points when they did succeed in dropping munitions. These considerations also figured prominently in the low effectiveness of the overall effort.

As the air war entered its fifth week, Clark admitted that Milosevic was still pouring reinforcements into Kosovo continuously and that "if you actually added up what's there on a given day, you might find that he's strengthened his forces in there."[53] Much as during some periods of Desert Storm, adverse weather at the five-week point had forced a cancellation or failure of more than half of all scheduled bombing sorties on 20 of the first 35 days of air attacks. Seemingly resigned to a waiting game as the air war appeared stalled after more than a month of continual bombing, a senior NATO diplomat confessed that it now felt as though Operation Allied Force "had been put on autopilot. Now we are basically waiting for something to crack in Belgrade."[54] In light of the stalled offensive, some saw the air war now threatening to stretch into summer 1999, if not longer.

---

[52]Bradley Graham and John Lancaster, "Most NATO Bombing Raids Target Previously Hit Sites," *Washington Post*, April 21, 1999. In fairness to NATO planners, some of those reattacks were valid, because a few especially large area targets entailed numerous individual aim points, some of which were missed in the initial attacks. The vast majority, however, merely entailed what many frustrated NATO crewmembers referred to as "bouncing rubble," having no practical effect and presenting considerable added risk to their own survivability. It was not uncommon for aircrews to complain vocally about having their "warm bodies sent out all over again to turn bricks into powder."

[53]Craig R. Whitney, "NATO Chief Admits Bombs Fail to Stem Serb Operations," *New York Times*, April 28, 1999.

[54]Neil King, Jr., "War Against Yugoslavia Lapses into Routine, but Clock Is Ticking," *Wall Street Journal*, May 6, 1999.

NATO FINALLY ESCALATES

In what proved in hindsight to be a watershed development for Operation Allied Force, the NATO summit that convened in Washington on April 23–25 to commemorate the alliance's 50th anniversary was pivotal in solidifying NATO's collective determination not to lose. As President Clinton's national security adviser, Samuel Berger, later attested, NATO's leaders unanimously agreed at the summit that "we will not lose. We will not lose. Whatever it takes, we will not lose."[55] Part of the mounting pressure on U.S. and NATO leaders to show greater resolution emanated from a public mood on both sides of the Atlantic that was growing increasingly sensitive to, and emboldened by, the horrific privations inflicted on helpless Kosovar Albanians by their Serb oppressors, shown daily on worldwide television—a public reaction, one might add, that calls into serious question the oft-heard assertion that Milosevic "won" the media campaign. The ugly spectacle of the ethnic cleansing push finally drove the allied leaders to turn the corner at the Washington summit, after which, as General Jumper later observed, "we really had the level of consensus we should have had to start this thing off. . . . After the Washington summit, there was no way that NATO was going to let itself fail."[56]

That consensus, along with the refugee crisis, occasioned an increased NATO willingness to attack major infrastructure targets. Eventually, thanks to this heightened inclination to ramp up the pressure, NATO's Master Target File grew from only 169 targets on the eve of the air effort to more than 976 by its end in early June.[57] Once the call for a substantially expanded target list had prevailed, the new goal became punishing Belgrade's political and military elites, weakening Milosevic's domestic power base, and demonstrat-

---

[55]Doyle McManus, "Clinton's Massive Ground Invasion That Almost Was," *Los Angeles Times*, June 9, 2000.

[56]General John Jumper, USAF, "Oral Histories Accomplished in Conjunction with Operation Allied Force/Noble Anvil."

[57]Dana Priest, "Target Selection Was Long Process," *Washington Post*, September 20, 1999. One must take care, however, not to confuse Master Target File growth with approved target growth. Although target *nominations* increased dramatically as the air war entered full swing, getting those targets individually approved remained a challenge throughout the air war to the very end.

ing by force of example that he and his fellow perpetrators of the abuses in Kosovo would find no sanctuary.

Even before the Washington summit, NATO's targeting efforts had already begun to focus gradually not just on dispersed and hidden enemy forces in Kosovo, but also on what NATO officials had come to characterize as the four pillars of Milosevic's power—the political machine, the media, the security forces, and the economic system. New targets added to the approved list included national oil refineries, petroleum depots, road and rail bridges over the Danube, railway lines, military communications sites, and factories capable of producing weapons and spare parts.[58] The first attacks against state radio and television stations in Belgrade took place on April 21, with three cruise missiles temporarily shutting down three channels run by Milosevic's wife, Mira Markovic, destroying the 12th through the 17th floors of the building, and killing several journalists and technicians, after NATO had issued a warning to employees to vacate the buildings. (Transmissions resumed 11 hours later, occasioning a reattack.) With that escalation, NATO finally brought the air war to Yugoslavia's political and media elite after weeks of hesitation, indicating that it was now emboldened enough to go directly after the business interests of Milosevic's family and friends. In the same attack, U.S. cruise missiles took out the offices of the political parties of Milosevic and his wife. Also on April 21, the Zezel bridge, the last remaining bridge over the Danube at Novi Sad, was dropped.

On April 28, a large, coordinated attack was launched against the Serb military airfield at Podgorica, with 30 munitions employed against such targets as hardened shelters, POL facilities, radar sites, and aircraft and helicopters parked in revetments. During that attack, a 4,700-lb GBU-28 "bunker-buster" was dropped for the first time in Allied Force by an F-15E on an underground aircraft and equipment storage hangar at the Pristina airfield. (By that point in the air war, F-15Es had begun flying seven-and-a-half-hour missions into Serbia directly from RAF Lakenheath in England.)[59] Having

---

[58]Eric Schmitt and Steven Lee Myers, "NATO Said to Focus Raids on Serb Elite's Property," *New York Times*, April 19, 1999.

[59]In the end, however, only some 10 percent of the 48th Fighter Wing's F-15E combat missions were flown out of Lakenheath. The remainder were flown out of the wing's

been repeatedly attacked before with less destructive munitions, that buried hangar and the remaining aircraft, munitions, and supplies kept in it were thought to have been taken out once and for all by this weapon, an assessment which later proved false.[60] Shortly thereafter, an attack was conducted against the national command center in Belgrade, a multistory facility buried more than 100 feet underground and known to have been one of Milosevic's occasional retreats.[61] Equipped with communications, medical facilities, living spaces, and enough food to last more than a month, it was designed to accommodate the entire Yugoslav general staff, top defense officials, and other civilian authorities.[62]

Despite these ramped-up attacks, however, the French leadership remained critical of many proposed strike options. In particular, President Jacques Chirac opposed any attacks against Belgrade's electrical power grid with high-explosive bombs that would physically render it inoperative for any length of time. In an effort to get around Chirac's resistance, U.S. planners worked behind the scenes with French officers in search of more palatable alternatives. As reported in a later U.S. press account, they finally came up with the idea of using the CBU-104(V)2/B cluster munition, formerly referred to by some U.S. Air Force officers as the CBU-94, which could shut down Belgrade's power source for at least a few hours by depositing carbon-graphite threads on the electrical grid, an option to which Chirac finally consented.[63]

Thanks to that modest breakthrough, in possibly the most consequential attack of the air war up to that point, USAF F-117s reportedly dropped CBU-104s on five transformer yards of Yugoslavia's electrical power grid—at Obrenovac, Nis, Bajina Basta, Drmno, and

---

forward operating location at Aviano. Conversation with USAF F-15E aircrews, 492nd Fighter Squadron, RAF Lakenheath, England, April 28, 2001.

[60]Robert Hewson, "Allied Force, Part II: Overwhelming Air Power," *World Air Power Journal*, Winter 1999/2000, p. 99.

[61]Paul Richter, "Bunker-Busters Aim at Heart of Leadership," *Los Angeles Times*, May 5, 1999.

[62]Ibid. The Pentagon's formal report to Congress later indicated that "some" hardened underground command bunkers had been destroyed.

[63]Dana Priest, "France Acted as Group Skeptic," *Washington Post*, September 20, 1999, and David A. Fulghum, "Russians Analyze U.S. Blackout Bomb," *Aviation Week and Space Technology*, February 14, 2000, p. 59.

Novi Sad—during the early morning hours of May 3, temporarily cutting off electricity to 70 percent of the country. These munitions were similar to weapons delivered by TLAMs against the Baghdad electrical power network during the opening hours of Operation Desert Storm. The effects were achieved by means of scattered reels of treated wire which unwound in the air after being released as BLU-114/B submunitions, draping enemy high-voltage power lines like tinsel and causing them to short out.[64] The announced intent of that escalated attack was to shut down the installations that provided electrical power to the VJ's 3rd Army in Kosovo to disrupt military communications and confuse Serb air defenses.[65] Very likely an unspoken intent was also to tighten the air operation's squeeze on the Serbian political leadership and rank and file.[66]

Whatever the case, the attack moved NATO over a new threshold and brought the war, for the first time, directly to the Serbian people. By the end of the seventh week, there began to be reports of Yugoslav officials openly admitting that the country was on the verge of widespread hardship because of the air war's mounting damage to the nation's economy, which had already been weakened by almost four years of international sanctions imposed for Serbia's earlier role in the war in Bosnia.[67] The destruction of one factory in Krujevac that produced automobiles, trucks, and munitions resulted in 15,000 people being put out of work, plus 40,000 more who were employed by the factory's various subcontractors. Attacks against other factories had similar effects on the Yugoslav economy. By the time Allied Force had reached its halfway point, the bombing of infrastructure targets had halved Yugoslavia's economic output and deprived more

---

[64]An inertial navigation system (INS)–guided version of the weapon, a variant of the wind-corrected munitions dispenser, is now said to be entering the U.S. munitions inventory. Fulghum, "Russians Analyze U.S. Blackout Bomb."

[65]David A. Fulghum, "Electronic Bombs Darken Belgrade," *Aviation Week and Space Technology*, May 10, 1999, p. 34.

[66]The results were more symbolic than strategically significant. After the May 3 attack, some 500 workers managed to clear the filaments sufficiently to restart the equipment within 15 hours. After a similar attack on May 8, the threads were cleared within 4 hours. William Arkin, "Smart Bombs, Dumb Targeting?" *Bulletin of the Atomic Scientists*, May/June 2000, p. 52.

[67]Robert Block, "In Belgrade, Hardship Grows Under Sustained Air Assault," *Wall Street Journal*, May 12, 1999.

than 100,000 civilians of jobs. Local economists reported that the effect was more damaging than that of the successive Nazi and allied bombing of Yugoslavia during World War II, when the country was far more rural in its economic makeup. A respected economist at Belgrade University who coordinated a group of economists from the International Monetary Fund (IMF) and World Bank, Mladjan Dinkic, called the results of the bombing an "economic catastrophe," adding that while the Serb population would not die of hunger, "our industrial base will be destroyed and the size of the economy cut in half."[68]

Only during the last two weeks of Allied Force, however, did NATO finally strike with real determination against Serbia's electrical power generating capability, a target set that had been attacked in Baghdad from the very first days of Desert Storm. The earlier "soft" attacks at the beginning of May with graphite filament bombs against the transformer yards of Yugoslavia's main power grid had caused a temporary disruption of the power supply by shorting out transformers and disabling them rather than destroying them. But this time, in perhaps the single most attention-getting strike of the entire air war up to that point, the Yugoslav electrical grid was severely damaged over the course of three consecutive nights starting on May 24. Those attacks, directed against electrical power facilities and related targets in Belgrade, Novi Sad, and Nis, the three largest cities in Serbia, shut off the power to 80 percent of Serbia, leaving millions without electricity or water service. They affected the heart of Yugoslavia's IADS, as well as the computers that ran its banking system and other important national consumers of electricity.[69]

As evidence that these infrastructure attacks were making their effects felt, the early street dancing and carefully orchestrated demonstrations of studied outrage against NATO in response to its earlier pinprick attacks became displaced by a manifest weariness on the part of most residents. Clark continued to stress that the top priority was to destroy the VJ's 3rd Army or run it out of Kosovo. He also ac-

---

[68]Steven Erlanger, "Economists Find Bombing Cuts Yugoslavia's Production in Half," *New York Times*, April 30, 1999.

[69]Philip Bennett and Steve Coll, "NATO Warplanes Jolt Yugoslav Power Grid," *Washington Post*, May 25, 1999.

knowledged, however, the goal of disrupting the everyday life of Serb citizens.[70] By late May, NATO military commanders had received authorization to attack Yugoslavia's civilian telephone and computer networks in an effort to sever communications between Belgrade and Kosovo.[71] In all of this, a long-discredited premise of classic air power theory, namely, that the bombing of civilian infrastructure would eventually prompt a popular reaction, seemed to be showing some signs of validity. Until that key turning point, Clark later observed, Operation Allied Force had been "the only air campaign in history in which lovers strolled down riverbanks in the gathering twilight and ate at outdoor cafes and watched the fireworks."[72]

FACING THE NEED FOR A GROUND OPTION

During the air war's initial weeks, administration officials continued to adhere to their initial hope that an air effort alone would eventually elicit the desired response from Milosevic. Even after Allied Force was well under way, Secretary General Solana announced that he was sure that the bombing would be over before the start of the long-planned Washington summit on April 23 to celebrate NATO's 50th birthday.[73] Deep doubts that the air attacks alone would suffice in forcing Milosevic to knuckle under, however, soon prompted a steady rise in military pressure—notably from some U.S. Air Force leaders directly involved with the air war—for developing at least a fallback option for a ground invasion.[74]

Indeed, even before the operation was a week old, indications had begun to mount that senior administration officials were starting to have second thoughts about the advisability of having peremptorily

---

[70]Ibid.

[71]William Drozdiak, "Allies Target Computer, Phone Links," *Washington Post*, May 27, 1999.

[72]Ignatieff, "The Virtual Commander," p. 35.

[73]James Gerstenzang and Elizabeth Shogren, "Serb TV Airs Footage of 3 Captured U.S. Soldiers," *Los Angeles Times*, April 1, 1999.

[74]On that account, Clark later acknowledged that his air commanders were no happier than he was with the absence of a ground threat, noting that it was "sort of an unnatural act for airmen to fight a ground war without a ground component." Ignatieff, "The Virtual Commander," p. 33.

ruled out a ground option before launching into Allied Force. The chairman of the JCS, General Shelton, for example, remarked that there were no NATO plans "right now" to introduce ground troops short of a peace settlement in Kosovo.[75] In a similarly hedged remark, Secretary Cohen pointed out that the Clinton administration and NATO had no plans to introduce any ground troops "into a hostile environment," leaving open the possibility that they might contemplate putting a ground presence into a Kosovo deemed "nonhostile" before the achievement of a settlement.[76] By the end of the second week, Secretary of State Albright went further yet toward hinting at the administration's growing discomfiture over having ruled out a ground threat when she allowed that NATO might change its position and put in ground troops should the bombing succeed in creating a "permissive environment."[77] Ultimately, the air war's continued indecisiveness led President Clinton himself to concede that he would consider introducing ground troops if he became persuaded that the bombing would not produce the desired outcome. In a clear contradiction to his earlier position on the issue, he asserted that he had "always said that . . . we have not and will not take any option off the table." That statement was later described by a U.S. official as testimony to an ongoing administration effort "to break out of a rhetorical box that we should never have gotten into."[78]

By the start of the third week, a consensus had begun to form in Washington that ground forces might well be needed, if only to salvage NATO's increasingly shaky credibility that was being steadily

---

[75]Paul Richter, "Use of Ground Troops Not Fully Ruled Out," *Los Angeles Times*, March 29, 1999.

[76]Rowan Scarborough, "Military Experts See a Need for Ground Troops," *Washington Times*, March 30, 1999.

[77]Rowan Scarborough, "Momentum for Troops Growing," *Washington Times*, April 5, 1999.

[78]John F. Harris, "Clinton Says He Might Send Ground Troops," *Washington Post*, May 19, 1999. In an earlier attempt at revisionism, Secretary of State Albright upbraided an interviewer by flatly declaring that "we never expected this to be over quickly," in complete contradiction to her categorical pronouncement the first night of the air war 11 days earlier that "I think that this is something, the deter and damage, is something that is achievable within a relatively short time." John Harris, "Reassuring Rhetoric, Reality in Conflict," *Washington Post*, April 8, 1999.

eroded by the air operation's lackluster performance.[79] That dawning realization led to two parallel escalation processes: one highly public—the substantial increase in the number of committed aircraft, the growing number of approved targets and heightened percentage of daily shooter sorties, and the hard attacks conducted against the Yugoslav power grid; and the other largely beneath public scrutiny—namely, more serious discussion within the U.S. government over the need to begin making concrete preparations for a ground intervention. Deputy Secretary of State Strobe Talbott conveyed a "very explicit" warning to Russian envoy Vladimir Chernomyrdin that President Clinton was seriously considering a ground option, a warning which we can assume Chernomyrdin duly passed on to Milosevic.

At the same time, a pronounced rift emerged between Clark and his Pentagon superiors over Clark's insistence on replacing talk with determined action in connection with preparations for a ground invasion. In his memoirs, Clark later gave candid vent to his frustration over this rift when he referred to the "divide between those in Washington who thought they understood war and those [of us] in Europe who understood Milosevic, the mainsprings of his power, and the way to fight on this continent."[80] Earlier in April, he had challenged U.S. and British officers at NATO headquarters to consider "what if" options for a potential ground war. Out of frustration over the refusal of both Washington and his NATO masters to countenance any serious consideration of a ground component to Allied Force, he also asked the Army, shortly after the air war began, to send him a half-dozen officers from the School of Advanced Military Studies at Fort Leavenworth, Kansas, to draw up secret plans for a broad spectrum of ground options, ranging from sending in peacekeepers to police any settlement that might be achieved singlehandedly by the air war to launching a full-fledged, opposed-entry land invasion if all else proved wanting. It soon became clear from

---

[79]Dan Balz, "U.S. Consensus Grows to Send in Ground Troops," *Washington Post*, April 6, 1999.

[80]Clark, *Waging Modern War*, p. 303. As a testament to the depth of his conviction on the criticality of getting serious about laying the groundwork for a land invasion, Clark in mid-May wrote a letter to Secretary General Solana which, he said, "demonstrated at length how moving into ground-force preparations would *exponentially* increase [NATO's] leverage against Milosevic." Ibid, pp. 307–308, emphasis added.

that inquiry that only about a dozen roads led into Kosovo from Albania. Like Kosovo's bridges, they were heavily mined and strongly
defended, with VJ troops well positioned on the high ground of the
most strategically crucial terrain. Accordingly, the study concluded
that the best invasion routes would be from Hungary and Croatia
into the flatter terrain of northern Serbia.

Several administration officials later commented that an invasion
threat from both east and west (namely, from Romania and Croatia
and from Hungary) would have been preferable to one from Albania
alone, where the transportation infrastructure was extremely primi-
tive and where wheeled vehicles would quickly bog down in wet
weather.[81] They further characterized the nascent ground threat as
pointed not just at Kosovo but at Serbia proper, since such an operation would aim directly at Milosevic's greatest vulnerability and, in so
doing, threaten to take down his regime. Secretary General Solana
later allowed that he had authorized NATO's military command to
revise and update plans for a possible ground invasion, while at the
same time indicating that the alliance was still far from any decision
to use ground forces and voicing his conviction that the air effort
would ultimately achieve its objectives.[82]

Throughout this secret ground-options planning, Clark was strongly
resisted by Secretary Cohen and White House security adviser
Berger. But he had the unwavering support of Britain's prime minister, Tony Blair, who had unsuccessfully raised the issue of ground
troops with Clinton at the NATO summit in late April. Not long
thereafter, apparently reflecting growing British concern that air attacks alone would prove insufficient to compel Milosevic to quit,
British Foreign Minister Robin Cook took the lead in mid-May in
proposing that allied ground troops be sent into Kosovo, even in the

---

[81]Interview by RAND staff, Washington, D.C., June 11, 2000. The UK Ministry of Defense's director of operations in Allied Force, Air Marshal Sir John Day, however, later
commented that there was never much military enthusiasm for a double envelopment
through Hungary. Conversation with Air Marshal Day, RAF Innsworth, United Kingdom, July 26, 2000.

[82]Thomas W. Lippman and Bradley Graham, "NATO Chief Asks Review of Invasion
Planning," *Washington Post*, April 22, 1999.

absence of a peace agreement, once the bombing had reduced VJ forces to a point where they could mount only scattered resistance.[83]

After a month of continued inconclusiveness in the air war, one began to hear talk not only at NATO headquarters but also in Washington regarding the need for a credible ground threat to evict the marauding Serb forces from Kosovo. As the end of the second month approached, NATO appeared more than ever headed toward conceding at least the possibility of a land invasion, even though the Clinton administration would still not brook even a hint of encouraging public debate over the subject. As one possible explanation for the administration's continued reluctance to embrace the growing need for a ground operation of some sort, polls taken during the air war's seventh week indicated that war fatigue was setting in, occasioning the first significant decline in U.S. public support. That support dropped from 65 percent in late April to 59 percent by mid-May, with opposition to the air war rising from 30 to 38 percent during the same period.[84]

By late May, with winter weather promising to become a limiting factor as early as the beginning of October, Clark had begun to stress that time was now critical with respect to planning for a ground invasion. On one occasion, he expressly warned NATO's civilian leaders and Washington alike: "Don't let the decision make itself."[85] In the British view, September 15 was absolutely the latest date on which a ground push could start, based on a determination that it would take a minimum of one month to complete the operation.[86]

By most accounts, the turning point in facing up to the need for a serious ground option came on May 27, when Cohen met secretly in Bonn with his four principal NATO counterparts, the British, French, German, and Italian defense ministers, in a six-and-a-half-hour ses-

---

[83]Eric Schmitt and Michael R. Gordon, "British Pressing Partners to Deploy Ground Troops," *New York Times*, May 18, 1999.

[84]Richard Morin, "Poll Shows Most Americans Want Negotiations on Kosovo," *Washington Post*, May 18, 1999.

[85]Carla Anne Robbins and Thomas E. Ricks, "Time Is Running Out If Invasion Is to Remain Option Before Winter," *Wall Street Journal*, May 21, 1999.

[86]Conversation with Air Marshal Sir John Day, RAF, UK Ministry of Defense director of operations in Allied Force, RAF Innsworth, United Kingdom, July 26, 2000.

sion convened expressly to consider what it would take to mount a land invasion and to weigh the merits and risks of such a course of action. By one informed account, that meeting was pivotal in getting the allies to come to closure once and for all on the need to begin serious preparations for a land invasion.[87] The chief of Britain's defense forces, General Sir Charles Guthrie, was an especially strong backer of a ground option, as was the British defense minister, George Robertson. The RAF also had agreed from the start that a ground option was needed. As but one indicator that acceptance of the need for such an option had, by that time, become all but a fait accompli, British planning had progressed to the point of actual reserve call-up and the booking of ferries and civil air transports to deliver British troops to the combat zone. The Bonn ministerial meeting thus took the process begun at the NATO summit a step further toward solidifying the idea that NATO was going to win, come what may, by extending that notion to include acceptance of a ground invasion should matters come to that.

By the end of May, NATO was generally acknowledged by the media as "inching ever closer to some kind of ground operation in the Balkans."[88] Lending further credence to that impression, several administration officials later acknowledged that Britain was on board with the United States by that time for a ground invasion if need be. They further acknowledged that most of the allies' concerns about attacking infrastructure targets had been largely put to rest, even though France remained an obstacle, and that it would have been easier to obtain NAC approval to go after increasingly sensitive targets with air attacks once the likelihood of a NATO ground invasion loomed larger.[89]

COUNTDOWN TO CAPITULATION

Following an inadvertent attack on a refugee convoy near Djakovica, Kosovo, on April 14—occasioned in part by a suspected visual misidentification by the participating USAF F-16 pilots (see Chapter

---

[87]Ibid.

[88]Richard J. Newman, "U.S. Troops Edge Closer to Kosovo," *U.S. News and World Report,* June 7, 1999.

[89]Interview by RAND staff, Washington, D.C., July 11, 2000.

Six)—the altitude floor of 15,000 ft that had been imposed at the start of the air war was eased somewhat in the southern portion, and NATO forward air controllers (FACs) flying over Kosovo were cleared to descend to as low as 5,000 ft if necessary, to ensure positive identification of ground targets in the KEZ.[90] Direct attacks on suspected VJ positions in Kosovo by B-52s occurred for the first time on May 5 and again the following day. Clark declared afterward that 10 enemy armor concentrations had been hit and that the Serbs were no longer able to continue their ethnic cleansing. NATO spokesmen further reported that enemy troops in the field were running low on fuel and that VJ and MUP morale had declined.[91] A day later, NATO claimed that it had destroyed 20 percent of the VJ's artillery and armor deployed in Kosovo. As for infrastructure attacks, only two of the 31 bridges across the Danube in Yugoslavia were said to be still functional by the end of the week. During the second week of May, however, enemy attack helicopters conducted an attack against the village of Kosari along the main supply route for the KLA. They also served as spotters for VJ artillery against KLA pockets of resistance.[92] Those operations indicated that NATO had done an imperfect job of preventing any and all enemy combat aircraft from flying.

On May 12, roughly 600 Allied Force sorties were launched all told, including the highest daily number of shooter sorties to date. (See Figure 3.3 for the overall trend line in U.S. and allied sorties flown over the 78-day course of Allied Force. Most of the troughs in that trend line indicate sortie drawdowns or cancellations occasioned by nonpermissive weather over Serbia.) The multiple waves of successive large force packages commenced with a sunrise launch of 36 aircraft, including USAF F-16s and A-10s, RAF Harrier GR. Mk 7s, French Jaguars and Super Etendards, Italian AMXs, and Canadian CF-18s. A subsequent late-morning launch featured 32 aircraft, consisting of RAF Tornado GR. Mk 1s, French Jaguars, and USAF

---

[90]The 15,000-ft restriction was never done away with over Serbia and Montenegro, however, and over Kosovo it was eased only for FACs and for some weapon deliveries in selected circumstances.

[91]Hewson, "Allied Force, Part II," p. 102.

[92]R. Jeffrey Smith and Dana Priest, "Yugoslavia Near Goals in Kosovo," *Washington Post*, May 11, 1999.

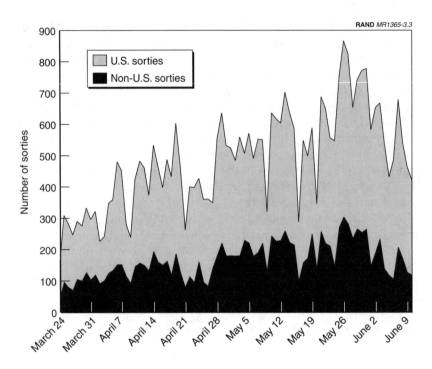

SOURCE: Hq USAFE/SA.

Figure 3.3—U.S. and Allied Sorties Flown

F-16s, followed by 30 F-15Es and 16 more later in the surge. A mid-afternoon strike with 28 jets was then followed by 24 more, with the day finally ending with a midnight package of 38 strikers, including B-1Bs and B-52s.[93]

Three days later, General Jumper declared that NATO had achieved de facto air superiority over Yugoslavia, enabling attacking aircraft to "go anywhere we want in the country, any time," even though the skies were admittedly "still dangerous."[94] Not long thereafter, an option became available to attack from the north with 24 F/A-18Ds of Marine Air Group 31 deployed to Taszar, Hungary. That option

---

[93]Hewson, "Allied Force, Part II," p. 109.

[94]Ibid., p. 110.

promised to further isolate Yugoslavia, make it appear surrounded, and force its remaining air defenses to work harder by having to look in more than one direction rather than mainly toward a single attack axis from the west. It also promised to avoid adding to the already severe air traffic congestion over the Adriatic and in other western approaches to Yugoslavia.

As allied air operations against VJ troops in the KEZ became more aggressive, a clear preference for the USAF's A-10 over the Army's AH-64 Apaches in Albania became evident because weather conditions over Kosovo had improved by that time, rendering the Apache's under-the-weather capability no longer pertinent and because enough of the Serb IADS had been deemed weakened or intimidated to make it safer to operate the A-10s at lower altitudes. Moreover, the Apaches were deemed to be more susceptible to AAA and infrared SAM threats than were the faster and higher-flying A-10s. President Clinton himself later reinforced those reservations when he commented in mid-May that the risk to the Apache pilots remained too great and that because of recent weather improvements, "most of what the Apaches could do [could now] be done by the A-10s at less risk."[95]

Later on in May, allied fighters and USAF heavy bombers committed against suspected enemy troop positions in the KEZ were joined for the first time by USAF AC-130 gunships, which offered an additional standoff capability against enemy vehicles and other ground targets with their accurate 40mm Bofors gun, 25mm Gatling gun, and 105mm howitzer. The AC-130, however, was only used over areas where there was no known or suspected presence of operational SAM batteries and always flew above the reach of IR SAMs and AAA. When targets of opportunity presented themselves on rare occasions, sensor platforms that detected ground vehicular movement would pass the coordinates and target characterization information to the

---

[95]Robert Burns, "Use of Apache Copters Is Not Expected Soon," *Philadelphia Inquirer*, May 19, 1999. In what may have been intended as an attempt to lessen the sting of this leadership ruling, one Army source suggested that sending the Apaches in had been meant all along merely as a scare tactic to induce Milosevic to negotiate. The source added that if they had really been intended to be used, the more modern and capable Apache Longbows would have been deployed instead. "Obviously, it was just for show, not for go." Rowan Scarborough, "Apaches Were Sent to Scare Serbs," *Washington Times*, May 21, 1999.

EC-130 ABCCC, which, in turn, would vector NATO attack aircraft into the appropriate kill box, first to confirm that the targets were valid and then to engage them. The ABCCC also controlled the ingress and egress of attacking fighters and maintained battlespace deconfliction throughout ongoing operations.

Once Serbia's air defenses became a less imminent threat, the air war also saw a heightened use of B-52s, B-1s, and other aircraft carrying unguided bombs.[96] By the end of May, some 4,000 free-fall bombs, around 30 percent of the total number of munitions expended altogether, had been dropped on known or suspected VJ targets in the KEZ. There was a momentary resurgence of Serb SAM activity later that month, with more than 30 SAMs reportedly fired on May 27, the greatest number launched any night in nearly a month.[97] That heightened activity was assessed as reflecting a determined last-ditch Serb effort to down at least one more NATO aircraft. (An F-117 had been shot down during the air war's fourth night, and a USAF F-16 had later been downed on the night of May 2.)[98]

---

[96] The Block D version of the B-1 employed in Allied Force was configured to carry the GBU-31 joint direct attack munition (JDAM), but only the B-2 actually delivered that still-scarce munition.

[97] It bears noting here that the highly effective GAU-8 30mm cannon carried by the A-10 saw use only 156 times in Allied Force because of the extreme slant range that was required by the 5,000-ft altitude restriction (comments on an earlier draft by Hq USAFE/SA, April 6, 2001). At that range, the principal problem for today's A-10 pilots is not hitting the target; it is *seeing* the target. At a 30-degree dive angle from 5,000 ft, the slant range to target is 10,000 ft.

[98] Glenn Burkins, "Serbs Intensify Effort to Down Allied Warplanes," *Wall Street Journal*, May 28, 1999. In the second instance, the ABCCC drew on instantly accessible satellite photos and maps maintained in a National Imagery and Mapping Agency computerized database to identify potential obstacles, such as power lines, in order to plot a safe course for the rescue helicopter that recovered the downed pilot. Bill Gertz and Rowan Scarborough, "Inside the Ring," *Washington Times*, May 19, 2000. Although there was definitely a pronounced increase in enemy SAM activity during the night of May 27 in an apparent effort to down a NATO pilot at any cost, it bears stressing that there were *no* nights during Allied Force without at least a few SAM shots, approximately 35 nights with 10 or more shots, and at least 13 nights with 20 or more shots. The highest number of shots observed (significantly higher than the number observed on May 27) was on the night of the F-16 loss. Overall, enemy SAM activity levels tracked closely with allied air attack levels. Low-observable and cruise-missile-only strikes prompted little enemy IADS reaction, whereas trolling for SAMs with F-16CJs and CGs and large conventional attack packages always generated a proportionately large enemy reaction. This trend remained consistent throughout the air war from start to finish. Comments on an earlier draft by Hq USAFE/IN, May 18, 2001.

In what was initially thought to have been a pivotal turn of events in the air effort against enemy ground forces, the newly enlarged and hastily trained KLA, estimated to have been equipped with up to 30,000 automatic weapons, including heavy machine guns, sniper rifles, rocket-propelled grenades, and antitank weapons, launched a counteroffensive on May 26 against VJ troops in Kosovo. That thrust, called Operation Arrow, involved more than 4,000 guerrillas of the 137th and 138th Brigades and drew artillery support from the Albanian army, with the aim of driving into Kosovo from two points along the province's southwestern border, seizing control of the highway connecting Prizren and Pec, and securing a safe route for the KLA to resupply its beleaguered fighters inside Kosovo.

Operation Arrow represented the first major assault by KLA rebels in more than a year. It was evidently intended to demonstrate both to Milosevic and to NATO that the KLA remained a credible fighting presence in Kosovo. The assault was thwarted at first by VJ artillery and infantry counterattacks, which indicated that the VJ still had plenty of fight in it despite 70 days of intermittent NATO bombing. Three days after launching their assault, the rebels found themselves badly on the defensive, with some 250 KLA fighters pinned down by 700 VJ troops near Mount Pastrik, a 6,523-ft peak just inside the Kosovo-Albanian border.

For abundant good reasons, not least of which was a determination to avoid even a hint of appearing to legitimize the KLA's independent actions, NATO had no interest in serving as the KLA's de facto air force and repeatedly refused to provide it with the equipment it would have needed for its troops to have performed directly as ground forward air controllers (FACs). The KLA did, however, receive allied support in other ways. There had been earlier unconfirmed reports going as far back as the air war's second week that KLA guerrillas had been covertly assisting NATO in the latter's effort to find and target VJ forces in Kosovo.[99] The first known direct NATO air support to the KLA occurred on the day that Operation Arrow commenced. It was confirmed both by KLA fighters in Albania and by military officials in Washington.

---

[99]Alessandra Stanley, "Albanian Fighters Say They Aid NATO in Spotting Serb Targets," *New York Times*, April 2, 1999.

Although the Clinton administration denied helping the KLA directly, U.S. officials did admit that NATO had responded to "urgent" KLA requests for air support to turn back the VJ counterattack against its embattled troops near Mount Pastrik. In addition to the support they attempted to provide at Mount Pastrik, NATO aircraft attacked VJ targets near the Kosovar villages of Bucane and Ljumbarda, enabling the rebels to capture those villages. The KLA kept NATO informed of its positions in part so that its troops would not be inadvertently bombed, which had occurred two weeks earlier in an accidental NATO attack on a KLA barracks in Kosari.[100] KLA guerrillas used cell phones to convey target coordinates to their base commanders, who, in turn, relayed that information to NATO military authorities.

Throughout most of Allied Force, NATO and the KLA fought parallel but separate wars against VJ and MUP forces in Kosovo, and both the U.S. government and the KLA denied coordinating their operations in advance. NATO did acknowledge, however, that rebel attacks on the ground had helped flush out VJ troops and armor and to expose them to allied air strikes on at least a few occasions, and that Clark had authorized the communication of KLA target location information to attacking NATO aircrews indirectly through the ABCCC. The KLA further acknowledged that NATO air strikes had helped its ground operations.[101] Despite NATO denials throughout the air war that it was aiding the KLA, it became evident that cooperation between the two was considerably greater than had been previously admitted. As reported by KLA soldiers, the KLA had begun as early as May 10 to supply NATO with target intelligence and other battlefield information at NATO's request, with the KLA's chief of staff, Agim Ceku, working with NATO officers in northern Albania. While refusing to elaborate on specifics, KLA spokesmen admitted that Ceku had been the KLA's principal point of contact with NATO. It was also Ceku who had participated in Croatia's 1995 Operation Storm offen-

---

[100]Dana Priest and Peter Finn, "NATO Gives Air Support to Kosovo Guerrillas," *Washington Post*, June 2, 1999.

[101]Marjorie Miller, "KLA Vows to Disarm If NATO Occupies Kosovo," *Los Angeles Times*, June 7, 1999.

sive that drove out the Krajina Serbs and helped end the fighting in Bosnia.[102]

Ultimately, VJ forces managed to repulse the KLA assault at Mount Pastrik. To do so, however, they had to come out of hiding and move in organized groups, making themselves potential targets, especially for A-10s, on those infrequent occasions when they were detected and approved for attack by the ABCCC or the CAOC.[103] When KLA actions forced VJ troops to concentrate enough tanks and artillery to defend themselves, NATO aircraft were occasionally able to detect and engage them. Enemy ground movements during the final two weeks were often first noted by the E-8 joint surveillance target attack radar system (Joint STARS) or other sensors, even though the VJ studiously sought to maneuver in small enough numbers to avoid being detected. The sensor operators would then transmit the coordinates of suspected enemy troop concentrations to airborne forward air controllers who, in turn, directed both unmanned aerial vehicles (UAVs) and fighters in for closer looks, and ultimately for attacks.[104] KLA ground movements were also displayed aboard the ABCCC, which was coordinating and controlling NATO attacks against VJ armored vehicles in Kosovo, deconflicting the attacking aircraft, and ensuring that KLA forces in close contact with the VJ were not inadvertently hit. Those operations represented classic instances of close air support, with KLA and enemy forces in close contact on the ground. The ABCCC and attacking NATO aircrews received commands directly from the allied CAOC in Vicenza, Italy, which, in at least one case, aborted an attack out of concern for hitting KLA fighters.[105]

Despite this heightened activity in the KEZ during the air war's final days, however, the attacks did better at keeping VJ and MUP troops

---

[102]Matthew Kaminski and John Reed, "NATO Link to KLA Rebels May Have Helped Seal Victory," *Wall Street Journal*, July 6, 1999.

[103]William Drozdiak and Anne Swardson, "Military, Diplomatic Offensives Bring About Accord," *Washington Post*, June 4, 1999.

[104]Tony Capaccio, "JSTARS Led Most Lethal Attacks on Serbs," *Defense Week*, July 6, 1999, p. 13.

[105]Michael R. Gordon, "A War out of the Night Sky: 10 Hours with a Battle Team," *New York Times*, June 3, 1999.

dispersed and hidden than they did at actually engaging and killing them in any significant numbers. Most attack sorties tasked to the KEZ did not release their weapons against valid military targets, but rather against so-called dump sites for jettisoning previously unexpended munitions, sites that were conveniently billed by NATO target planners as "assembly areas." Even the B-52s and B-1s, for all the free-fall Mk 82 bombs they dropped during the final days, were tasked with delivering a high volume of munitions without causing any collateral damage. After the air war ended, it was never established that any of the bombs delivered by the B-52s and B-1s had achieved any militarily significant destructive effects, or that NATO's cooperation with the KLA had yielded any results of real operational value. The steadily escalating attacks against infrastructure targets in and around Belgrade that were taking place at the same time, however, were beginning to produce a very different effect on Serb behavior.

THE ENDGAME

On June 2, with Operation Allied Force working at peak intensity and with weather and visibility for NATO aircrews steadily improving, Russia's envoy to the Balkans, former Prime Minister Viktor Chernomyrdin, and Finland's President Martti Ahtisaari, the European Union representative, flew to Belgrade to offer Milosevic a plan to bring the conflict to a close. Ahtisaari's inclusion in the process was said by one informed observer to have grown out of a suggestion by Chernomyrdin that value might be gained from including a respected non-NATO player on his mission.[106] The same day, after the two emissaries had essentially served him with an ultimatum that had been worked out and agreed to previously by the United States, Russia, the European Union, and Ahtisaari, Milosevic accepted an international peace proposal. Under the terms of the proposed agreement, he would accede to NATO's demands for a withdrawal of all VJ, MUP, and Serb paramilitary forces from Kosovo; a NATO-led security force in Kosovo; an unmolested return of the refugees to

---

[106]Comments on an earlier draft by Ivo Daalder of the Brookings Institution, Washington, D.C., March 15, 2001. Daalder previously served as director for European affairs on the National Security Council staff in 1995 and 1996, where he was responsible for coordinating U.S. policy for Bosnia.

their homes; and the creation of a self-rule regime for the ethnic Albanian majority that acknowledged Yugoslavia's continued sovereignty over Kosovo. NATO would continue bombing pending the implementation of a military-to-military understanding that had been worked out between NATO and Yugoslavia on the conditions of Yugoslavia's force withdrawal. The agreement, which came on the 72nd day of the air effort, was ratified the day after, on June 3, by the Serb parliament and was rationalized by Milosevic's Socialist Party of Serbia on the ground that it meant "peace and a halt to the evil bombing of our nation."[107]

Milosevic later met with loyalist and opposition leaders to explain the reasons for his decision to accept the peace plan. That was as strong an indicator as any to date that the United States and NATO were at the brink of success in their effort to get Yugoslavia's 40,000 troops removed from Kosovo, the Kosovar refugees returned to their homes, and NATO-dominated peacekeepers on Kosovo's soil to ensure that the agreement was honored by Milosevic. The agreement stipulated that once all occupying VJ and MUP personnel had departed Kosovo, an agreed-upon contingent of Serbs—numbering only in the hundreds, not thousands—could return to Kosovo to provide liaison to the various peacekeeping entities commanded by British Army Lieutenant General Sir Michael Jackson, help clear the minefields that they had earlier laid, and protect Serb interests at religious sites and border crossings.

The two-page draft agreement further called for removing all Serb air defense equipment and weapons deployed within 15 miles of the Kosovo border by the first 48 hours so that NATO aircraft could verify the troop withdrawals unmolested by any threats. The plan envisaged a U.S. sector to be controlled, first, by 1,900 Marines with light vehicles and helicopters standing by aboard three ships in the Aegean and, later, by the full American force complement made up largely of Army tank and infantry units to be brought in from Germany. U.S. forces, including the Marines from the 26th Marine Expeditionary Unit at sea and three Army battalions from the 1st Infantry Division in Germany, would make up 15 percent of the overall

---

[107]Daniel Williams and Bradley Graham, "Yugoslavs Yield to NATO Terms," *Washington Post*, June 4, 1999.

Kosovo Force (KFOR). The agreement similarly provided for British, French, Italian, and German sectors.

NATO refused to commit itself to an early halt to its air attacks, since its leaders knew that it would be extremely difficult to resume the bombing once the refugees began coming home. During the negotiations over the terms of Serb withdrawal, however, NATO pilots were under orders not to attack any enemy positions unless in direct response to hostile acts. After the Serb parliament agreed to the ceasefire, no bombs fell on Belgrade for three consecutive nights. B-52 strikes against dispersed VJ forces, however, continued.

No sooner had this accord been reached in principle than NATO and Serb military officials failed to reach an understanding on the conditions for VJ and MUP withdrawal. The talks quickly degenerated into haggling over when NATO would halt its air attacks and whether Serbia would have more than a week to get its troops out of Kosovo. The proximate cause of the breakdown in talks was a Serb demand that the UN Security Council approve an international peacekeeping force *before* NATO troops entered Kosovo. That heel-dragging suggested that the Serbs were seeking to soften some of the terms of the settlement or, perhaps, were looking for more time to continue their fight with the KLA. Secretary Cohen and General Shelton allowed that extending the Yugoslav withdrawal by several days would be acceptable but that they would not countenance any deliberate attempts at delay. More specifically, the implementation of the Serb withdrawal was hung up on differences over the sequencing of four events: the start of the enemy pullout, a pause in NATO bombing, the passage of a UN resolution, and the entry of international peacekeepers with a "substantial NATO content." In response to this willful foot-dragging, NATO's attacks, which initially had been scaled back after Milosevic accepted the proposed peace plan, resumed their previous level of intensity.

On June 7, at the same time as the talks were under way, VJ forces launched a renewed counterattack against the KLA in an area south of Mount Pastrik, where the two sides had been locked in an artillery duel since May 26. For a time, a major breakthrough in NATO's air effort was thought to have occurred when the defending KLA forces flushed out VJ troops who had been dispersed around Mount Pastrik, creating what NATO characterized as a casebook target-rich environment. Thanks to improved weather, a noticeable degradation of Serb air defenses, and the effective role thought to have been played by the KLA in forcing VJ troops to come out of hiding, two B-52s and two B-1Bs dropped a total of 86 Mk 82s on an open field in a daytime raid near the Kosovo-Albanian border where VJ forces were believed to have been massed.[108] The initially estimated number of enemy troops caught in the open by the attack was 800 to 1,200, with early assessments suggesting that fewer than half had survived the attack.[109] It later appeared, however, that the number of enemy casualties was considerably less than originally believed—if, indeed, the attacking bombers had killed a significant number of VJ troops at all.

Whatever the case, the following day the United States, Russia, and six other member-states agreed on a draft UN Security Council resolution to end the conflict. The resolution called for a complete withdrawal of Serb troops, police, and paramilitary forces from Kosovo and for all countries to cooperate with the war crimes tribunal that had indicted Milosevic.[110] The sequence finally agreed to was that the Serb force withdrawal would commence, NATO would concurrently halt its bombing, and only *after* those two actions occurred would the Security Council vote on the text of the agreement. The last provision was a token concession to Russia and China, whose representatives had insisted that the bombing be stopped before any Security Council vote was taken.

In the end, the VJ acceded to a six-page agreement that permitted a KFOR presence of 50,000 peacekeepers commanded by a NATO general and having sweeping occupation powers over Kosovo. By the terms of the agreement, Serb forces would withdraw along four designated routes over 11 days, under the constant threat of resumed bombing in case of any willful delays.[111] (Belgrade had asked for 17

---

[108]R. Jeffrey Smith and Molly Moore, "Plan for Kosovo Pullout Signed," *Washington Post*, June 10, 1999.

[109]William Drozdiak, "Yugoslav Troops Devastated by Attack," *Washington Post*, June 9, 1999.

[110]Smith and Moore, "Plan for Kosovo Pullout Signed."

[111]At one point in the negotiations, the VJ military delegation leader, Colonel General Svetozar Marjanovic, abruptly walked out of the talks, stating that he needed to

days.) Kosovo was to be ringed by a 5-km buffer zone, and NATO was to provide for the safe return of all refugees. After 78 days of continual bombing by NATO, the agreement was finally signed on June 9 in a portable hangar at a NATO airfield in Kumanovo, Macedonia, five miles south of the Yugoslav border. The 11 days granted to Yugoslavia for the troop withdrawal was another diplomatic concession, considering that NATO had initially insisted that the withdrawal be completed in 7 days.

NATO finally stopped the bombing upon verifying that the Serb withdrawal had begun, after which the UN Security Council approved, by a 14-0 vote with China abstaining, a resolution putting Kosovo under international civilian control and the peacekeeping force under UN authority. With that, President Clinton declared that NATO had "achieved a victory."[112]

Once NATO peacekeeping forces moved in on the ground in Kosovo, they began discovering the full extent of Serb atrocities committed against the Kosovar Albanians. Among other things, they found an interrogation center in Pristina that had been used by Serb police, in which thousands of Kosovar suspects were said to have been "processed." Inside the bowels of the building, they came across garrotes with wooden handles, brass knuckles, broken baseball bats, chainsaws, and leather manacles and straps. They also were told by surviving Kosovars that the Serb police had spent three days burning records before the British paratroopers finally arrived.[113] Later, the British government estimated that some 10,000 ethnic Albanians had died at the hands of marauding Serbs during the course of Operation Allied Force.[114]

As the last of some 40,000 VJ and MUP personnel exited Kosovo on June 20 a few hours ahead of NATO's deadline, NATO declared a formal end to the air war. The bombing had earlier been suspended

---

"consult with authorities in Belgrade." He made it only to a border post and returned to the negotiating table within an hour.

[112]Tim Weiner, "From President, Victory Speech and a Warning," *New York Times*, June 11, 1999.

[113]See Julian Barger, "Bloody Paper Chain May Link Torture to Milosevic," *The Guardian*, June 18, 1999.

[114]Ian Black and John Hooper, "Serb Savagery Exposed," *The Guardian*, June 18, 1999.

informally for 10 days when the first Serb troops began leaving Kosovo. The departure of the last Serb forces and the arrival of the KFOR peacekeepers effectively brought an end to Yugoslav control over a province that had been a special and even sacred preserve of Serbia for centuries.

Initial estimates just before the cease-fire went into effect claimed that the air war had taken out 9 percent of Serbia's soldiers (10,000 of 114,000), 42 percent of its aircraft (more than 100 of 240), 25 percent of its armored fighting vehicles (203 of 825), 22 percent of its artillery pieces (314 of 1,400), and 9 percent of its tanks (120 of 1,270).[115] After the cease-fire, the Pentagon claimed that the operation had destroyed 450 enemy artillery pieces, 220 armored personnel carriers, 120 tanks, more than half of Yugoslavia's military industry, and 35 percent of its electrical power-generating capacity.[116] General Shelton reported that 60 percent of the infrastructure of the Yugoslav 3rd Army, the main occupying force in Kosovo, had been destroyed, along with 35 percent of the 1st Army's infrastructure and 20 percent of the 2nd Army's.[117] The U.S. Air Force's deputy chief of staff for air and space operations, Lieutenant General Marvin Esmond, announced that the allied bombing effort had destroyed a presumed 80 percent of Yugoslavia's fixed-wing air force, zeroed out its oil refining capability, and eliminated 40 percent of its army's fuel inventory and 40 percent of its ability to produce ammunition. Many of these initial assessments were later discovered to have been overdrawn by a considerable margin.

In the final tally, allied aircrews flew 38,004 out of a planned 45,935 sorties in all, of which 10,484 out of a planned 14,112 were strike sorties.[118] A later report to Congress by Secretary Cohen and General Shelton claimed that more than 23,300 combat missions, including

[115]Michael R. Gordon and Eric Schmitt, "Shift in Targets Let NATO Jets Tip the Balance," *New York Times*, June 5, 1999.

[116]Weiner, "From President, Victory Speech and a Warning."

[117]Bradley Graham, "Air Power 'Effective, Successful,' Cohen Says," *Washington Post*, June 11, 1999.

[118]Operation Allied Force and Operation Joint Guardian briefing charts dated August 19, 1999, provided to the author by Air Marshal Sir John Day, RAF, UK Ministry of Defense director of operations in Allied Force, RAF Innsworth, United Kingdom, July 25, 2000.

defensive counterair patrols and defense suppression attacks, were flown altogether, entailing weapon releases against roughly 7,600 desired mean points of impact (DMPIs) on fixed targets and slightly more than 3,400 presumed mobile targets of opportunity.[119] As for the air war's intensity over time, what started out as little more than 200 combat and combat-support sorties a day eventually rose to over 1,000 sorties a day by the time of the cease-fire.[120] All told, 28 percent of the sorties flown were devoted to direct attack, with 12 percent going to SEAD, 13 percent to attacks against dispersed enemy forces in Kosovo, 16 percent to defensive counterair patrols, 20 percent to inflight refueling, and 11 percent to other combat support missions (including AWACS, Joint STARS, ABCCC, EC-130 jammers, airlift, and combat search and rescue).[121]   Figure 3.4 shows the breakout of U.S. sorties flown by aircraft type.

According to the final air operations database later compiled by Hq USAFE, 421 fixed targets in 11 categories were attacked over the 78-day course of Allied Force, of which 35 percent were believed to have been destroyed, with another 10 percent sustaining no damage and the remainder suffering varying degrees of damage from light to severe. The largest single fixed-target category entailed ground-force facilities (106 targets), followed by command and control facilities (88 targets) and lines of communication, mostly bridges (68 targets). Other target categories included POL-related facilities (30 targets), industry (17 targets), airfields (8 targets), border posts (18 targets), and electrical power facilities (19 targets). In addition, 7 so-called counterregime targets were assessed as having sustained overall light damage. Finally, 60 targets were associated with Serb air defenses in two categories (radars and launch equipment), out of which two of

---

[119]Secretary of Defense William S. Cohen and Chairman of the Joint Chiefs of Staff General Henry H. Shelton, *Kosovo/Operation Allied Force After-Action Report*, Washington, D.C., Department of Defense, Report to Congress, January 31, 2000, p. 87.

[120]Ibid., p. 68.

[121]Operation Allied Force and Operation Joint Guardian briefing charts dated August 19, 1999.

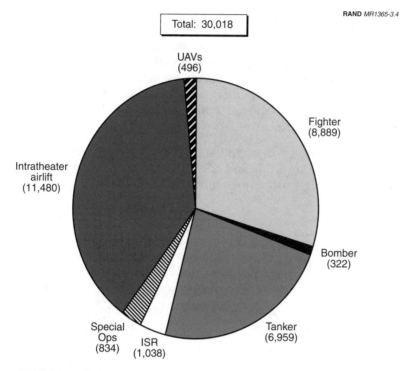

SOURCE: AWOS Fact Sheet.

Figure 3.4—USAF Sortie Breakdown by Aircraft Type

three SA-2s, 11 of 16 SA-3s, and 3 of 25 STRAIGHT FLUSH radars associated with the SA-6 were assessed as having been destroyed.[122]

---

[122]"AWOS Fact Sheet," Hq USAFE/SA, December 17, 1999. See also William M. Arkin, "Top Air Force Leaders to Get Briefed on Serbia Air War Report," *Defense Daily*, June 13, 2000, p. 1. As attested by cockpit display videotapes released to the press throughout the air war, allied air attacks succeeded in taking out quite a few more SA-6 launchers than those accounted for here. However, since the STRAIGHT FLUSH radar formed the core of an SA-6 battery, the battery was considered operational until the STRAIGHT FLUSH was destroyed. Comments on an earlier draft by Hq USAFE/IN, May 18, 2001.

As for the 28,018 munitions (excluding TLAMs) that were expended altogether, a full one-third were general-purpose Mk 82 unguided bombs dropped by B-52s and B-1s during the war's final two weeks. Figure 3.5 presents the trend of U.S. and allied munitions expenditure over the 78-day course of Allied Force. Figure 3.6 shows the number of precision weapons and nonprecision weapons delivered daily over the same period. Of that number, the United States delivered 83 percent, or all but 4,703 (see Figure 3.7).

In a telling reflection of the sparse intelligence available on the location of enemy SAMs and of NATO's determination to avoid losing even a single aircrew member, some 35 percent of the overall

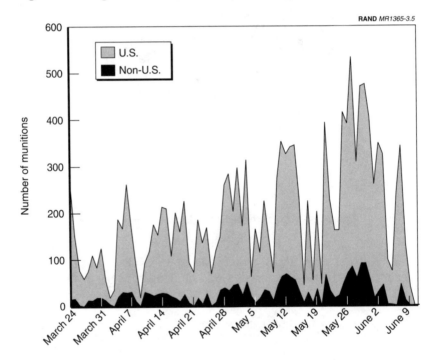

SOURCE: Hq USAFE/SA.

Figure 3.5—U.S. and Allied Ground-Attack Munitions Expended (excluding TLAM)

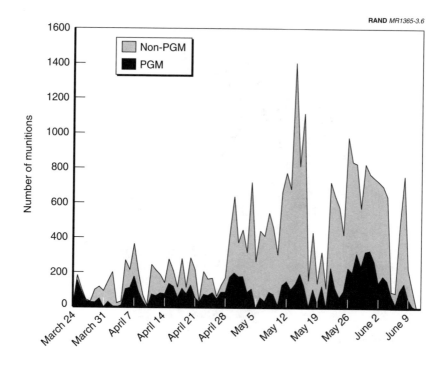

SOURCE: Hq USAFE/SA.

Figure 3.6—U.S. and Allied Munitions Expenditures by Type

effort (including both direct attack and mission support) was directed against enemy air defenses. Thanks in part to the weight of that effort, only two allied aircraft were downed and not a single friendly fatality was incurred, save for two AH-64 pilots who were killed in a training accident in Albania (see Chapter Five for more on these incidents). Even at that, however, enemy SAMs were effectively suppressed but not often destroyed.

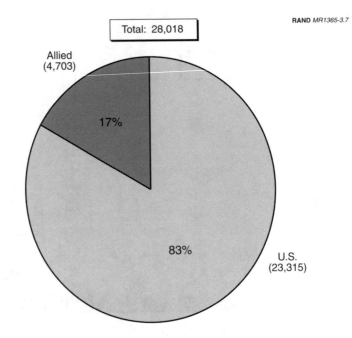

RAND *MR1365-3.7*

SOURCE: AWOS Fact Sheet.

Figure 3.7—Total Numbers of Munitions Expended

Stealth bomber. Used for the first time in combat during Allied Force after having been in line service since 1993, a USAF B-2 prepares to take on fuel midway across the Atlantic Ocean during one of two preplanned tanker hookups en route to target. The low-observable bomber, operating nonstop from its home base in the United States, was the first allied aircraft to penetrate Serb defenses on opening night.

Safe recovery. An F-117 stealth attack aircraft lands at Aviano Air Base, Italy, just after sunrise following a night mission into the most heavily defended portions of Serbia. During the air war's fourth night, an F-117 was downed just northwest of Belgrade, most likely by a lucky SA-3 shot, in the first-ever loss of a stealth aircraft in combat. (The pilot was promptly retrieved by CSAR forces.)

Heavy players. A venerable USAF B-52H bomber stands parked on the ramp at RAF Fairford, England, as a successor-generation B-1B takes off on a mission to deliver as many as 80 500-lb Mk 82 bombs or 30 CBU-87 cluster bomb units against enemy barracks and other area targets. An AGM-86C CALCM fired from standoff range by a B-52 was the first allied weapon to be launched in the war.

Final checks. Two Block 40 F-16CGs from the 555th Fighter Squadron at Aviano taxi into the arming area just short of the runway for one last look by maintenance technicians before taking off on a day mission to drop 500-lb GBU-12 laser-guided bombs on "flex" targets of opportunity in Serbia or Kosovo, as directed by airborne FACs and as approved, in some cases, by the CAOC.

Burner takeoff. An F-15E from the 494th Fighter Squadron home-based at RAF Lakenheath, England, clears the runway at Aviano in full afterburner, with CBU-87 cluster munitions shown mounted on its aftmost semiconformal fuselage weapons stations. Eventually, some F-15E strike sorties into Serbia and Kosovo were flown nonstop to target and back directly from Lakenheath.

On the cat. A U.S. Navy F/A-18C assigned to Fighter/Attack Squadron 15 is readied for a catapult launch for an Allied Force day combat mission from the aircraft carrier USS *Theodore Roosevelt* cruising on station in the Adriatic Sea. On April 15, carrier-based F/A-18s figured prominently in a major CAOC-directed air strike on the Serb air base at Podgorica, Montenegro.

SAM hunter. This Block 50 F-16CJ in the arming area at Aviano shows an AGM-88 high-speed anti-radiation missile (HARM) mounted on the left intermediate wing weapons station, with an AIM-9M air-to-air missile on the outboard station and an AIM-120 AMRAAM on the wingtip missile rail. The USAF's F-16CJ inventory was stressed to the limit to meet the SEAD demand of Allied Force.

Combat support. U.S. Navy and Marine Corps EA-6B Prowler electronic warfare aircraft, like this one shown taxiing for takeoff at Aviano, provided extensive and indispensable standoff jamming of enemy early warning and IADS fire-control radars to help ensure unmolested allied strike operations, including B-2 and F-117 stealth operations, against the most heavily defended enemy targets in Serbia.

Task Force Hawk. A U.S. Army AH-64 Apache attack helicopter flares for landing at the Rinas airport near Tirana, Albania, following a ferry flight from its home base at Illesheim, Germany. In all, 24 Apaches were dispatched to Albania with the intent to be used in Operation Allied Force, but none saw combat in the end because of concerns for the aircraft's prospects for survival in hostile airspace.

Cramped spaces. This USAF C-17 parked on the narrow ramp at Rinas airport, incapable of accommodating the larger C-5, was one of many such aircraft which provided dedicated mobility service to TF Hawk. In more than 500 direct-delivery lift sorties altogether, C-17s moved 200,000-plus short tons of equipment and supplies to support the Army's deployment within the span of just a month.

Eagle eye. Ground crewmen at RAF Lakenheath prepare a LANTIRN targeting pod to be mounted on an F-15E multirole, all-weather fighter. The pod, also carried by the Navy F-14D and the USAF F-16CG, contains a forward-looking infrared (FLIR) sensor for target identification at standoff ranges day or night, as well as a self-contained laser designator for enabling precision delivery of LGBs.

Deadly force. Munitions technicians at RAF Fairford prepare a CBU-87 cluster bomb unit for loading into a USAF B-1B bomber in preparation for a mission against fielded Serbian forces operating in Kosovo. With a loadout of 30 CBU-87s—more than five times the payload of an F-15E—the B-1 can fly at fighter-equivalent speeds more than 4,200 nautical miles unrefueled.

Help from an ally. One of 18 CF-18 Hornet multirole fighters deployed in support of Allied Force from Canadian Forces Base Cold Lake, Alberta, Canada, is parked in front of a hardened aircraft shelter at Aviano. The aircraft mounts two 500-lb GBU-12 laser-guided bombs on the outboard wing pylons and two AIM-9M air-to-air missiles on the wingtip rails.

Force protection. A security guard stands watch over a USAF C-17 airlifter at the Rinas airport in support of the U.S. Army's Apache attack helicopter deployment to Albania. For a time, reported differences between on-scene Air Force and Army commanders with respect to who was ultimately responsible for the airfield made for discomfiting friction within the U.S. contingent.

Flexing into the KEZ. An AGM-65 Maverick-equipped A-10 from the USAF's 52nd Fighter Wing stationed at Spangdahlem Air Base, Germany, takes off from Gioia del Colle to provide an on-call capability against possible Serb targets detected in Kosovo by allied sensors, including the TPQ-36 and TPQ-37 firefinder radars operated by the U.S. Army on the high ground above Tirana, Albania.

Round-the-clock operations. An F-16 pilot readies himself for a night mission over Serbia, his helmet shown fitted with a mount for night-vision goggles. Used in conjunction with compatible cockpit lighting, NVGs made possible night tactics applications, including multiaircraft formations and simultaneous bomb deliveries, which otherwise could only have been conducted during daylight.

Night refueling. A USAF F-15C air combat fighter, shown here through a night-vision lens, moves into the precontact position to take on fuel from a KC-135 tanker before resuming its station to provide offensive counterair protection for attacking NATO strikers. With a loss of six MiGs in aerial combat encounters the first week, Serb fighters rarely rose thereafter to challenge NATO's control of the air.

Splash one Fulcrum. A team of U.S. military personnel examines the remains of an enemy MiG-29 fighter (NATO code name Fulcrum) which was shot down in Bosnian airspace by a USAF F-15C on the afternoon of March 26, 1999. The downed aircraft, which appeared to have strayed from its planned course due to a loss of situation awareness by its pilot, brought to five the number of MiG-29s destroyed in early Allied Force air encounters.

Hard-target killer. This F-15E pilot, a USAF major assigned to the 494th Fighter Squadron, looks over a 4,700-lb electro-optically-guided GBU-28 bunker-buster munition mounted on his aircraft's centerline stores station. The aircraft, one of a two-ship flight of F-15Es (call sign Lance 31 and 32), delivered the weapon on April 28, 1999, against an underground hangar at the Serb air base at Podgorica.

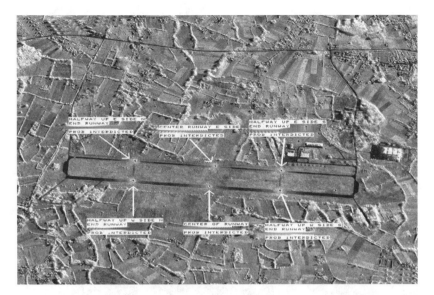

Precision attack. In April 1999, a single B-2 achieved six accurately placed GBU-31 JDAM hits against six runway-taxiway intersections at the Obvra military airfield in Serbia, precluding operations by enemy fighters until repairs could be completed. This post-strike image graphically shows the B-2's ability with JDAM to achieve the effects of mass without having to mass, regardless of weather.

A bridge no more. Another post-strike battle-damage assessment image shows this bridge in Serbia cut in two places by a precision bombing attack. Sometimes enemy bridges were dropped at the behest of NATO target planners to prevent the flow of traffic over them. At other times, they were attacked and damaged to sever key fiber-optic communications lines that were known to run through them.

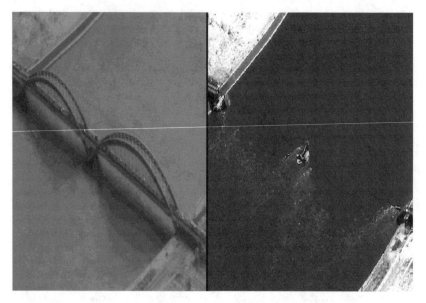

Before and after. This bridge over the Danube River near Novi Sad in Serbia, shown here in both pre- and post-strike imagery, was all but completely demolished by precision bombing on Day 9 of Allied Force as Phase III of the air war, for the first time, ramped up operations to include attacks against not only Serbian IADS and fielded military assets but also key infrastructure targets.

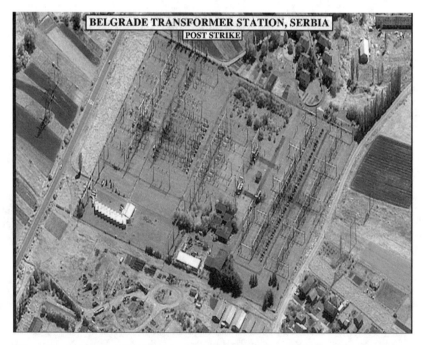

Effects-based targeting. For three consecutive nights beginning on May 24, U.S. aircraft struck electrical power facilities in Belgrade, Novi Sad, and Nis, the three largest cities in Serbia, shutting off electrical power to 80 percent of Serbia. This transformer yard in Belgrade was one such target that was attacked in what was arguably the most influential strike of Allied Force to that point.

Chapter Four

WHY MILOSEVIC GAVE UP WHEN HE DID

As might have been predicted, disagreements arose after the cease-fire went into effect over which of the air war's target priorities (fielded forces or infrastructure assets) was more crucial to producing the outcome. Contention also arose over the more basic question of the extent to which the air effort as a whole had been the cause of Milosevic's capitulation. On the one hand, there was the view of those air power proponents who were wont to conclude up front that "for the first time in history, the application of air power alone forced the wholesale withdrawal of a military force from a disputed piece of real estate."[1] On the other hand, there was the more skeptical view offered by the commander of the international peacekeeping forces in Kosovo, British Army Lieutenant General Sir Michael Jackson, who suggested that "the event of June 3 [when the Russians backed the West's position and urged Milosevic to surrender] was the single event that appeared to me to have the greatest significance in ending the war." Asked about the effects of the air attacks, Jackson, an avowed critic of air power, replied tartly: "I wasn't responsible for the air campaign; you're asking the wrong person."[2]

---

[1]John A. Tirpak, "Lessons Learned and Re-Learned," *Air Force Magazine*, August 1999, p. 23.

[2]Andrew Gilligan, "Russia, Not Bombs, Brought End to War in Kosovo, Says Jackson," *London Sunday Telegraph*, August 1, 1999. To his credit, Jackson did later testify to the Commons Defense Committee of Britain's parliament that "the effect of the strategic bombing, I suspect, was much weightier than the damage being done to the [Serb] army in Kosovo." "General Admits NATO Exaggerated Bombing Success," *London Times*, May 11, 2000.

We may never know for sure what mix of pressures and inducements ultimately led Milosevic to admit defeat, at least until key Serb archival materials become available or those closest to Milosevic during the air war become disposed to offer first-hand testimony. Asked by a reporter why Milosevic folded if the bombing had not defeated him militarily, Clark, who knew the Serb dictator well from previous negotiating encounters, replied: "You'll have to ask Milo-sevic, and he'll never tell you."[3] Yet why Milosevic gave in and why he did so when he did are by far the most important questions about the air war experience, since the answers, insofar as they are know-able, will help to lay bare the coercive dynamic that ultimately swung the outcome of Allied Force. It need hardly be said that such insight can be of tremendous value in informing any strategy ultimately chosen by the United States and its allies for future interventions of that sort. Accordingly, it behooves analysts to make every effort to delve further into this innermost mystery of the air war, since even approximate answers, if buttressed by valid evidence, are almost certain to be more useful to senior policymakers than most "lessons" of a more technical nature regarding how specific systems worked and how various procedural aspects of the operation could have been handled better, important as the latter questions are.

In the search to understand what ultimately occasioned NATO's success, one can, of course, insist that air power alone was the cause of Milosevic's capitulation in the tautological sense that Allied Force was an air-only operation and that in its absence, there would have been no reason to believe that he would have acceded to NATO's demands.[4] Yet as crucial as the 78-day bombing effort was in bringing Milosevic to heel, there is ample reason to be wary of any intimation that NATO's use of air power produced that ending with-out any significant contribution by other factors. On the contrary, numerous considerations in addition to the direct effects of the bombing in all likelihood interacted to produce the Serb dictator's eventual decision to cave in. As Ivo Daalder and Michael O'Hanlon have remarked, in a balanced reflection on this point, "air power

---

[3]Michael Ignatieff, "The Virtual Commander: How NATO Invented a New Kind of War," *The New Yorker*, August 2, 1999, p. 31.

[4]See, for example, Rebecca Grant, "Air Power Made It Work," *Air Force Magazine*, November 1999, pp. 30–37.

might best be thought of as the force driving Milosevic into a dead-end corner and threatening to crush him against the far wall. But had NATO not remained unified, Russia not joined hands with NATO in the diplomatic endgame, and the alliance not begun to develop a credible threat of a ground invasion, Milosevic might have found doors through which to escape from the corridor despite the aerial punishment."[5]

CONSIDERATIONS IN ADDITION TO THE BOMBING

Beyond the obvious damage that was being caused by NATO's air attacks and the equally obvious fact that NATO could have continued bombing indefinitely and with virtual impunity, another likely factor behind Milosevic's capitulation was the fact that the sheer depravity of Serbia's conduct in Kosovo had stripped it of any remaining vestige of international support—including, in the end, from its principal backers in Moscow. Although Milosevic's loss of Russian support may not have been the determining factor behind his capitulation, it was, without question, a contributing factor. A high-level official in the Clinton administration who was directly involved in setting policies for Operation Allied Force later commented that with respect to the numerous ongoing diplomatic efforts to backstop the coercive bombing, Russia was "a key arrow in the quiver."[6] That became most clearly apparent when Russian President Boris Yeltsin called Clinton on April 25, the last the day of the NATO summit, and, in an unprecedentedly long 75-minute conversation, expressed his concerns over the escalating air war and offered to send former Russian Prime Minister Chernomyrdin as his personal envoy to help find a negotiated solution. Once Milosevic came face to face with the realization that Russia had joined the West in pressing for a settlement of

---

[5]Ivo H. Daalder and Michael E. O'Hanlon, *Winning Ugly: NATO's War to Save Kosovo*, Washington, D.C., The Brookings Institution, 2000, p. 184.

[6]This official, in an interview with RAND staff members in Washington on June 11, 2000, further claimed that the White House was not surprised when Milosevic accepted the deal on June 3, since the administration was confident that once Chernomyrdin had agreed to NATO's terms, it was merely a matter of time before a successful denouement would be reached, considering that Chernomyrdin knew Milosevic's bottom line and would not have signed up for any arrangement that he knew Milosevic would not accept. What *was* surprising, the official said, was that Milosevic did not first seek to buy time by proffering more "half-loaf" compromise deals.

the Kosovo standoff, he knew that he had lost any remaining trace of international backing.

On top of that was the sense of walls closing in that Milosevic must have had when he was indicted as a war criminal by a UN tribunal only a week before his loss of Moscow's support. On May 27, that tribunal charged Milosevic and four of his senior aides—including General Dragoljub Ojdanic, the Yugoslav army chief, and Vlajko Stojilkovic, the interior minister responsible for the MUP—with crimes against humanity for having deported more than 700,000 ethnic Albanians and having allegedly murdered 340 innocents, mostly young men. Even if that indictment did not give Milosevic pause in and of itself, it almost surely closed the door on any remaining chance that Russia might change course and resume its support for him.

Yet a third factor, this one a direct second-order result of the bombing, may have been mounting elite pressure behind the scenes. As the air attacks encroached more on Belgrade proper, Secretary Cohen reported that senior VJ leaders had begun sending their families out of Yugoslavia, following a similar action earlier by members of the Yugoslav political elite and reflecting possible concern among top-echelon commanders that Milosevic had led them down a blind alley in choosing to take on the United States and NATO.[7] U.S. officials indicated that during the last week of the air war, VJ leaders had swung from supporting Milosevic on Kosovo to openly rebelling and pressuring the Serb dictator to agree to NATO's terms. Cohen's report of increasing demoralization among the VJ's most senior leaders as they helplessly watched the escalating destruction all around them gave rise to hopes within the Clinton administration that Milosevic might be looking for a face-saving way out.[8] The fact that the bombing effort caused more infrastructure damage during its last week than during its entire first two months was thought by some to have reawakened old tensions between Milosevic and an army leadership that was said to have never fully trusted him.

---

[7]Daniel Williams and Bradley Graham, "Milosevic Admits to Losses of Personnel," *Washington Post*, May 13, 1999.

[8]Interview with Secretary of Defense William S. Cohen, "Milosevic Is Far Weaker Now," *USA Today*, May 14, 1999.

A related factor may have been mounting heat from Milosevic's cronies among the Yugoslav civilian oligarchy, prompted by the continued bombing of military-related industries, utilities, and other infrastructure targets in and around Belgrade in which they had an economic stake and whose destruction increasingly threatened to bankrupt them.[9] On that point, administration officials remarked that among other things, the dropping of bridges throughout Serbia by NATO air attacks had hindered the activities of smugglers who represented a key source of income for those cronies. Moreover, CIA and other allied intelligence organizations were said to have been gathering information on the bank accounts and business interests of Milosevic and his closest partners, the latter of whom were starting to pressure him to call it quits.[10]

Finally, U.S. psychological operations could have been a contributing factor, although the evidence for that remains both spotty and less than convincing. One report to that effect suggested that Milosevic's wife was becoming "increasingly hysterical" as the bombing intensified and that Milosevic himself was finally pushed over the edge after the United States, via a "friendly intermediary," shipped him a videotape showing what a fuel-air explosive could do to his forces—at roughly the same time as the KLA's counteroffensive in Kosovo forced VJ troops into the open and exposed them to NATO fire.[11] Apart from the fact that fuel-air explosives are not currently maintained in the U.S. munitions inventory, this claim presumed that the

---

[9]Paul Richter, "Officials Say NATO Pounded Milosevic into Submission," *Los Angeles Times,* June 5, 1999. The possible effects of the bombing on what one might call second-tier Serb leaders are especially noteworthy, in that they suggest that the elite substructure of an enemy's hierarchy may make for more lucrative leadership targets than the "big guys." Unlike the topmost political leaders, these second-tier individuals have "retirement plans," in that they have options to recoup their interests under a new regime. They thus may be more malleable than their bosses, even as they are often critical to their bosses' survival. I am grateful to Colonel Robert Owen, USAF, for having suggested this intriguing idea to me.

[10]Doyle McManus, "Clinton's Massive Ground Invasion That Almost Was," *Los Angeles Times,* June 9, 2000. A persistent concern that tended to inhibit a truly aggressive use of such information entailed the liability implications of information attacks against foreign bank accounts, as well as official worries about the Pandora's box that might be opened if the United States began playing that game, thus rendering its own economy susceptible to similar measures in return.

[11]Tom Walker, "Bomb Video Took Fight out of Milosevic," *London Sunday Times,* January 30, 2000.

VJ's troops were a particularly valued asset for Milosevic, which, by all indications, they were not.

THE PROSPECT OF A GROUND INVASION

Among the many considerations that converged to produce Milosevic's eventual capitulation, the most discomfiting to him over the long run—apart from the bombing itself—may well have been what he perceived, rightly or wrongly, to be the prospect of an eventual NATO ground intervention. Whatever NATO's declared stance on the ground-war issue may have been, its actions as the air war progressed spoke louder than its words.

To begin with, Operation Allied Harbor, set in motion as early as April 8, aimed at putting some 8,000 NATO ground troops into Macedonia to help with refugee aid efforts. More significantly, a 32,000-person NATO Stabilization Force (soon to number 50,000) patrolling Bosnia-Herzegovina, and 7,500 additional NATO troops in Albania deployed to perform humanitarian work there made for an undeniable signal that a NATO ground presence was forming in the theater. That presence included 2,400 combat-ready U.S. Marines aboard three warships in the Adriatic to provide force protection for the Marine F/A-18s that were operating out of the former Warsaw Pact air base at Taszar. In addition, some 5,000 U.S. Army troops, with a substantial artillery and armor complement, accompanied the 24 AH-64 Apache helicopters that were sent to Albania in late April. There is every reason to believe that this deployment, along with NATO's subsequent decision to enlarge the Kosovo peacekeeping force (KFOR) to as many as 50,000 troops, was assessed by Milosevic as an indication that a NATO ground option was at least being kept open.

Taking advantage of a covert relationship between the CIA and the KLA, NATO also had begun probing the capability and extent of the VJ's ground defenses, an inquiry that most likely did not escape Milosevic's attention. In a related development, NATO engineers on May 31 began widening and reinforcing a key access road from Durres to Kukes on the Kosovo-Albanian border so that it could support the weight of a main battle tank. Earlier, Clark had authorized the engineers to strengthen the road to handle refugee traffic only, but they made it strong enough to support the Bradley armored fighting vehicle (AFV). This time, only three days before Milosevic finally called it quits, Washington gave Clark permission to send in another engineering battalion to make the road capable of supporting M1A2 Abrams tanks and artillery.[12]

Beyond that, Milosevic may have gotten wind of a secret NATO plan for a massive ground invasion code-named Plan B-minus, which was slated to be launched the first week of September if approved by NATO's political leaders. In support of this plan, Britain had agreed to contribute the largest single national component up to that time (50,000 troops) to an envisaged 170,000-man contingent; the United States would have contributed at least 100,000 more. Developed by a secret planning team at NATO's military headquarters in Mons, Belgium, Plan B-minus relied heavily on previous plans going back to June 12, 1998, which featured six land-attack options, including a full invasion of Serbia itself (Plan Bravo, with 300,000 NATO troops). The chief of Britain's defense staff, General Sir Charles Guthrie, later confirmed the outlines of this plan.[13] Milosevic was said by a well-placed NATO source to have been at least broadly informed of NATO thinking with respect to it. Indeed, as the UK Ministry of Defense's director of operations in Allied Force, RAF Air Marshal Sir John Day, later commented, "the decision to increase KFOR was militarily right in itself, but it was also a form of heavy breathing on Milosevic and a subtle way of moving to B-minus while keeping the coalition together. The move also had the effect of shortening our timelines for B-minus. It is true that the forces that were being prepared for KFOR-plus were the core elements of what would then have become B-minus, the full ground invasion."[14]

In a sign that such indicators may have begun to affect Milosevic's risk calculus, VJ units were reported in mid-May to be digging in along likely attack routes from Macedonia and Albania and fortifying the border, in a distinct shift in effort from expelling ethnic Albanians to preparing for a possible showdown with NATO on the ground. In

---

[12]Dana Priest, "A Decisive Battle That Never Was," *Washington Post*, September 19, 1999.

[13]Patrick Wintour and Peter Beaumont, "Revealed: The Secret Plan to Invade Kosovo," *London Sunday Observer*, July 18, 1999.

[14]Peter Beaumont and Patrick Wintour, "Leaks in NATO—and Plan Bravo Minus," *London Sunday Observer*, July 18, 1999.

particular, VJ troops were observed laying mines and attempting to block potential ground attack routes from Skopje and Kumanovo in Macedonia, in a pattern of activity suggesting that the allied bombing effort had not yet come close to breaking their cohesion and fighting spirit.[15]

Moreover, earlier on the same day that Milosevic eventually capitulated, President Clinton held a widely publicized meeting with his service chiefs for the express purpose of airing options for land force employment in case NATO decided it had no choice but to approve a ground invasion.[16] That was his first meeting with all four chiefs at any time during the course of Operation Allied Force. Immediately after the meeting, which left the issue unresolved, Clinton was said to have been planning to inform the chiefs that he was now ready to sign on to a ground invasion should developments leave no alternative.[17] In what he later described as "a pretty depressing memo" to the president, Berger wrote that "we basically should go ahead with what Clark had proposed if the [Ahtisaari-Chernomyrdin] mission failed." In that memo, Berger listed three options. The first, to arm the Kosovars, would create a multitude of undesirable downstream consequences that would persist for years and thus was ruled out as a nonstarter. The second, to wait until spring, was equally unacceptable because it would oblige NATO to supply and protect the Kosovar refugees in Albania throughout the winter. That left only the third option, a massive ground invasion by 175,000 NATO troops, some 100,000 of whom would be American.[18] Taken together, these developments made for a compelling pattern of evidence suggesting that both Washington and its chief NATO allies had crossed the Rubicon when it came to facing up to the land-invasion issue, and that they had become determined by the end of May to commit to a

---

[15]Michael R. Gordon, "NATO Says Serbs, Fearing Land War, Dig In on Border," *New York Times,* May 19, 1999.

[16]Jane Perlez, "Clinton and the Joint Chiefs to Discuss Ground Invasion," *New York Times,* June 2, 1999.

[17]For details, see Steven Erlanger, "NATO Was Closer to Ground War in Kosovo Than Is Widely Realized," *New York Times*, November 7, 1999.

[18]McManus, "Clinton's Massive Ground Invasion That Almost Was." NATO commanders were asking for three months to assemble the invasion force.

forced entry on the ground if the bombing did not produce an acceptable settlement soon.

Some, however, have made more of this sequence of events than the evidence warrants. In the early wake of the successful conclusion of Operation Allied Force, revisionist claims began emanating from some quarters suggesting that the air effort had been totally ineffective and that, in the end, it had been Milosevic's fear of a NATO ground invasion that induced him to capitulate.[19] Clark himself, in his memoirs, indicated his belief that by mid-May, NATO "had gone about as far as possible with the air strikes" and that in the end, it had been the Apache deployment and the prospect of a NATO ground intervention that, "*in particular*, pushed Milosevic to concede."[20] That notwithstanding the all-but-conclusive evidence Clark presented elsewhere throughout his book that NATO's top political leaders were nowhere near having settled on a definitive invasion plan—let alone decided to proceed with such a plan should the bombing prove unavailing.[21] Even viewed in the most favorable light conceivable, such far-reaching claims on behalf of the implied ground threat defy believability because any NATO land invasion, however possible it may eventually have been, would have taken months, at a minimum, to prepare for and successfully mount.

In contrast, Milosevic was living with the daily reality of an increasingly brutal air war that showed no sign of abating. Although Clark's

---

[19]A recent example of this countercontention dismissed the claims of unspecified "air power enthusiasts" and posited instead that "the decision to commit ground forces [a decision which, in fact, had *not* been made at the time of Milosevic's capitulation] was critical to NATO's success." Brigadier General Huba Wass de Czege, USA (Ret.) and Lieutenant Colonel Antulio J. Echevarria II, USA, "Precision Decisions: To Build a Balanced Force, the QDR Might Consider These Four Propositions," *Armed Forces Journal International*, October 2000, p. 54.

[20]General Wesley K. Clark, *Waging Modern War: Bosnia, Kosovo, and the Future of Combat,* New York, Public Affairs, 2001, pp. 305, 425, emphasis added.

[21]The most compelling of such evidence cited by Clark was the May 28 statement by Secretary of Defense Cohen, made less than a week before Milosevic capitulated, that "there is no consensus for a ground force. And until there is a consensus, we should not undertake any action for which we could not measure up in the way of performance. . . . And so, there is a very serious question in terms of trying to push for a consensus that you really diffuse or in any way diminish the commitment to the air campaign. The one thing we have to continue is to make sure we have the allies consolidated in strong support of the air campaign. They are. And they are in favor of its intensification. So that's where we intend to put the emphasis." Ibid, p. 332.

effort to find and attack dispersed and hidden VJ forces in Kosovo was consuming the preponderance of shooter sorties while accomplishing little by way of tangible results, more and more infrastructure targets were also being approved and struck every day.[22] In a revealing admission of what was uppermost among his concerns on the day he elected to settle, Milosevic asked Chernomyrdin directly on June 3 in response to NATO's ultimatum: "Is this what I have to do to get the bombing stopped?" Chernomyrdin replied in the affirmative, with Ahtisaari adding: "This is the best you can get. It's only going to get worse for you." To which Milosevic responded: "Clearly I accept this position."[23]

There is no question that by the end of May, NATO had yielded to the inevitable and embraced in principle the need for a ground invasion should the bombing continue to prove indecisive. There also is every reason to believe that awareness of that change in NATO's position on Milosevic's part figured importantly in his eventual decision to capitulate. There is *no* basis, however, for concluding that the mere threat of a land invasion somehow overshadowed the continuing, here-and-now reality of NATO's air attacks as the preeminent consideration accounting for that decision. There also is little benefit to be gained from the misguided efforts by air and land power partisans alike to argue the relative impact of the air attacks and ground threat in simplistic either-or terms. It detracts not in the least from the air war's signal accomplishments to concede that developments on the land-invasion front almost surely were part of the chemistry of Milosevic's concession decision. Although any impending ground intervention was months away at best, there is no question that both the Clinton administration and the principal NATO allies had made up

---

[22]However, by dispersing their assets and selectively emitting with their radars, Serb IADS operators forced NATO aircrews to remain wary to the very end and denied them the freedom to operate at will in hostile airspace. Although the Serbs' repeated attempts to bring down NATO aircraft frequently came in the form of ineffective ballistic launches, the launches were amply disconcerting to allied pilots, who were forced to threat-react—often aggressively—to ensure their own safety. Many guided shots in accordance with IADS doctrine were also fired against attacking allied aircraft, requiring even more aggressive and hair-raising countertactics by the targeted aircraft. A first-hand account of one such episode is reported in Dave Moniz, "Eye-to-Eye with a New Kind of War," *Christian Science Monitor*, March 23, 2000.

[23]Quoted in Tyler Marshall and Richard Boudreaux, "Crisis in Yugoslavia: How an Uneasy Alliance Prevailed," *Los Angeles Times*, June 6, 1999.

their minds on the need to do something along those lines should the air war continue to prove unavailing. In light of that, as two RAND colleagues have suggested, "in assessing NATO air attacks on Serbia, analysts should focus not on the role air power played *instead of* a ground invasion . . . but on the role it played in combination with the possibility of one."[24]

MILOSEVIC'S PROBABLE DECISION CALCULUS

To better understand the interaction of influences that most likely persuaded Milosevic to concede, it may be instructive to view Allied Force as it unfolded not through our own frame of reference, but rather through Serbian eyes. Those who planned and ran the air operation understandably tended to fixate on such negative aspects as target-list restrictions and what many considered to be excessive fretfulness on the part of the alliance's political leaders over the possibility of causing collateral damage. For them, the air war's dominant hallmarks were such sources of daily frustration as repeated delays in the target approval process and the consequent inefficiency of the overall effort. Naturally, in their view, the performance of air power in Operation Allied Force left a great deal to be desired.

Yet to those on the operation's receiving end far removed from such concerns, it must have seemed, certainly by the end of the second month, as though NATO was prepared to keep escalating and to continue bombing indefinitely. From Milosevic's viewpoint, new targets were being attacked with mounting regularity after the NATO summit of April 23–25, and ever more infrastructure targets were being hit with seemingly no end in sight. Moreover, one might surmise that even the inadvertent Chinese embassy bombing played an indirect part in inducing Milosevic to capitulate. Whatever U.S. and NATO officials said about that incident for the public record, Milosevic may have thought that the bombing had been intentional and that it presaged both a lifting of NATO's target limitations and worse damage yet to come. As if to affirm that fear after the fact, USAFE's commander, General John Jumper, later disclosed that with the increased number of strike aircraft that had become available in the-

---

[24]Daniel L. Byman and Matthew C. Waxman, "Kosovo and the Great Air Power Debate," *International Security*, Spring 2000, p. 15.

ater by late May, the operation's intent was to employ FACs and begin attacking kill boxes all throughout Serbia, not just in Kosovo, and to go at will after tunnels, bridges, storage areas, and other military targets of interest.[25]

The almost universal belief among air warfare professionals that a more aggressive effort starting on opening night, in consonance with a more doctrinally pristine strategy, would have yielded the same result more quickly may have been correct as far as it went, but that conviction was based solely on faith in the intrinsic power of the air weapon, not on any evidence directly related to the case at hand. The only way a more intensive and resolute air campaign would have caused Milosevic to fold substantially sooner than he did would have been for the air war's effects to persuade him that much earlier that his strategy had no chance of succeeding.

In fact, as RAND colleague Stephen Hosmer has argued, Milosevic's decision to capitulate hinged on developments that necessarily took time to unfold and mature.[26] To begin with, the Serb dictator, just like NATO, pursued a concrete, if also flawed, strategy from the very start. He knew that the terms levied by the United States at Rambouillet, if implemented, would have replaced Serb dominance over Kosovo with a NATO military presence that claimed rights of access to all of Yugoslavia. They also would have raised the distinct possibility that Kosovo's future would be decided by a NATO-enforced referendum, an event which could only have resulted in a loss for Serbia.[27] Those two threatened outcomes, along with additional downside consequences, would have put at risk not only Serbian control over Kosovo, but also the foundations of Milosevic's personal rule, and hence his political—and perhaps even physical—survival.

---

[25]General John Jumper, USAF, "Oral Histories Accomplished in Conjunction with Operation Allied Force/Noble Anvil."

[26]Stephen T. Hosmer, *The Conflict over Kosovo: Why Milosevic Decided to Settle When He Did*, Santa Monica, California, RAND, MR-1351-AF, 2001.

[27]The latter of these two concerns was more an issue for Milosevic than the former. Had he been seriously worried about a NATO presence that might actually encroach into Serbia, as opposed to just taking effective control of Kosovo (his real fear), he would have sought to head off that possibility at Rambouillet. He never did. I am grateful to Ivo Daalder of the Brookings Institution for bringing this point to my attention.

In addition, Milosevic probably convinced himself that if he hunkered down and stoically endured the bombing, he could undermine NATO's persistence and cohesion by ensuring the eventual occurrence of noncombatant civilian fatalities and extracting the fullest propaganda value from collateral-damage incidents. Indeed, he most likely balked at Rambouillet in full expectation that he would be bombed by NATO, yet only symbolically and for a token period of time, convinced that NATO would lack the stomach to continue bombing for very long. On this point, Stojan Cerovic, a Serb journalist working in Washington, suggested that Milosevic at first saw no danger to himself from the bombing and operated on the assumption that other nations would become so incensed over NATO's perceived attempts at hegemony that they would rally behind the Serb cause.[28] No doubt expecting nothing more than a replay of the ineffectual pinprick attacks that had been carried out by U.S. forces against Iraq since the preceding December, he evidently calculated that he could easily wait out any punitive air strikes that NATO might bring itself to carry out.

Where Milosevic blundered even more grievously than did NATO (in the latter's faulty assumption that just a few days of bombing would suffice) was in unleashing the full brunt of his ethnic cleansing campaign almost immediately after Allied Force began. No doubt he calculated that Operation Horseshoe would quickly empty Kosovo of its ethnic Albanian populace and thus enable him to move directly against the KLA, eliminate it as a continued factor affecting any ultimate political outcome, and, along the way, solve his ethnic problem in Kosovo with a fait accompli. Alternatively, or perhaps in addition, he may also have been trying to signal his own determination to NATO, although there is no "smoking-gun" evidence to this effect. After all, the main lesson he likely drew from Deliberate Force in 1995 was that he gave up the fight just a few days too early. Most assessments of Deliberate Force include arguments that NATO was approaching the end of its rope politically and militarily because of a

---

[28]Justin Brown, "Why U.S. Bombs Failed to Topple Milosevic," *Christian Science Monitor*, March 24, 2000.

lack of additional approved targets.[29] In light of that perception, Milosevic, in addition to working on his Kosovar Albanian problem, may simply have been trying to tell everyone that this time it would not be so easy. Whatever the case, his depredations instead merely galvanized NATO's resolve and ensured that the allies would continue bombing until their objectives were met. By throwing down a gauntlet to NATO and, in effect, challenging it to see who could hold out longer, Milosevic forced NATO to recognize that its own credibility and existence as an alliance were now on the line.[30]

There is no way of knowing for sure from the evidence currently available why June 3 was the date on which Milosevic finally elected to give in. There is a strong presumptive case to be made, however, that by the end of May, he had come to realize that any remaining countercoercive leverage he had over NATO was almost nonexistent. As Hosmer concluded, once the Serb dictator became convinced that future attacks would be unconstrained, a settlement at the earliest possible moment became not just an option but an imperative. Continued bombing during the negotiations over implementation of the agreement, moreover, closed the door to any possibility of his backsliding. Milosevic further had every reason to assume by that time that any terms of a settlement agreement would never look better, and that the time was propitious for a loss-cutting move while he could retain at least the polite fiction of having extracted concessions from NATO.

As for disincentives against holding out any longer, Milosevic also had every reason to believe that continued resistance on his part would only lead to continued, and quite probably escalated, bombing. Even in the absence of an imminent NATO ground assault, he knew that the air war could have continued for many more weeks, even indefinitely. With the possibility that electrical power and water supplies to Belgrade might be cut off at any time, the approach of

---

[29]See, in particular, Colonel Robert Owen, USAF, ed., *Deliberate Force: A Case Study in Effective Air Campaigning*, Maxwell AFB, Alabama, Air University Press, January 2000, pp. 455–522.

[30]Stephen Hosmer has pointed out that the ethnic cleansing hardened NATO's resolve in another way as well: Only a NATO military presence in Kosovo would have convinced the refugees to go back to their homes, and no outcome short of the latter would have been acceptable to NATO.

winter offered the prospect of making daily life horrendously difficult for Serbia's leaders and rank and file alike. Worse yet, the mere thought of a NATO land invasion occurring at some indeterminate future point had the most ominous implications, in that it could have meant Serbia's loss of Kosovo for good, posing the direst threat to Milosevic's survival. In light of those mutually reinforcing facts, he evidently convinced himself that although his own continued liveli-hood required his capitulation, he could convert his tactical defeat into a long-term loss for NATO by swallowing his temporary setback in Kosovo while remaining in power to fight another day.

In sum, although it did not achieve a military victory over Belgrade in the classic sense, NATO unquestionably prevailed over Milosevic in a high-stakes contest of wills. Diplomacy and coercive bombing to-gether convinced the Serb dictator that he had failed to split NATO and that Russia would not act to stop the air war. At the same time, they allowed him enough maneuver room to maintain at least a fig leaf of a claim to credibility in the eyes of his compatriots that he had not yielded to NATO on all fundamentals. As Barry Posen concluded, "all of the principal wedges into NATO's cohesion had been tested. Further testing would prove very expensive in terms of damage to Serbia's infrastructure and economy."[31]

In the end, however inefficient the air war may have been because of its need to honor U.S. and NATO domestic political realities, the manner in which it was conducted (avoiding friendly fatalities and minimizing noncombatant enemy casualties) nevertheless effec-tively countered and ultimately neutralized Milosevic's strategy by keeping NATO's cohesion intact to the very end. In response, the Serb dictator most likely opted to accept NATO's demands simply out of a rational calculation that he had nothing to gain and much to risk by holding out any longer. Indeed, as the endgame neared, one can imagine how he may even have begun to harbor dark visions of being gunned down in the street, in the grim manner of the Ceauces-

---

[31]Barry R. Posen, "The War for Kosovo: Serbia's Political-Military Strategy," *International Security*, Spring 2000, p. 75. One can, however, question Posen's subsequent suggestion that Milosevic achieved "some political success" by holding out as long as he did, considering that he lost control of Kosovo, suffered heavy damage to his infra-structure and economy, and ultimately was defeated in a fair election, arrested, and jailed for having committed crimes against the state.

cus after their control over Romania collapsed in 1991. Said a source close to the Yugoslav government: "I can't pinpoint an exact moment when Milosevic finally listened, but there was tremendous pressure from all sides; the West, his inner circle, and his wife. It was building up, and eventually he just let go."[32]

THE DETERMINING ROLE OF THE AIR WAR

To repeat a point stressed at the beginning of this chapter, it would be reductionist to a fault to conclude that Milosevic was bombed into submission by air attacks to the exclusion of any other contributing factors. However, the bombing did create political conditions in Belgrade that enabled Milosevic to negotiate.[33] Insofar as the bombing may have been insufficient to produce his capitulation in and of itself, it bears underscoring that those conditions were all indirect effects of the air war. Had it not been for Allied Force and its direct effects, the additional stimuli would never have materialized. As General Clark later remarked, "the indispensable condition for all other factors was the success of the air campaign itself."[34]

From the Yugoslav perspective, there must have been a nagging sense of the inexorability of NATO's eventual victory as the air war neared the end of its second month. The truculent early defiance that was so studiously expressed by Belgrade's citizens before the war began affecting them personally soon turned into sullen resignation under the mounting duress caused by the bombing of infrastructure targets. For a time, the half-hearted bombing during the first month actually seemed to rally public determination to withstand the offensive and to increase public support for the widely unpopular Milosevic. However, the spontaneous street celebrations that erupted immediately *after* the cease-fire suggested that the Yugoslav rank and file had begun to doubt Milosevic's stewardship in having led the country into an unwinnable contest of wills against the world's most powerful alliance. Possibly reflecting mounting

---

[32]"NATO's Game of Chicken," *Newsweek*, July 26, 1999, p. 59.

[33]For detailed amplification on this point, see Hosmer, *The Conflict over Kosovo: Why Milosevic Decided to Settle When He Did*.

[34]Quoted in John T. Correll, "Lessons Drawn and Quartered," *Air Force Magazine*, December 1999, p. 2.

popular weariness of the bombing, Deputy Prime Minister Vuk Draskovic declared as early as April 25 that "Yugoslavia should recognize that it cannot defeat NATO and that it must face the reality of a world standing against Yugoslavia."[35]

The precise and measured nature of the attacks that were being conducted against leadership and infrastructure targets in the heart of the Yugoslav capital on a daily basis only became fully apparent to outside observers after they had a chance to inspect the results up close. As one American reporter who visited Belgrade after the war remarked tellingly: "Like ice-pick punctures in the neck, the chilling quality of the strikes was not their size but their placement. We stopped at an intersection in the heart of the city. At each corner of the intersection, but only at each corner, there were ruins. The Serbian government center, the foreign ministry and two defense ministry buildings had been reduced to rubble or were fire-gutted shells. The precision of the destruction suggested a war with an invisible, all-seeing enemy and a city helpless to protect itself."[36]

In what may have been read by Milosevic as an ominous indicator that the bombing was coming ever closer to the most senior national leadership, General Ljubisa Velichkovic, the former air force chief of staff, was killed in an air attack on Day 70 while visiting VJ troops in the field. Velichkovic, who had been removed from office by Milosevic the previous year as a part of a purge of the military leadership and been given the honorific title of deputy chief of staff, was identified as the highest-ranking casualty since Operation Allied Force began.[37] It is entirely possible that Milosevic had come to fear by that point that a similar fate could befall him at any moment.

Viewed in hindsight, the bombing seems to have had two outcome-determining effects. First, it eventually persuaded Milosevic that

---

[35]Quoted in Robert Hewson, "Allied Force, Part II: Overwhelming Air Power," *World Air Power Journal*, Winter 1999/2000, p. 97. Three days later, Draskovic was fired by Prime Minister Momir Bulatovic for having made that statement.

[36]Blaine Harden, "The Milosevic Generation," *New York Times Magazine*, August 29, 1999, p. 34.

[37]"Sacked Yugoslav Air Chief Killed," *London Times*, June 2, 1999. See also William Drozdiak and Steven Mufson, "NATO Sending Tough Terms to Belgrade," *Washington Post*, June 2, 1999.

NATO not only would not relent, but also was determined to prevail and had both the technical and political wherewithal to do so. Second, given the incapacity of the Serb IADS to shoot down significant numbers of allied aircraft, it further convinced him that his own defeat sooner or later was inevitable. Although its resolve was slow in coming, NATO finally showed that it would not be moved by the public outcry over collateral damage and could sustain the bombing indefinitely, at a negligible cost in terms of friendly losses. As with Iraq's forces during Operation Desert Storm, the VJ's leaders, no less than Milosevic, must have found NATO's ability to inflict unrelenting damage on their country with virtual impunity to be profoundly demoralizing. Before June 3, the commander of the VJ's 3rd Army in Kosovo, General Nebojsa Pavkovic, had argued that his forces remained more or less intact and that they could defend Serbia if put to the test. After Ahtisaari and Chernomyrdin delivered NATO's ultimatum on June 2 and a cease-fire was agreed to, however, he reportedly declared to a group of disconcerted VJ reservists that Serbia's leaders had been put on notice by the Russians that if NATO's terms were rejected, "every city in Serbia would be razed to the ground. The bridges in Belgrade would be destroyed. The crops would all be burned. Everyone would die."[38]

True enough, thanks to the improved flexible targeting procedures (that is, procedures for responding promptly to mobile or pop-up targets that had been detected by allied sensors) that had been implemented by late April (see Chapters Six and Seven) and the clearer weather that had begun to develop the following month, NATO's ability to get at dispersed and hidden enemy forces in Kosovo improved perceptibly during the air war's final week. In all likelihood, however, NATO broke Milosevic's will and that of his political supporters primarily because it had convincingly shown that it could also destroy such key infrastructure targets as hardened bunkers, bridges, electrical power stations, and other targets directly tied to Yugoslav society and the regime's control over it. By all indications, those attacks played the central role in bringing Milosevic to accept NATO's demands and created the political conditions in Serbia that

---

[38]Quoted in Chris Hedges, "Angry Serbs Hear a New Explanation: It's All Russia's Fault," *New York Times*, July 16, 1999.

allowed Milosevic to abandon Belgrade's physical presence in Kosovo in exchange for a cessation of the bombing.

As one may recall, manipulation of the Kosovo issue and Serbia's strong emotional attachment to the province had figured prominently in Milosevic's rise to power and in his continued hold on it since 1989. For that reason, acceding to NATO's demands as expressed in the proposed Rambouillet accords would, in all likelihood, have meant political suicide for him. By June 1999, the opposite had become true: Milosevic's continued survival seemed to depend on finding a way to stop the bombing and to extricate himself gracefully from his growing predicament. Although Ahtisaari and Chernomyrdin provided him with the ready pretext that he needed, it was the air war's steadily increasing encroachment on Serbia's core equities that most likely prompted the decisive shift in his political calculus, as perhaps best attested by his own plaintive question to Chernomyrdin on June 2 cited earlier.[39] In contrast, by Clark's own admission after the cease-fire, the attempted attacks against dispersed and hidden VJ forces in Kosovo caused the latter little significant pain or inconvenience. That suggests, by elimination, that whatever one may believe was Milosevic's most critical vulnerability, the bombing of Clark's target priorities in the KEZ was *not* what mainly swung his decision to capitulate. [40]

On this still-contentious issue, defense analyst William Arkin, who led a private bomb damage assessment mission for Human Rights Watch for three weeks in August 1999 and who visited more than 250 targeted sites in the process, perhaps offered the most helpful and

---

[39]Indeed, from a low of fewer than 100 daily strike sorties flown during the air war's fifth night, the bombing effort intensified steadily and uninterruptedly to almost three times that number by the eve of Milosevic's capitulation on June 3. Briefing by the chairman of the Joint Chiefs of Staff, June 10, 1999, cited in Major General Eitan Ben-Eliahu, commander, Israeli Air Force, "Air Power in the 21st Century: The Impact of Precision Weapons," *Military Technology*, April 2000, p. 40.

[40]It bears acknowledging here, however, that only the authoritative report of NATO's intent to proceed with an eventual ground invasion, should the bombing alone fail to dislodge Milosevic, finally convinced Moscow to play its constructive role in June 1999. Russia's deploying of Chernomyrdin helped negotiate an international military presence in Kosovo, thus warding off a NATO-only presence and preserving at least some Russian influence in the Balkans. On this point, see the informed comment offered by former Russian foreign ministry Balkan official Oleg Levitin, "Inside Moscow's Kosovo Muddle," *Survival*, Spring 2000, p. 138.

incontestable perspective when he observed: "It was not *what* we bombed, but *that* we bombed. The coalition didn't crumble, the Russians didn't bail Belgrade out, China was unable to affect the war. At some point it was clear to Milosevic that he wasn't going to be able to wait out the bombing, that NATO wasn't going to go away, and that progressively Serbia was being destroyed, he chose to get the best negotiated settlement he could. To say it was this or that target that was important to Milosevic is just to engage in mirror-image speculation."[41]

---

[41]William Arkin, "Yugoslavia Trip Report," September 8, 1999. In a similar vein, Karl Mueller suggested that "while it was not clear how NATO was going to win, it certainly would continue the effort until it managed to do so. From this perspective, it was not *what* NATO was bombing that mattered, but the fact that it was *continuing* to bomb. . . ." Karl Mueller, "Deus ex Machina? Coercive Air Power in Bosnia and Kosovo," unpublished paper, School of Advanced Air Power Studies, Maxwell AFB, Alabama, November 7, 1999, p. 10.

Chapter Five

ACCOMPLISHMENTS OF THE AIR WAR

A number of "firsts" were recorded during NATO's air war for Kosovo. To begin with, Operation Allied Force was the first air war in which all three currently deployed U.S. Air Force heavy bomber types saw combat use. Those bombers constituted a major part of the overall strike force. Of some 700 U.S. combat aircraft committed to the operation altogether, a mere 21 heavy bombers (10 B-52s, 5 B-1s, and 6 B-2s) delivered 11,000 out of the more than 23,000 U.S. air-to-ground munitions that were expended over the operation's 78-day course.[1]

There also was an unprecedented use of precision-guided munitions in the air war. In Desert Storm, only 10 percent of the participating U.S. strike aircraft were PGM-capable. That number rose to 69 percent in Operation Deliberate Force and shot up to 90 percent in Allied Force.[2] Thanks to the heavy use of PGMs in the interest of both operational efficiency and avoiding unintended collateral damage, a full three-quarters of the more than 400 fixed targets attacked in Serbia were assessed as having sustained moderate to severe damage.[3] Some 64 percent of the 9,815 aim points altogether were hit by PGMs, for a total hit rate of 58 percent.[4] Figure 5.1 shows the

---

[1]David Atkinson, "B-2s Demonstrated Combat Efficiency over Kosovo," *Defense Daily*, July 1, 1999, p. 1.

[2]Comments on an earlier draft by Hq USAFE/SA, April 6, 2001.

[3]*Kosovo: Lessons from the Crisis*, Report to Parliament by the Secretary of State for Defense, The Stationery Office, London, England, June 2000, p. 36.

[4]"AWOS Fact Sheet," Hq USAFE/SA, December 17, 1999.

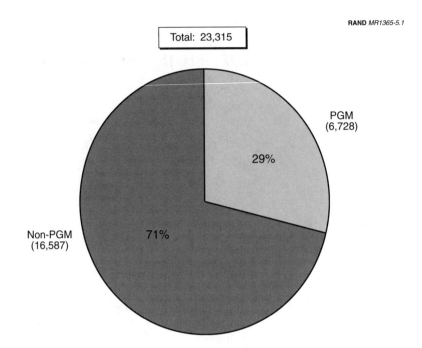

RAND *MR1365-5.1*

SOURCE: AWOS Fact Sheet.

Figure 5.1—U.S. Precision and Nonprecision Munitions Expended

proportion of precision munitions and nonprecision munitions delivered by U.S. combat aircraft over the 78-day course of the bombing effort. At nearly a third of the total number of ground-attack
munitions expended altogether, PGM use in Allied Force greatly
overshadowed that in Operation Desert Storm nearly a decade earlier. In that conflict, the proportion of PGMs delivered by U.S. forces
compared to nonprecision munitions was less than 10 percent.

In addition, more than in any previous U.S.-led air operation, UAVs
were used in Allied Force for combat support, most notably for locating VJ troops dispersed in the KEZ.[5] In yet another precedent, the

_____

[5]The qualification "U.S.-led" is appropriate here, considering that the Israeli Air Force
has made regular and highly effective use of UAVs over southern Lebanon for nearly
two decades, going back to the Beka'a valley air campaign of 1982.

USAF's air expeditionary force (AEF) concept was first successfully exercised in a full-up combat setting, with expeditionary fighter squadrons deploying to Aviano Air Base, Italy, from the continental United States and from U.S. bases in Europe and folding into the anchor 31st Air Expeditionary Wing stationed there, which, at its peak, operated a record 175 combat aircraft.[6] Relatedly, the assignment of tactical control of 12 C-17s directly to USAFE roundly validated that aircraft's "direct delivery" status and reflected a major step forward in the employment of air mobility forces as global assets. Finally, as the discussion below will sketch out in more detail, Operation Allied Force saw the most extensive use of space systems in combat to date, with more than 50 U.S. and European satellites directly involved in support of USEUCOM and NATO intelligence, coordination, and attack activities.

THE COMBAT DEBUT OF THE B-2

Of major note, Allied Force finally saw the long-awaited combat debut of the USAF's B-2 stealth bomber, which was the first manned aircraft to penetrate Serb air defenses the first night.[7] As the final countdown drew near, expectations ran high throughout the Air Force that the regional combatant commanders in chief around the world, who had long resisted the B-2's use in earlier air power applications because of their distrust of unproven systems, would finally be won over by a record of unblemished accomplishment by the aircraft over Serbia and Kosovo. Those expectations were more than vindicated. Of 19 B-2s all told that had been delivered to the aircraft's parent 509th Bomb Wing at Whiteman AFB, Missouri, only 9 were available to USEUCOM for combat operations, with the other 10 undergoing avionics upgrades to the aircraft's definitive Block 30 status.[8] Nevertheless, to the surprise of many, the B-2 turned out to be the most consistently effective performer of the entire air war. According to the 509th commander at the time, Brigadier General

---

[6]The wing had most of the essential support assets on hand, so deploying squadrons did not need to bring much by way of logistics overhead.

[7]Dale Eisman, "Over Balkans, It's Beauty vs. the Beast," *Norfolk Virginian-Pilot*, April 26, 1999.

[8]Vince Crawley, "B-2s See Combat over Yugoslavia," *Defense Week*, March 29, 1999, p. 6.

Leroy Barnidge, B-2 operations demonstrated a 96-percent weapons effectiveness rate.

Since only six of the nine available aircraft were actually used on combat missions, the average turn time per aircraft was two days.[9] There was never a shortage of capability to meet USEUCOM's targeting needs, however. Some B-2s were turned in the time it took to refuel them. The only reported case of a B-2 component having failed during a combat mission was a malfunction of a rotary bomb launcher, which was promptly repaired upon the aircraft's return to base.[10] The chief maintenance drivers were said to have been the aircraft's low-observable treatment, its flight control system, its synthetic-aperture radar, and engine accessory drives.

Each B-2 flew nonstop to its targets in its final Block 30 configuration directly from Whiteman on 28- to 32-hour round-trip missions, delivering up to 16 global positioning system (GPS)-guided GBU-31 joint direct-attack munitions (JDAMs) from 40,000 ft, usually through cloud cover, against enemy targets including hardened command bunkers and air defense facilities. Those missions typically entailed 15-hour legs out and back, with two inflight refuelings per leg. Two aircraft were launched on 15 nights and just a single aircraft on 19 nights. The aircrews quickly adjusted to these unprecedentedly long missions and coped with them adequately. They also quickly adapted to the demands of real-time targeting changes en route. Although the USAF bomber community, by virtue of its traditional nuclear focus, had long been predisposed to do things in a carefully preplanned way, USAFE's commander, General John Jumper, traveled to Whiteman and personally talked to B-2 aircrews about the need for rapid adaptability. After just a few hours of intense operator-to-operator brainstorming, any residual doubts some B-2 pilots may have harbored regarding the merits of replacing traditional cold-war practices with real-time improvisation as needed to meet current demands were put to rest. The first time the ensuing air ef-

---

[9]Of the nine available B-2s at Whiteman, one was kept aside for training, one was undergoing final upgrades to Block 30 status, and one was in extensive maintenance. "Missouri-to-Kosovo Flights for B-2 Not a Concern to Wing Commander," *Inside the Air Force,* July 2, 1999, p. 12.

[10]"B-2 Performed Better in Kosovo Than USAF Expected," *Inside the Pentagon,* July 8, 1999, p. 11.

fort attempted to apply what came to be called "flex" (for flexible) targeting against enemy assets that had been detected and identified only on short notice, the B-2s took out two SA-3 sites that had been assigned to them only a few hours prior to their planned arrival over target.[11]

In all, 49 B-2 combat sorties were launched out of Whiteman, of which 45 made it to target and were cleared to drop munitions. Although that was less than half a percent of the 9,500 strike sorties flown in Allied Force altogether, the B-2 dropped 11 percent (some 700) of the bombs delivered against fixed targets in Serbia and Kosovo. It also dropped a full third of all precision munitions expended during the air effort.[12] In addition to its normal load of JDAMs, the B-2 was also configured to carry the GPS-guided GBU-37 for special missions against deeply buried or superhardened targets.[13] A total of 652 JDAMs and 4 GBU-37s were dropped, with more than 80 percent of the B-2's assigned targets being hit on a single pass.[14] In a major improvement in the combat leverage and versatility of the American air weapon, the aircraft proved itself capable of operating effectively above weather that grounded all other allied combat aircraft. It also consistently achieved up to 16 separate target hits per sortie.

It bears emphasizing here that the B-2 did not merely drop weapons preprogrammed to home in on assigned coordinates, but used its onboard synthetic aperture radar (SAR) to take two successive images of the target during its initial approach. By so doing, the B-2 was able to eliminate the largest target error source in the JDAM, namely, the error in the exact location of the aim point in GPS space. As a result, the B-2's average miss distance with JDAM was less than half the 13 meters stipulated for unassisted JDAMs.[15]

---

[11] "Jumper on Air Power," *Air Force Magazine*, July 2000, p. 43.

[12] Paul Richter, "B-2 Drops Its Bad PR in Air War," *Los Angeles Times*, July 8, 1999.

[13] Adam Hebert, "Air Force Follows Roadmap in Employment of Bombers Against Serbia," *Inside the Air Force*, April 2, 1999, p. 2.

[14] Barry D. Watts, "The EA-6B, E-8C, and B-2 in Operation Allied Force," Northrop Grumman Analysis Center briefing, Rosslyn, Virginia, May 8, 2000.

[15] Barry D. Watts, *The Military Use of Space: A Diagnostic Assessment,* Washington, D.C., Center for Strategic and Budgetary Assessments, February 2001, p. 42.

On most nights, penetrating B-2s received standoff jamming support from Navy or Marine EA-6Bs, as well as SEAD support from orbiting F-16CJs standing by as needed as a precautionary measure. On at least one occasion, however, B-2 strikes occurred without *any* offboard jamming support. Thanks to the aircraft's third-generation stealth properties, it did not require such support to ensure its survivability, and EA-6B jamming for both the B-2 and the F-117 was said to have been "indirect." Supporting EA-6B and F-16CJ pilots were provided with time blocks and rough areas within which the stealthy aircraft would be concurrently operating, but not the exact routing of those aircraft. In the absence of those mission specifics, they relied on time and space deconfliction to maintain safe separation.[16] Because of their low observability and the persistence of overlapping and unlocated enemy SAM defenses, only the B-2s and F-117s were committed against targets in downtown Belgrade for the first 58 days of the operation.[17]

Since every B-2 mission, save one or two, benefited from dedicated offboard electronic countermeasures (ECM) support and was flown against less than top-of-the-line enemy defenses, it remains unclear as to what extent the aircraft's stealth properties were truly tested in modern combat. However, by all accounts the aircraft was never tracked by enemy radar, let alone shot at by enemy SAMs. Unlike all other aircraft that flew combat missions in Allied Force, the B-2 operated autonomously. It simply checked in with the ABCCC as it approached the target area, received a go/no-go code, and pressed ahead to its assigned targets in radio silence. If a target change was required en route, the Combined Air Operations Center (CAOC) could pass essential information to ingressing B-2 aircrews as much as an hour and 45 minutes before the aircraft's scheduled time on target (TOT). That ability to select new targets while airborne enabled the aircraft to take out some enemy SA-3s and their radars shortly after they were located and identified by allied sensors.[18] The

---

[16]Watts," The EA-6B, E8C, and B-2 in Operation Allied Force."

[17]Colonel Tony Imondi, 509th Operations Group commander, quoted in Bill Sweetman, "B-2 Is Maturing into a Fine Spirit," *Jane's International Defense Review*, May 2000.

[18]Brigadier General Randy Gelwix, USAF, "Oral Histories Accomplished in Conjunction with Operation Allied Force/Noble Anvil."

B-2's onboard GPS-aided targeting system (GATS) and SAR also allowed the aircraft to find, identify, and successfully attack imprecisely located targets.

As the air war unfolded, former Secretary of the Air Force Donald Rice observed that the B-2, although one of the most controversial weapons in the U.S. inventory, was "proving to be the nation's single most cost-effective attack aircraft."[19] Rice further pointed out that the much-derided stealth treatments on the aircraft had proven themselves durable and reliable and that the aircraft had been consistently flying through inclement weather and returning home in serviceable condition. As for identified shortcomings, the B-2 was found to need a direct satellite link to national intelligence agencies to provide its crew with a more current picture of the electronic battlefield so that the aircraft could be rerouted in near-real time to avoid any pop-up SAM threats that might have been detected after it had taken off. It also became apparent, at least to some observers, that the 509th Bomb Wing's crew ratio of two two-pilot crews per aircraft might need to be increased to four crews, or else that provisions might need to be made for future combat contingencies to allow the B-2 to operate out of airfields closer to the battlespace in the interest of reducing mission times.[20]

Through its consistently effective performance in Allied Force, the B-2 finally validated the "global reach, global power" concept first articulated by the USAF more than a decade earlier. Along with the B-52 and B-1, it showed the value of combat aircraft that are not dependent on bases near the theater of operations. In addition, its consistently successful use of JDAM in near-precision attacks against

---

[19]Donald B. Rice, "No Stealth to Pentagon's Bias Against the B-2," *Los Angeles Times*, May 9, 1999.

[20]David A. Fulghum, "Lessons Learned May Be Flawed," *Aviation Week and Space Technology*, June 14, 1999, p. 205. A serious limiting factor affecting the first of these suggested solutions is that doubling the B-2's crew ratio would require either doubling the number of training sorties and hours flown by the Air Force's limited B-2 inventory or reducing the number of sorties and flying hours made available for each B-2 crew member—to a point where their operational proficiency and expertise would be unacceptably compromised. Alternatively, the Air Force is now taking a close look at using RAF Fairford, England, and the island bases of Diego Garcia and Guam as forward staging areas from which to conduct B-2 operations in future regional contingencies worldwide.

high-priority fixed targets irrespective of weather may, at long last, have presaged an end to the six-year U.S. habit of routinely resorting to expensive cruise missiles as a seemingly risk-free way of delivering precision ordnance. Before the start of Allied Force, the Clinton administration had expended nearly 800 cruise missiles, all told, in various punitive attacks against presumed terrorist targets and against Iraq. At a price penalty of as much as $1.5 million a shot in sunk costs, that added up to enough to pay for the purchase of 50,000 JDAMs (for a 62:1 cost ratio).[21]

UAV EMPLOYMENT

Also for the first time in American combat experience, UAVs offered commanders and planners the frequent advantage of real-time video imagery without any accompanying danger of aircrew losses. Some UAVs were flown as low as 1,000 ft above VJ troop positions to gather real-time imagery, which, in turn, occasionally enabled prompt and effective attacks by A-10s and F-16s against the often fleeting targets. Several UAVs were lost when commanders requested closer looks, forcing the drones to descend into the lethal envelopes of Serb AAA and man-portable air defense systems (MANPADS). These losses did not evoke great concern, however, since the UAVs were intentionally sent out on missions that were known ahead of time to be especially risky, including highly classified missions to collect and downlink evidence on Serb atrocities.[22]

The USAF's RQ-1A Predator, with a 24-hour endurance capability, mounted a synthetic-aperture radar that enabled it to track targets through clouds and thereby augment the two E-8 Joint STARS aircraft that were operating adjacent to Kosovo out of Germany. Predator also offered the wherewithal for collecting signals intelligence (SIGINT) through its ability to approach threat emitters more closely than manned aircraft and to monitor low-power transmis-

---

[21]William M. Arkin, "In Praise of Heavy Bombers," *Bulletin of the Atomic Scientists,* July–August 1999. Another 218 U.S. and British TLAMs were fired during Operation Allied Force.

[22]"Despite Losses, Backers Say Unmanned Systems Excelling Over Kosovo," *Inside the Pentagon,* June 10, 1999, p. 1.

sions, such as those from cell phones and portable radios operated by enemy ground troops.[23]

The most-advanced Predator was not available when Operation Allied Force began. The USAF initially elected to keep those aircraft at their home base at Indian Springs near Nellis AFB, Nevada, rather than commit them to USEUCOM, owing to its reluctance to accept their delivery from the manufacturer without the accompanying technical manuals it needed to maintain and effectively operate them. (Earlier-generation Predators already operating in the theater were frequently prevented from flying because of their susceptibility to icing.)[24] The USAF finally sent three advanced Predators to its UAV facility at the Tuzla airfield in Bosnia. It took more than a week to get the first Predator airborne over Kosovo, however, because of undisclosed technical difficulties. In the meantime, USEUCOM and NATO were obliged to rely on satellites and higher-flying UAVs for targeting and battle damage assessment (BDA).[25]

One new procedure demonstrated operationally for the first time in Kosovo entailed a clever fusion of UAV sensor and specialized command and control procedures, in which two Predators orbiting at 5,000 ft would provide electro-optical and infrared identification of mobile targets and a third Predator would then use its laser designator and mapping software to provide geolocation, after which orbiting A-10s or F-16s could be called in on the detected target. Several confirmed hits on VJ tanks were made possible by this technique.

Interestingly, Predator was not always used in Operation Allied Force in the manner in which it was originally designed to be used. In addition to target search and intelligence collection, the UAV was also often employed to validate pilot reports of possible SAM or ground-force targets on the move, since the rules of engagement of-

---

[23]John D. Morrocco, David Fulghum, and Robert Wall, "Weather, Weapons Dearth Slow NATO Strikes," *Aviation Week and Space Technology*, April 5, 1999, p. 29.

[24]"Air Force Reluctant to Deploy All-Weather Predator UAVs to Balkans," *Inside the Air Force*, April 2, 1999, p. 1. Another concern had to do with a larger requirements debate within the Air Force over whether UAVs developed under a fast-track acquisition process, as was Predator, should be managed like a more expensive fighter program.

[25]Jane Perlez, "Serbs Try to Empty Disputed Province, NATO Aides Assert," *New York Times*, March 29, 1999.

ten required two sets of eyes on a potential target. As General Jumper later explained, those who planned and executed the air effort soon learned that they "had to make forward air controllers out of what had previously been intelligence collectors."[26] The original intended Predator mission was to find targets. What happened as the air war unfolded, however, was that Predator was used instead in the collateral-damage management loop and sent out to put real-time eyes on candidate targets that had already been located but not identified, so as to verify that they were valid military targets.[27]

The U.S. Army's Hunter UAVs operated from the Skopje airfield in Macedonia, with their first operational mission into Kosovo taking place on April 4. Hunter imagery was first downlinked to ground controllers in Skopje and then forwarded either to the CAOC in Vicenza, Italy, or to NATO headquarters in Belgium and to the Pentagon as appropriate.[28] Normally used as a corps asset, Hunter in this instance transmitted real-time video imagery via orbiting satellites and downlinked it directly to the Joint Broadcast System in the United States, which then transmitted it to the CAOC, making for only a one-second delay. Its targets were normally objects of tactical interest against which commanders would not risk a manned aircraft, such as artillery emplacements and dispersed VJ units in the KEZ, which had organic self-protection air defense assets. Much like Predator, Hunter flew whenever the weather allowed. It often would loiter in the vicinity of hot targets to observe munitions impacts and provide real-time BDA.[29]

Both Predator and Hunter operators soon discovered that better sensors were needed for the drones to identify ground targets positively from above 8,000 ft. They also learned that better integration of UAV and manned aircraft operations was essential for minimizing the

---

[26]"Jumper on Air Power," p. 42.

[27]One problem pointed up by this mode of operation was the slow flying speed of the aircraft. At a maximum airspeed of only 70 nautical miles per hour, Predator typically required considerable time to get to a previously located target candidate, by which time the latter may have moved to a new location.

[28]Elizabeth Becker, "They're Unmanned, They Fly Low, and They Get the Picture," *New York Times*, June 3, 1999.

[29]Tim Ripley, "Task Force Hunter," *World Air Power Journal*, Winter 1999/2000, p. 122.

danger of midair collisions. As a stopgap toward that end, UAVs were restricted to operating in specially designated airspace, where they experienced a heightened likelihood of being shot at because of their frequency of flight over the same terrain.[30] In all, 25 UAVs operated by all allies went down over the 78-day course of Allied Force as a result either of enemy action or of mechanical failure. The United States lost four Predators, eight Hunters (three to infrared SAMs, one to a radar SAM, and the others for mechanical reasons), and four Pioneers. Germany and France lost a total of six Canadian-built CL-289 drones and two French Crecerelles, most of them in a single week.[31]

After Allied Force ended, General Jumper revealed that had combat operations continued into the summer, the USAF would have started employing a new tactic whereby Predators equipped with laser designators would have been flown under the weather near enemy targets to designate those targets for LGBs once the latter had been released by allied fighters flying at safer altitudes above the cloud cover. Jumper further disclosed that UAVs, having successfully undergone a rigorous operational shakedown over Kosovo, would in the future be used more in the targeting loop than in the intelligence collection loop—patrolling aggressively and making the most of their extended loiter time to seek out and identify hidden targets.[32]

THE CONTRIBUTIONS OF SPACE

Among the many U.S. and European space systems that were involved in supporting the planning and execution of air attacks, the most pivotal were classified U.S. satellites that provided imagery support, including transmissions directly through new National Reconnaissance Office (NRO) data reception hardware which had been

---

[30]David A. Fulghum, "Joint STARS May Profit from Yugoslav Ops," *Aviation Week and Space Technology*, July 26, 1999, p. 74.

[31]William M. Arkin, "Top Air Force Leaders to Get Briefed on Serbia Air War Report," *Defense Daily*, June 13, 2000, p. 1. For further details on UAV operations, see Lieutenant Commander J. D. Dixon, "UAV Employment in Kosovo: Lessons for the Operational Commander," paper submitted to the Naval War College, Newport, Rhode Island, February 8, 2000.

[32]David A. Fulghum, "Kosovo Conflict Spurred New Airborne Technology Use," *Aviation Week and Space Technology*, August 23, 1999, p. 30.

installed in the 31st Air Expeditionary Wing's Tactical Integrated Planning (TIP) center at Aviano Air Base, Italy; Defense Meteorological Support Program (DMSP) satellites that provided weather imagery down to 1,000-ft resolution; the GPS satellite constellation which enabled the consistently accurate delivery of JDAMs by B-2s; and various NRO data relay and SIGINT spacecraft. Other allied space assets used in Operation Allied Force included the NATO-4 communications satellite, a British Skynet satellite, the French Telesat Syracuse system, U.S. Defense Satellite Communications System (DSCS) satellites, and ultra-high-frequency (UHF) follow-on satellites.[33] After the effort ended, U.S. Space Command estimated that 80 percent of the spaceborne communications used during Operation Allied Force had been transmitted via commercial satellite systems.[34]

At least five notable space success stories came out of the Allied Force experience. The first was the effective use of the Multisource Tactical System (MSTS) on the B-52 and B-1, which gave bomber crews real-time situation awareness updates. The system had existed before but had never previously been used in combat. The second major success story was the highly successful use of GPS-guided munitions described earlier, most notably JDAM on the B-2 and the Navy's TLAM II. Third was the use of the Defense Support Program (DSP) satellite constellation for providing real-time battle damage indications (BDI) as an input into the BDA process. New procedures toward that end were created and refined for Allied Force that had never before been used.[35] Fourth, the Hook 112 survival radio was available for use by U.S. aircrews, making an important new role for space-enabling systems in CSAR.[36] Finally, command and control

---

[33]Craig Covault, "Military Space Dominates Air Strikes," *Aviation Week and Space Technology*, March 29, 1999, pp. 31–32.

[34]Peter Grier, "The Investment in Space," *Air Force Magazine*, February 2000, p. 50.

[35]On the other hand, cockpit multifunction display videotapes showing successfully impacting munitions were *not* used in the BDA process by the Joint Analysis Center at RAF Molesworth, resulting in numerous revisits to targets that were already known by attacking pilots to have been struck before to good effect. Conversation with Lieutenant Colonel Ray Dissinger, Aviano AB, Italy, June 12, 2000.

[36]The Hook 112 was developed by the Air Force for use between downed aircrew members and CSAR forces to eliminate a problem presented by the previous survival radio, which allowed enemy monitors to locate the downed crewmember's position by

personnel in the CAOC coordinated the tasking of terrestrial intelligence, surveillance, and reconnaissance (ISR) assets—notably the USAF's U-2s and RC-135 Rivet Joint electronic intelligence (ELINT) aircraft—with space-based ISR assets (that is, national satellite systems) to a level never before achieved in a wartime operational setting.[37] In all, reported the USAF's chief provider of operational space support to warfighters at all levels, space integration into Allied Force was "the most extensive seen to date." But there was still ample room for further improvement in such areas as space doctrine, better education regarding the nation's space capabilities for prospective users, and better integration of these capabilities into the contingency plans of air component commanders worldwide.[38]

---

triangulating on the relatively lengthy voice exchanges required to coordinate a rescue by CSAR teams. The Hook 112 communicates the downed crewmember's position by means of an encrypted burst transmission that denies enemy monitors the ability to triangulate. A GPS receiver incorporated in the Hook 112 automatically transmits the crewmember's exact location, along with any coded transmissions the downed crewmember may wish to communicate. Major General Gary Dylewski, "The USAF Space Warfare Center: Bringing Space to the Warfighter," in Peter L. Hays et al., eds, *Spacepower for a New Millennium: Space and U.S. National Security,* New York, McGraw-Hill, 2000, p. 96.

[37]"Space Support to Operation Allied Force: Preliminary Lessons Learned," briefing to the author by Colonel Robert Bivins, director of operations, U.S. Air Force Space Warfare Center, Schriever AFB, Colorado, February 25, 2000.

[38]Major General Robert Hinson, commander, 14th Air Force, "Space Doctrine Lessons from Operation Allied Force," command briefing, Vandenberg AFB, California, December 16, 1999.

Chapter Six

FRICTION AND OPERATIONAL PROBLEMS

Although NATO's use of air power in Allied Force must, in the end, be adjudged a success, some troubling questions arose well before the air war's favorable outcome over a number of unexpected and disconcerting problems encountered along the way. Some of those problems, most notably in the area of what air planners came to call "flex" targeting of elusive VJ troops on the move in Kosovo, were arguably as much a predictable result of prior strategy choices as a reflection of any inherent deficiencies in the air weapon itself.[1] Of more serious concern were identified shortcomings that indicated needed fixes in the realm of tactics, techniques and procedures, and, in some cases, equipment. Beyond the problem of locating, identifying, and engaging dispersed and hidden light infantry targets, the shortcomings arousing the greatest consternation included assessed deficiencies in SEAD, excessively lengthy information and intelligence cycle time, inadvertent civilian casualties, and some serious deficiencies in alliance interoperability. Also of special concern were the many problems spotlighted by the U.S. Army's plagued deployment of its AH-64 Apache helicopters to Albania and the full extent of U.S. global military overcommitment that the Allied Force experience brought to light.

---

[1]The "flex" targeting effort entailed the launching of combat aircraft without specific assigned target locations and coordinates, although tasked to seek out various classes of targets, either through free search or upon being directed to a specific area of known or suspected enemy activity by the CAOC or an airborne forward air controller.

FRUSTRATIONS WITH THE SEAD EFFORT

In contrast to the far more satisfying SEAD experience in Desert Storm, the initial effort to suppress Serb air defenses in Allied Force did not go nearly as well as expected. The avowed going-in objective of the SEAD operation was to neutralize as many of Serbia's SAMs and AAA sites as possible, particularly its estimated 16 SA-3 LOW BLOW and 25 SA-6 STRAIGHT FLUSH fire control radars. Another early goal was to take out or suppress long-range surveillance radars that could provide timely threat warning to MANPADS operators carrying shoulder-fired infrared SAMs like the SA-7.

The Serbs, however, kept their SAMs defensively dispersed and operating in an emission control (EMCON) mode, prompting concern that they were attempting to draw NATO aircraft down to lower altitudes where they could be more easily engaged. Before the initial strikes, there were reports of a large-scale dispersal of SA-3 and SA-6 batteries from nearly all of the regular known garrisons. The understandable reluctance of enemy SAM operators to emit and thus render themselves cooperative targets made them much harder to find and attack, forcing allied aircrews to remain constantly alert to the radar-guided SAM threat throughout the air war.[2] It further had the effect of denying some high-risk targets for a time, increasing force package size, and increasing overall SEAD sortie requirements.

Moreover, unlike in the more permissive Desert Storm operating environment, airspace availability limitations in the war zone typically made for high predictability on the part of attacking NATO aircraft, and collateral damage avoidance considerations frequently prevented the use of the most tactically advantageous attack headings. The resulting efforts to neutralize the Serb IADS were, according to retired U.S. Navy Admiral Leighton Smith, the commander of NATO forces in Bosnia from 1994 to 1996, "like digging out potatoes one at a time."[3] The commander of USAFE, General Jumper, later added that the CAOC could never get NATO political clearance to attack the most troublesome early warning radars in Montenegro,

---

[2]Dana Priest, "NATO Unlikely to Alter Strategy," *Washington Post*, March 26, 1999.

[3]Dana Priest, "NATO Pilots Set to Confront Potent Foe," *Washington Post*, March 24, 1999.

which meant that the Serbs knew when attacks were coming most of the time.[4] In other cases, the cumbersome command and control arrangements and the need for prior CAOC approval before fleeting pop-up IADS targets detected by Rivet Joint or other allied sensors could be attacked resulted in many lost opportunities and few hard kills of enemy SAM sites.

Operation Allied Force drew principally on 48 USAF F-16CJs and 30 Navy and Marine Corps EA-6B Prowlers, along with Navy F/A-18s and German and Italian electronic-combat role (ECR) Tornados, to conduct the suppression portion of allied counter-SAM operations. Land-based Marine EA-6Bs were tied directly to attacking strike packages and typically provided ECM support for missions conducted by U.S. aircraft. Navy Prowlers aboard the USS *Theodore Roosevelt* supported carrier-launched F-14 and F/A-18 raids and strike operations by allied fighters. The carrier-based Prowlers each carried two AGM-88 high-speed antiradiation missiles (HARMs). Those operating out of Aviano, in contrast, almost never carried even a single HARM, preferring instead to load an extra fuel tank because of their longer route to target. This compromise was often compensated for by teaming the EA-6B with HARM-shooting F-16CJs or Luftwaffe Tornado ECR variants.[5]

The USAF's EC-130 Compass Call electronic warfare aircraft was used to intercept and jam enemy voice communications, thereby allowing the EA-6Bs to concentrate exclusively on jamming enemy early warning radars. The success of the latter efforts could be validated by the RC-135 Rivet Joint ELINT aircraft, which orbited at a safe distance from the combat area. The biggest problem with the EA-6B was its relatively slow flying speed, which prevented it from keeping up with ingressing strike aircraft and diminished its jamming effectiveness as a result. On occasion, the jamming of early warning radars forced Serb SAM operators to activate their fire-control radars, which in turn rendered them susceptible to being

---

[4]General John Jumper, USAF, "Oral Histories Accomplished in Conjunction with Operation Allied Force/Noble Anvil."

[5]Robert Wall, "Sustained Carrier Raids Demonstrate New Strike Tactics," *Aviation Week and Space Technology*, May 10, 1999, p. 37.

attacked by a HARM. Accordingly, enemy activation of SAM fire-control radars was limited so as to increase their survivability.[6]

SEAD operations conducted by F-16CJs almost invariably entailed four-ship formations. The spacing of the formations ensured that the first two aircraft in the flight were always looking at a threat area from one side and the other two were monitoring it from the opposite side. That enabled the aircraft's HARM Targeting System (HTS), which only provided a 180-degree field of view in the forward sector, to maintain 100-percent sensor coverage of a target area whenever allied strike aircraft were attempting to bomb specific aim points within it. According to one squadron commander, the F-16CJs would arrive in the target area ahead of the strikers and would build up the threat picture before the strikers got close, so that the latter could adjust their ingress routes accordingly. In so doing, the F-16CJs would provide both the electronic order of battle and the air-to-air threat picture as necessary. The squadron commander added that enemy SAM operators got better at exploiting their systems at about the same rate that the F-16CJ pilots did, resulting in a continuous "cat and mouse game" that made classic SAM kills "hard to come by."[7]

As noted in Chapter Three, only a few SAMs were reported to have been launched against attacking NATO aircraft the first night. The second night, fewer than 10 SA-6s were fired, with none scoring a hit. Later during Allied Force, enemy SAMs were frequently fired in large numbers, with dozens launched in salvo fashion on some nights but only a few launched on others. Although these ballistic launches constituted more a harassment factor than any serious challenge to NATO operations, numerous cases were reported of allied pilots being forced to jettison their fuel tanks, dispense chaff, and maneuver violently to evade enemy SAMs that were confirmed to be guiding.[8]

---

[6]Robert Wall, "Airspace Control Challenges Allies," *Aviation Week and Space Technology*, April 26, 1999, p. 30.

[7]Tim Ripley, "Viper Weasels," *World Air Power Journal*, Winter 1999/2000, p. 102. The standard F-16CJ weapons loadout was two AGM-88 HARMs and four AIM-120 advanced medium-range air-to-air missiles (AMRAAMs).

[8]Richard J. Newman, "In the Skies over Serbia," *U.S. News and World Report*, May 24, 1999, p. 24. It bears noting here that 10 or more pilots operating in a target area might report an observed SAM shot as ballistic, while the one pilot on whose helmet the

Indeed, the SAM threat to NATO's aircrews was far more pronounced and harrowing than media coverage typically depicted, and aggressive jinking and countermaneuvering against airborne SAMs was frequently necessary whenever the Serbs sought to engage NATO aircraft. The Supreme Allied Commander in Europe, U.S. Army General Wesley Clark, later reported that there had been numerous instances of near-misses involving enemy SAM launches against NATO aircraft, and General Jumper added that a simple look at cockpit display videotapes would show that "those duels were not trivial."[9] From the very start of NATO's air attacks, Serb air defenders also sought to sucker NATO aircrews down to lower altitudes so they could be brought within the lethal envelopes of widely proliferated MANPADS and AAA systems. A common Serb tactic was to fire on the last aircraft in a departing strike formation, perhaps on the presumption that those aircraft would be unprotected by other fighters, flown by less experienced pilots, and low on fuel, with a consequent limited latitude to countermaneuver.

The persistence of a credible SAM threat throughout the air war meant that NATO had to dedicate a larger-than-usual number of strike sorties to the SEAD mission to ensure reasonable freedom to operate in enemy airspace. In turn, fewer sorties were available for NATO mission planners to allocate against enemy military and infrastructure targets—although the limited number of approved targets at any one time tended to minimize the practical effects of that consequence. Moreover, the Block 50 F-16CJ, which lacked the ability to carry the LANTIRN targeting pod, was never used for night precision bombing because it could not self-designate targets.

One of the biggest problems to confront attacking NATO aircrews on defense-suppression missions was target location. Because of

---

missile was figuratively guiding would be actively reacting to it. Shortly thereafter, 10 pilots would recover to widely dispersed home bases and report nonthreatening ballistic launches, while only one would return with the evidence of a guided shot. This drove a perception among Allied Force leaders that "most" of the SAM shots observed were ballistic. Once all the pertinent information was fused and duplicate reporting was factored out, however, it turned out that a substantial number of SAM launches (perhaps as many as a third) were guided. Comments on an earlier draft by Hq USAFE/IN, May 18, 2001.

[9]Cited in "Ground Troops Lauded," *European Stars and Stripes*, August 6, 1999, and "Jumper on Air Power," *Air Force Magazine*, July 2000, p. 41.

Kosovo's mountainous terrain, the moving target indicator (MTI) and SAR aboard the E-8 Joint STARS could not detect objects of interest in interspersed valleys that were masked from view at oblique look angles, although sensors carried by the higher-flying U-2 often compensated for this shortfall.[10] The cover provided to enemy air defense assets by the interspersed mountains and valleys was a severe complicating factor. Similarly, efforts to attack the internetted communications links of the Yugoslav IADS were hampered by the latter's extensive network of underground command sites, buried land lines, and mobile communications centers. Using what was called fused radar input, which allowed the acquisition and tracking of NATO aircraft from the north and the subsequent feeding of the resulting surveillance data to air defense radars in the south, this internetting enabled the southern sector operations center to cue defensive weapons (including shoulder-fired man-portable SAMs and AAA positions) at other locations in the country where there was no active radar nearby. That may have accounted, at least in part, for why the F-16CJ and EA-6B were often ineffective as SAM killers, since both employed the HARM to home in on enemy radars that normally operated in close proximity to SAM batteries.[11]

In all, well over half of the HARM shots taken by allied SEAD aircrews were preemptive targeting, or so-called PET, shots, with a substantial number of these occurring in the immediate Belgrade area.[12] Many HARM shots, however, were reactive rather than preplanned, made in response to transitory radar emissions as they were detected.[13]

Yugoslavia's poorly developed road network outside urban areas may also have worked to the benefit of NATO attackers on more than a few occasions because enemy SAM operators depended on road

---

[10]Further mitigating this constraint, the limited surveillance range of Joint STARS caused by interposed ridge lines restricted E-8 operations primarily with regard to Kosovo, which harbored only a limited SAM threat (only one of the 5 SA-6 regiments and no SA-2s or SA-3s). Most of the enemy IADS targets were assessed to lie outside Kosovo. Moreover, the U-2 and Rivet Joint typically performed well and did not suffer the same problems that sometimes plagued the E-8. Comments on an earlier draft by Hq USAFE/IN, May 18, 2001.

[11]Wall, "Airspace Control Challenges Allies."

[12]Brigadier General Randy Gelwix, USAF, "Oral Histories Accomplished in Conjunction with Operation Allied Force/Noble Anvil."

[13]Wall, "Airspace Control Challenges Allies," p. 30.

transportation for mobility and towed AAA tended to bog down when driven off prepared surfaces and into open terrain. NATO pilots therefore studiously avoided flying down roads and crossed them when necessary at 90-degree angles to minimize their exposure time. By remaining at least 5 km from the nearest road, they often were able to negate the AAA threat, albeit at the cost of making it harder to spot moving military vehicles.

Whenever available intelligence permitted, the preferred offensive tactic entailed so-called DEAD (destruction of enemy air defense) attacks aimed at achieving hard kills against enemy SAM sites using the Block 40 F-16CG and F-15E carrying LGBs, cluster bomb units (CBUs), and the powered AGM-130, rather than merely suppressing SAM radar activity with the F-16CJ and HARM.[14] For attempted DEAD attacks, F-16CGs and F-15Es would loiter near tankers orbiting over the Adriatic to be on call to roll in on any pop-up SAM threats that might suddenly materialize.[15] The unpowered AGM-154 Joint Standoff Weapon (JSOW), a "near-precision" glide weapon featuring inertial and GPS guidance and used by Navy F/A-18s, was also effective on at least a few occasions against enemy acquisition and tracking radars using its combined-effects submunitions.[16]

One problem with such DEAD attempts was that the data cycle time had to be short enough for the attackers to catch the emitting radars before they moved on to new locations. One informed report observed that supporting F-16CJs were relatively ineffective in the reactive SEAD mode because the time required for them to detect an impending launch and get a timely HARM shot off to protect a striker

---

[14]The AGM-130 could be fired from a standoff range of up to 30 nautical miles. It featured GPS guidance, enhanced by terminal homing via man in the loop through live video feed data-linked to the attacking aircraft from the guiding weapon.

[15]The Block 50/52 F-16CJs used for defense suppression were equipped to carry the AGM-65 Maverick missile, but they did not employ that munition in Allied Force because the pilots, given their predominant focus on making the most of the AGM-88 HARM, had not sufficiently trained for its use.

[16]Gelwix, "Oral Histories." JSOW was employed only infrequently during Allied Force. Many of the targets assigned to the Navy were inappropriate for attack by the AGM-154's cluster-bomb variant because of collateral damage concerns and the lengthy timelines associated with attacks against mobile targets and with the munition's lack of a precise impact timeline. William M. Arkin, "Fleet Praises JSOW, Lists Potential Improvements," *Defense Daily*, April 26, 2000.

invariably exceeded the flyout time of the SAM aimed at the targeted aircraft. As a result, whenever attacking fighters found themselves engaged by a SAM, they were pretty much on their own in defeating it. That suggested to at least some participating aircrews the value of having a few HARMs uploaded on selected aircraft in every strike package so that strikers could protect themselves as necessary without having to depend in every case on F-16CJ or EA-6B support.[17]

The commander of the Marine EA-6B detachment at Aviano commented that there was no single-solution tactic that allied SEAD assets could employ to negate enemy systems. "If we try to jam an emitter in the south," he said, "there may be a northern one that can relay the information through a communications link and land line. They are fighting on their own turf and know where to hide."[18] The detachment commander added that Serb SAM operators would periodically emit with their radars for 20 seconds, then shut down the radars to avoid swallowing a HARM.

In all, more than 800 SAMs were reported to have been fired at NATO aircraft, both manned and unmanned, over the course of the 78-day air war, including 477 SA-6s and 124 confirmed man-portable infrared missiles (see Figure 6.1 for a depiction of reported enemy SAM launches by type).[19] A majority of the fixed SAMs were fired without any radar guidance. Yet despite that expenditure of assets, only two NATO aircraft, an F-117 and an F-16, were shot down by enemy fire, although another F-117 sustained light damage from a nearby SA-3 detonation and two A-10s were hit by enemy AAA fire but not downed.[20] There also were two reported cases of short-range infrared (IR)-guided missiles hitting A-10s, one of which apparently struck the bottom of the aircraft, defused itself, and bounced off

---

[17]Lieutenant Colonel Philip C. Tissue, USMC, "21 Minutes to Belgrade," *Proceedings*, U.S. Naval Institute, September 1999, p. 40.

[18]Michael R. Gordon, "NATO to Hit Serbs from 2 More Sides," *New York Times*, May 11, 1999.

[19]"AWOS Fact Sheet," Hq USAFE/SA, December 17, 1999. See also William M. Arkin, "Top Air Force Leaders to Get Briefed on Serbia Air War Report," *Defense Daily*, June 13, 2000, p. 1.

[20]David A. Fulghum, "Kosovo Report to Boost New JSF Jamming Role," *Aviation Week and Space Technology*, August 30, 1999, p. 22.

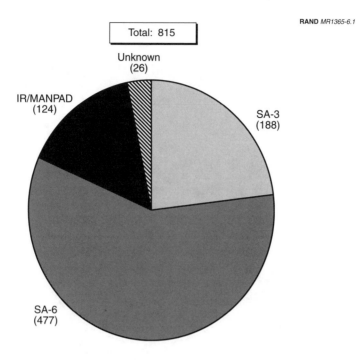

RAND *MR1365-6.1*

Total: 815

Unknown
(26)

IR/MANPAD
(124)

SA-3
(188)

SA-6
(477)

SOURCE: AWOS Fact Sheet.

Figure 6.1—Enemy SAM Launches Reported

harmlessly.[21] At least 743 HARMs were fired by U.S. and NATO aircraft against the radars supporting these enemy SAMs (Figure 6.2 provides a detailed breakout of HARM expenditure by target type).[22] Yet enough of the Serb IADS remained intact to require NATO fighters to operate above the 15,000-ft hard deck for most of the air effort. The main reason for this requirement was the persistent AAA and MANPADS threat. Although the older SA-7 could be effectively

---

[21]"Washington Outlook," *Aviation Week and Space Technology*, September 20, 1999, p. 25.

[22]"AWOS Fact Sheet," Hq USAFE/SA, December 17, 1999.

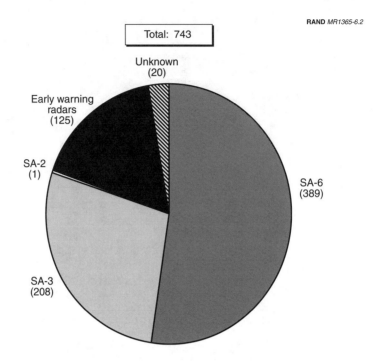

RAND *MR1365-6.2*

SOURCE: AWOS Fact Sheet.

Figure 6.2—HARM Expenditures by Target Type

countered by flares if it was seen in time, the SA-9/13, SA-14, SA-16, and SA-18 presented a more formidable threat.

In the end, as noted above, only two aircraft (both American) were brought down by enemy SAM fire, thanks to allied reliance on electronic jamming, the use of towed decoys, and countertactics to negate enemy surface-to-air defenses.[23] However, NATO never fully succeeded in neutralizing the Serb IADS, and NATO aircraft operating over Serbia and Kosovo were always within the engagement envelopes of enemy SA-3 and SA-6 missiles—envelopes that extended

[23]In all, 1,479 ALE-50 towed decoys were expended by U.S. aircraft during Allied Force.

to as high as 50,000 ft. Because of that persistent threat, mission planners were forced to place such high-value ISR platforms as the U-2 and Joint STARS in less-than-ideal orbits to keep them outside the lethal reach of enemy SAMs. Even during the operation's final week, NATO spokesmen conceded that only three of Serbia's approximately 25 known mobile SA-6 batteries had been confirmed destroyed.[24]

In all events, by remaining dispersed and mobile, and activating their radars only selectively, the Serb IADS operators yielded the short-term tactical initiative in order to present a longer-term operational and strategic challenge to allied air operations. The downside of that inactivity for NATO was that opportunities to employ the classic Wild Weasel tactic of attacking enemy SAM radars with HARMs while SAMs were guiding on airborne targets were "few and far between."[25] The Allied Force air commander, USAF Lieutenant General Michael Short, later indicated that his aircrews were ready for a wall-to-wall SAM threat like that encountered over Iraq during Desert Storm, but that "it just never materialized. And then it began to dawn on us that . . . they were going to try to survive as opposed to being willing to die to shoot down an airplane."[26] In fact, the survival tactics employed by Serb IADS operators were first developed and applied by their Iraqi counterparts in the no-fly zones of Iraq that have been steadily policed by Operations Northern and Southern Watch ever since the allied coalition showed its capability against active SAM radars during the Gulf war. That should not have come as any great surprise to NATO planners, and it is reasonable to expect more of the same as potential future adversaries continue to monitor U.S. SEAD capabilities and operating procedures and to adapt their countertactics accordingly.

---

[24]Comments on an earlier draft by Hq USAFE/IN, May 18, 2001.

[25]Tim Ripley, "'Serbs Running Out of SAMs,' Says USA," *Jane's Defense Weekly,* June 2, 1999.

[26]Interview with Lieutenant General Michael Short, USAF, PBS *Frontline,* "War in Europe," February 22, 2000. Serb IADS operators may have been able to trade short-term effectiveness for longer-term survivability because allied aircraft were typically unable to find and successfully attack VJ fielded forces and other mobile ground targets. Had they been able to do so and to kill VJ troops in large numbers, the VJ's leadership would have insisted on a more aggressive air defense effort. That would have enabled NATO to kill more SAMs, but at the probable cost of more friendly aircraft lost. I am indebted to my RAND colleague John Stillion for this insight.

The dearth of enemy radar-guided SAM activity may also have been explainable, at least in part, by reports that the Air Force's Air Combat Command had been conducting information operations by inserting viruses and deceptive communications into the enemy's computer system and microwave net.[27] Although it is unlikely that U.S. information operators were able to insert malicious code into enemy SAM radars themselves, General Jumper later confirmed that Operation Allied Force had seen the first use of offensive computer warfare as a precision weapon in connection with broader U.S. information operations against enemy defenses. As he put it, "we did more information warfare in this conflict than we have ever done before, and we proved the potential of it." Jumper added that although information operations remained a highly classified and compartmented subject about which little could be said, the Kosovo experience suggested that "instead of sitting and talking about great big large pods that bash electrons, we should be talking about microchips that manipulate electrons and get into the heart and soul of systems like the SA-10 or the SA-12 and tell it that it is a refrigerator and not a radar."[28] Such pioneering attempts at offensive cyberwarfare pointed toward the feasibility of taking down SAM and other defense systems in ways that would not require putting a strike package or a HARM missile on critical nodes to neutralize them.

During Desert Storm, by means of computer penetration, high-speed decrypting algorithms, and taps on land lines passing through friendly countries, the United States was reportedly able to intercept and monitor Iraqi email and digitized messages but engaged in no manipulation of enemy computers. During Allied Force, however, information operators were said to have succeeded in putting false targets into the enemy's air defense computers to match what enemy controllers were predisposed to believe. Such activities also reportedly occasioned the classic operator-versus-intelligence conundrum from time to time, in which intelligence collectors sought to preserve enemy threat systems that were providing them with streams of in-

---

[27]David A. Fulghum, "Serb Threat Subsides, but U.S. Still Worries," *Aviation Week and Space Technology*, April 12, 1999, p. 24.

[28]"Jumper on Air Power," p. 43.

formation while operators sought to attack them and render them useless in order to protect allied aircrews.[29]

Fortunately for NATO, the Serb IADS did not include the latest-generation SAM equipment currently available on the international arms market. There were early unsubstantiated reports, repeatedly denied by the Russian Ministry of Foreign Affairs, that several weeks before the start of the bombing effort, Russia had provided Yugoslavia with elements of between six and ten S-300PM (NATO code-name SA-10) long-range SAM systems, which had been delivered without their 36D6 Clam Shell low-altitude acquisition radars.[30] Had those reports been valid, even the suspected presence of SA-10 and SA-12 SAMs in the enemy IADS inventory would have made life far more challenging for attacking NATO aircrews. Milosevic reportedly pressed the Russians hard for such equipment repeatedly, without success. Deputy Secretary of State Strobe Talbott later stated that the Yeltsin government had been put on the firmest notice by the Clinton administration that any provision of such cutting-edge defensive equipment to Yugoslavia would have had a "devastating" effect on Russian-American relations.[31]

All of this raised basic questions about the adequacy of U.S. SEAD tactics and suggested a need for better real-time intelligence on mobile enemy IADS assets and a means of getting that information to pilots quickly enough for them to act on it, as well as for greater standoff attack capability.[32] The downings of both the F-117 and F-16 were attributed to breakdowns in procedures aimed at detecting

---

[29]David A. Fulghum, "Yugoslavia Successfully Attacked by Computers," *Aviation Week and Space Technology*, August 23, 1999, pp. 31–34.

[30]Zoran Kusovac, "Russian S-300 SAMs 'In Serbia,'" *Jane's Defense Weekly*, August 4, 1999.

[31]Michael Ignatieff, *Virtual War: Kosovo and Beyond*, New York, Henry Holt and Company, Inc., 2000, p. 109.

[32]For example, the SA-10 and SA-12, now available on the international arms market for foreign military sale, are lethal out to a slant range of some 80 nautical miles, five times the killing reach of the earlier-generation SA-3 (David A. Fulghum, "Report Tallies Damage, Lists U.S. Weaknesses," *Aviation Week and Space Technology*, February 14, 2000, p. 34). One SA-10/12 site in Belgrade and one in Pristina could have provided defensive coverage of all of Serbia and Kosovo, as well as threatened Compass Call and the ABCCC operating outside enemy airspace.

enemy IADS threats in a sufficiently timely manner and ensuring that pilots did not fly into lethal SAM envelopes unaware of them. Other factors cited in the two aircraft downings were faulty mission planning and an improper use of available technology (see below for more on the F-117 downing). Although far fewer aircraft were lost during Allied Force than had been expected, these instances pointed up some systemic problems in need of fixing. As one Air Force general observed, "there had to be about 10 things that didn't go right. But the central issue is an overall lack of preparedness for electronic warfare."[33]

One of the first signs of this insidious trend cropped up as far back as August 1990, when half of the Air Force's ECM pods being readied for deployment to the Arabian peninsula for Desert Storm were found to have been in need of calibration or repair. Among numerous later sins of neglect with respect to electronic warfare (EW) were Air Force decisions to make operational readiness inspections (ORIs) and Green Flag EW training exercises less demanding, decisions that naturally resulted in an atrophying of the readiness inspection and reporting of EW units, along with a steady erosion of EW experience at the squadron level. "Now," said the Air Force general cited above, "they only practice reprogramming [of radar warning receivers] at the national level. Intelligence goes to the scientists and says the signal has changed. Then the scientists figure out the change for the [ECM] pod and that's it. Nobody ever burns a new bite down at the wing."[34]

During the years since Desert Storm, the response time for SEAD challenges has become longer, not shorter, owing to an absence of adequate planning and to the disappearance of a talent pool of Air Force leaders skilled in EW. One senior Air Force Gulf War veteran complained that "we used to have an XOE [operational electronic

---

[33]David A. Fulghum, "NATO Unprepared for Electronic Combat," *Aviation Week and Space Technology*, May 10, 1999, p. 35. A thorough and detailed account of the many problems and concerns identified and highlighted with respect to the USAF's current SEAD and electronic warfare repertoire is contained in the summary report of an Air Force–commissioned study by RAND's Natalie Crawford and seven senior retired Air Force general-officer electronic warfare experts, "USAF EW Management Process Study," briefing charts, October 1, 1999.

[34]Fulghum, "NATO Unprepared for Electronic Combat," p. 35.

warfare] branch in the Air Staff. That doesn't exist any more. We used to reprogram [ECM] pods within the wings. They don't really do that any more." During a subsequent colloquium on the air war and its implications, former Air Force chief of staff General Michael Dugan attributed these problems to the Air Force's having dropped the ball badly in 1990, when it failed to "replace a couple of senior officers in the acquisition and operations community who [oversaw] the contribution of electronic combat to warfighting output. The natural consequence was for this resource to go away."[35]

A particular concern prompted by the less-than-reassuring SEAD experience in Allied Force was the need for better capabilities for accommodating noncooperative enemy air defenses and, more specifically, countering the enemy tactic whereby Serb SAM operators resorted to passive electro-optical rather than active radar tracking. That tactic prompted Major General Dennis Haines, Air Combat Command's director of combat weapons systems, to spotlight the need for capabilities other than relying on radar emissions to detect SAM batteries, as well as to locate and fix on enemy SAM sites more rapidly when they emitted only briefly.[36] Looking farther downstream, one might also suggest that in the long run, the answer is not to continue getting better at SEAD but rather to move to improved low-observability capabilities and to the use of UCAVs (unmanned combat air vehicles), with a view toward rendering SEAD increasingly unnecessary.

Such concerns have occasioned a growing sense among SEAD specialists that the management of EW should be taken out of the domain of information operations, where it was pigeonholed for convenience after the retirement of the EF-111 and F-4G, and returned to its proper home at the USAF Air Warfare Center at Nellis AFB, Nevada. As one senior officer complained in this respect, electronic combat after Desert Storm found itself "buried in with information operations and information attack. What got lost was the critical issue that EW is a component of combat aircraft survivability."[37] One

---

[35]"Washington Outlook," *Aviation Week and Space Technology*, August 23, 1999, p. 27.

[36]Robert Wall, "SEAD Concerns Raised in Kosovo," *Aviation Week and Space Technology*, June 26, 1999, p. 75.

[37]"Washington Outlook," *Aviation Week and Space Technology*, June 7, 1999, p. 23.

side result of this neglect of the EW mission by the Air Force was that maintenance technicians could no longer reprogram quickly (that is, in 24 hours or less) ECM pods and radar warning receivers to counter newly detected enemy threats. That problem first arose in 1998, when several planned U-2 penetrations into hostile airspace had to be canceled at the last minute because USAF radar warning systems could not recognize some IADS signals emanating from Iraq and Bosnia.

Yet another problem highlighted by the IADS challenge presented in Allied Force was the disconcertingly small number of F-16CJs and EA-6Bs available to perform the SEAD mission. Aircraft and aircrews were both stretched extremely thin, even with the modest help provided by German and Italian Tornado ECR variants. This shortage of SEAD assets prompted a proposal for backfitting the HARM targeting system carried by the F-16CJ onto older F-16s and F-15Es. Another fix suggested for the shortfall in SEAD capability was to begin supplementing existing capabilities and tactics, which rely on the small-warhead HARM, with PGMs and attack tactics aimed at achieving hard kills against IADS targets for the duration of a campaign, essentially a very different approach. Most telling of all, the uneven results of the SEAD experience in Allied Force induced Air Combat Command to seek an increase in its planned acquisition of new F-16CJs from 30 to 100.[38]

THE F-117 SHOOTDOWN

It did not take long for the problems connected with the air war's SEAD effort to register their first toll. On the fourth night of air operations, in the first combat loss ever of a stealth aircraft, an F-117 was downed at approximately 8:45 p.m. over hilly terrain near Budanovici, about 28 miles northwest of Belgrade, by an apparent barrage of SA-3s. Fortunately, the pilot ejected safely and, against formidable odds, was recovered before dawn the next day by a

---

[38]"Washington Outlook," *Aviation Week and Space Technology*, May 24, 1999, p. 27.

combat search and rescue team using MH-53 Pave Low and MH-60 Pave Hawk helicopters, and directed by a flight of A-10s.[39]

There was a flurry of speculation afterward as to how such an unexpected event might have taken place. Experts at Lockheed Martin Corporation, the aircraft's manufacturer, reported that unlike earlier instances of F-117 combat operations, the missions flown over Yugoslavia had required the aircraft to operate in ways that may have compromised its stealth characteristics. By way of example, they noted that even a standard banking maneuver can increase the aircraft's radar cross-section (RCS) by a factor of 100 or more—and such turns were unavoidable in the constricted airspace within which the F-117s were forced to fly.[40] Another unconfirmed report suggested that the RC-135 Rivet Joint aircraft monitoring enemy SAM activity may have been unable to locate the SA-3 battery that was thought to have downed the F-117 and may additionally have failed to relay to the appropriate command and control authorities timely indications of enemy SAM activity. Lending credence to that interpretation, the commander of Air Combat Command, General Richard Hawley, commented that "when you have a lot of unlocated threats, you are at risk even in a stealth airplane."[41]

Although the Air Force has remained understandably silent as to what confluence of events it believes occasioned the F-117's downing, press reports claimed that Air Force assessors had concluded, after conducting a formal postmortem, that a lucky combination of low-technology tactics, rapid learning, and astute improvisation had

---

[39]Although some criticism was voiced afterward as to how CSAR had been shown to be "broken" because of problems that cropped up during the rescue operation (apparently, one of the helicopters was forced to disengage, refuel, and penetrate enemy airspace a second time before it could find and finally retrieve the downed pilot), genuine acts of heroism were displayed during the mission. It ended up a brilliant success and had the welcome effect of turning a propaganda coup for Milosevic almost instantly into a propaganda coup for NATO. On the criticism expressed, see Rowan Scarborough, "Air Force Search and Rescue Operations Called 'Broken,'" *Washington Times*, September 13, 1999.

[40]James Peltz and Jeff Leeds, "Stealth Fighter's Crash Reveals a Design's Limits," *Los Angeles Times*, March 30, 1999.

[41]"Washington Outlook," *Aviation Week and Space Technology*, May 3, 1999, p. 21. Asked whether the aircraft's loss was caused by a failure to observe proper lessons from earlier experience, Hawley added: "That's an operational issue that is very warm."

converged in one fleeting instant to enable an SA-3 not operating in its normal, radar-guided mode to down the aircraft. Enemy spotters in Italy doubtless reported the aircraft's takeoff from Aviano, and IADS operators in Serbia, as well as perhaps in Bosnia and along the Montenegran coast, could have assembled from scattered radars enough glimpses of its position en route to its target to cue a SAM battery near Belgrade to fire at the appropriate moment. The aircraft had already dropped one laser-guided bomb near Belgrade, offering the now-alerted air defenders yet another clue. (The Air Force is said to have ruled out theories hinging on a stuck weapons bay door, a descent to below 15,000 ft, or a hit by AAA.)[42]

At least three procedural errors were alleged to have contributed to the downing.[43] The first was the reported inability of ELINT collectors to track the changing location of the three or four offending SAM batteries. Three low-frequency Serb radars that at least theoretically could have detected the F-117's presence were reportedly not neutralized because U.S. strike aircraft had earlier bombed the wrong aim points within the radar complexes. Also, F-16CJs carrying HARMs and operating in adjacent airspace could have deterred the SA-3 battery from emitting, but those aircraft had been recalled before the F-117 shootdown.

The second alleged procedural error entailed an EA-6B support jammer that was said to have been operating not only too far away from the F-117 (80 to 100 miles) to have been of much protective value, but also out of proper alignment with the offending threat radars, resulting in inefficient jamming.

Last was the reported fact that F-117s operating out of Aviano had previously flown along more or less the same transit routes for four nights in a row because of a SACEUR ban on overflight of Bosnia to

---

[42]Eric Schmitt, "Shrewd Serb Tactics Downed Stealth Jet, U.S. Inquiry Shows," *New York Times*, April 11, 1999. In subsequent testimony before the Senate Armed Services Committee, Secretary of the Air Force F. Whitten Peters did confirm that the aircraft had been downed by enemy SAMs. See Vince Crawley, "Air Force Secretary Advocates C-130, Predators," *Defense Week*, July 26, 1999, p. 2.

[43]See David A. Fulghum and William B. Scott, "Pentagon Gets Lock on F-117 Shootdown," *Aviation Week and Space Technology*, April 19, 1999, pp. 28–30, and Paul Beaver, "Mystery Still Shrouds Downing of F-117A Fighter," *Jane's Defense Weekly*, September 1, 1999.

avoid jeopardizing the Dayton accords. That would have made their approach pattern into Yugoslav airspace predictable. Knowing from which direction the F-117s would be coming, Serb air defenders could have employed low-frequency radars for the best chance of getting a snap look at the aircraft. Former F-117 pilots and several industry experts acknowledged that the aircraft is detectable by such radars when viewed from the side or from directly below. U.S. officials also suggested that the Serbs may have been able to get brief nightly radar hits while the aircraft's weapons bay doors were fleetingly open.

Heated arguments arose in Washington and elsewhere in the immediate aftermath of the shootdown over whether USEUCOM had erred in not aggressively having sought to destroy the wreckage of the downed F-117 in order to keep its valuable stealth technology out of unfriendly hands and eliminate its propaganda value, which the Serbs bent every effort to exploit.[44] Said a former commander of Tactical Air Command, General John M. Loh: "I'm surprised we didn't bomb it, because the standing procedure has always been that when you lose something of real or perceived value—in this case real technology, stealth—you destroy it."[45] The case for at least trying to deny the enemy the wreckage was bolstered by Paul Kaminski, the Pentagon's former acquisition chief and the Air Force's first F-117 program manager during the 1970s. Kaminski noted that although the F-117 had been operational for 15 years, "there are things in that airplane, while they may not be leading technologies today in the United States, are certainly ahead of what some potential adversaries have." Kaminski added that the main concern was not that any exploitation of the F-117's low-observable technology would enable an enemy to put the F-117 at greater risk, but rather that it could help him eventually develop his own stealth technology in due course.[46] Reports indicated that military officials had at first considered attempting to destroy the wreckage but opted in the end not to follow

---

[44]To bolster their case, some noted that when an F-117 had crashed earlier at an air show near Baltimore in 1998, the Air Force had thoroughly sanitized the area and hauled off the wreckage to prevent its most sensitive features from being compromised.

[45]Vago Muradian, "Stealth Compromised by Not Destroying F-117 Wreckage," *Defense Daily*, April 2, 1999.

[46]Ibid.

through with the attempt because they could not have located it quickly enough to attack it before it was surrounded by civilians and the media.[47] Those issues aside, whatever the precise explanation for the downing, it meant not merely the loss of a key U.S. combat aircraft but the dimming of the F-117's former aura of invincibility, which for years had been of incalculable psychological value to the United States.

PROBLEMS WITH FLEXIBLE TARGETING

Yet another disappointment in the air war's performance centered on what turned out to be NATO's almost completely ineffective efforts to attack mobile VJ forces in the KEZ. By the end of the third week, despite determined attempts by allied aircrews over the preceding week, NATO analysts were unable to confirm the destruction of a single VJ tank or military vehicle, owing to the success of enemy ground units at dispersing and concealing their armor. That disappointment underscored the limits of conducting air operations against dispersed and hidden enemy troops in conditions in which weather, terrain, and tactics all favored the enemy and where no friendly ground combat presence was on hand to compel those forces to concentrate and expose themselves. Had Serb commanders any reason to fear a NATO ground invasion, they would have had little alternative but to position their tanks to cut off roads and other avenues of attack, thus making their forces more easily targetable by NATO air power. Instead, having dispersed and hidden their tanks and armored personnel carriers (APCs), Serb army and paramilitary units were free to go in with just 20 or more troops in a single vehicle to terrorize a village in connection with their ethnic cleansing campaign.

---

[47]On April 2, the Yugoslav government announced its intention to hand over pieces of the downed F-117 to Russian authorities. Robert Hewson, "Operation Allied Force: The First 30 Days," *World Air Power Journal*, Fall 1999, p. 18. For the record, it should be noted that USAF F-15Es were immediately put on alert to destroy the wreckage with AGM-130s after the F-117 downing was confirmed, but by the time the wreckage location could be positively determined, CNN was on the scene and collateral damage issues precluded the attack. Comments on an earlier draft by Hq USAF/XOXS, July 9, 2001.

Indeed, the opportunity to get at fielded enemy ground units with air power alone had been essentially lost by NATO even before Operation Allied Force commenced. As General Jumper later recalled, during the Rambouillet talks in early March 1999, "we watched 40,000 Serbian troops mass north of Kosovo, we watched them infiltrate down into Kosovo, we watched heavy armor come down into there, all under the umbrella of the peace conference, and we weren't able to react."[48] Once those forces had completed their massing on March 15 and had begun a substantial incursion into Kosovo, any chance for allied air power to be significantly effective against them promptly disappeared. Once safely dispersed, VJ units simply turned off the engines of their tanks and other vehicles to save fuel, hid their vehicles in barns, churches, forests, and populated areas, hunkered down, and hoped to wait the air effort out. By the end of April, General Clark frankly conceded that after six weeks of bombing, there were more VJ, MUP, and Serb paramilitary forces in Kosovo than there had been when Allied Force began. That attested powerfully to the latter's near-total ineffectiveness, at least up to that point, in halting the Serbian ethnic cleansing rampage throughout Kosovo.

Once the targeting of enemy troops in Kosovo became a SACEUR priority at the start of the third week, Yugoslavia was divided into four large search sectors. The two USAF E-8 Joint STARS aircraft that had been committed to supporting the air effort were tasked with searching for ground targets in the KEZ and with providing near-real time intelligence and targeting information to the CAOC in Vicenza and to the EC-130 ABCCC. Depending on the possibility of collateral damage, Joint STARS was sometimes cleared to communicate directly to airborne FACs and to direct NATO strikes against fleeting targets of opportunity, with the goal of getting target information and coordinates to orbiting strike aircraft within minutes.[49]

---

[48]General John Jumper, USAF, "Oral Histories Accomplished in Conjunction with Operation Allied Force/Noble Anvil."

[49]Robert Wall, "Joint STARS Changes Operational Scheme," *Aviation Week and Space Technology*, May 3, 1999, pp. 25–27.

Before long, three broad approaches to what came to be called "flex" targeting emerged for prompt employment against mobile VJ and MUP forces operating in Kosovo and against pop-up IADS assets deployed in Serbia. In the first, called "alert flex" targeting, combat aircraft were apportioned from the very outset as designated "flex" sorties in the ATO and reserved for launch on short notice against any pop-up targets that might be detected and identified within the ATO cycle. Initially, such designated aircraft were kept on ground alert. Later in the operation, they were placed on airborne tanker alert, which reduced their response times by as much as two hours.

The second approach entailed redirecting aircraft already en route to preplanned fixed targets. Strikers would be diverted either to alternate high-value fixed targets in Serbia or to recently detected mobile targets in Serbia or Kosovo. Because of the large number of NATO fighters already preapportioned and available on call for use as alert flex assets, however, such en route diversions occurred only rarely. All three heavy bombers (the B-52s, B-1s, and B-2s) were also diverted to new targets on occasion, requiring real-time changes in their preplanned ingress routes.

The third category of flexible targeting involved dedicated sorties launched into holding orbits for on-call attacks against detected mobile VJ forces in Kosovo after the KEZ was declared on Day 20 of the air effort. This approach, which evolved progressively over time, entailed the use of F-16s, A-10s, or Tornados serving as airborne forward air controllers. Their FAC-qualified pilots would search for ground targets in predesignated kill boxes, attempt a visual identification of any suspected target candidates, and assess the potential for collateral damage after determining that the target candidates were valid. Depending on the prevailing rules of engagement, the FAC pilots would first request ABCCC or CAOC approval to attack the target and then, upon being cleared to release weapons, would drop their munitions on the approved target while directing their wingmen to drop on adjacent targets. In the event that multiple targets were detected and approved, additional strike aircraft would be called in if they were close at hand. Because NATO had no fielded ground forces in the combat zone, the FACs could not request ground assistance and were on their own in locating and identifying mobile targets.

As noted earlier, a major problem that inhibited the effectiveness of Joint STARS in support of these missions was Kosovo's mountainous terrain, which required the aircraft to fly unusually close to enemy territory so its sensor operators could look into valleys and minimize the enemy's opportunities to take advantage of terrain masking. Even then, the high ridgelines often made it impossible for Joint STARS crews, from their standoff orbits, to peer into some valleys where VJ forces were thought to have been concentrated. Joint STARS also had only a limited ability to detect and monitor ground targets in dense woods and built-up areas. Because of these constraints, NATO had little by way of wide-area airborne surveillance and cueing of the sort that had made coalition operations against enemy ground forces so effective in Desert Storm. That deficiency placed a doubly high premium on hitting enemy ground-force targets as they moved into open areas and were visually detected by airborne FACs. It also, in effect, ceded the tactical initiative to VJ forces, since the latter could decide when and where to reposition themselves. The net result was a need for large numbers of combat aircraft continuously orbiting over the KEZ but producing little tactical return, compounded—indeed, largely caused—by the absence of a NATO ground threat to force enemy troops into more predictable patterns of behavior.[50]

The performance of Joint STARS against dispersed and hidden enemy forces was less than satisfactory not only because of the constraints described above, but also because of an unfortunate failure by air operations managers to make the most of the aircraft's inherent capabilities for supporting counterland operations. That failure partly reflected a continuing slowness on the part of the U.S. Air Force to develop and institutionalize a detailed appreciation for how land forces operate and, in turn, to acquire the conceptual wherewithal that is essential for making air power more effective in defeating those forces. Surprisingly little progress was registered by the Air Force over the nine years since Desert Storm in developing a concept of operations for using Joint STARS in a surveillance and control team that also includes AWACS, Rivet Joint, airborne FACs, and UAVs, all working as a synergistic collective against elusive enemy ground forces.

---

[50]I am indebted to my colleague John Stillion for developing these points.

As one telling testament to this failure, the inclusion of Joint STARS in the air war's equipment roster had been requested by the Army, not by the Air Force.[51] Because of the predominant USAF focus on attacking fixed infrastructure targets, few in the Air Force fully appreciated the E-8's capability for providing wide-area, all-weather standoff coverage of the KEZ and its resultant ability to provide USEUCOM's and NATO's operational-level commanders with real-time situation awareness regarding the status and activity of VJ forces. It took days for Joint STARS even to be included in the ATO. Once there, the aircraft was typically thought of as a surveillance platform operating in the service of the intelligence community, rather than as a strike support asset working to provide direct and immediate assistance to NATO aircrews conducting flexible targeting missions. With the right teaming, connectivity, and practice, the use of Joint STARS to cue UAVs might have reduced, if not eliminated, the "searching-through-a-soda straw" problem, lessened UAV exposure to hostile fire, and helped maintain tactical surprise for NATO aircrews engaged in the search for VJ targets of opportunity. No measures of that sort, however, were attempted until quite late in Allied Force.

Yet another complicating influence on the air effort's attempts against dispersed and hidden enemy forces stemmed from the command and control arrangements that had been hastily cobbled together at the operational and tactical levels once it became clear that NATO was committed to an air war for the long haul. Although the CAOC eventually worked out a means of using real-time imagery to detect fielded VJ forces in the KEZ and to "flex" allied air assets to attack those newly developed targets in an orderly fashion, those doing the "flex" decisionmaking during the first half of Allied Force did so with no apportionment or targeting guidance whatever. As one expert observer noted, "if the detected target was militarily significant, it was struck, regardless of [General Short's] priorities or intentions. There was no link to an assessment mechanism, so that once a target was struck, there was no way to link it to what unit it had been associated with, so no effective degradation was re-

---

[51]Personal communication to the author from Price Bingham, Northrop Grumman Corporation, Melbourne, Florida, December 20, 1999.

corded."[52] As a result, combat aircraft were sometimes diverted from scheduled ATO targets of clear operational significance to attack "flex" targets of highly dubious tactical, let alone operational or strategic, worth. Moreover, owing to the absence of any feedback mechanism, aircraft were often committed against targets that had already been successfully struck, forcing the CAOC either to re-role aircraft on short notice or else to expose aircrews needlessly to enemy IADS threats a second time. For most of the air war, roughly half of General Short's available surface-attack sorties were committed against targets in the KEZ. Of those, a significant percentage were "flexed" in this haphazard manner.[53]

Weather was still another complicating factor in the effort against dispersed VJ forces. From the 15,000-ft altitude floor above which NATO aircrews typically operated, the cloud cover over Kosovo was greater than 50 percent for more than 78 percent of the air war's duration. That allowed unimpeded strike operations on only 24 of the air war's 78 days. The impact of these conditions on the flexible targeting effort was considerable. In all, 3,766 planned sorties, including 1,029 designated close air support sorties, had to be canceled because of weather.

Even on clear days, another factor preventing the kill box system from being as effective as it might otherwise have been was the tight rules-of-engagement regime that had been imposed after the Djakovica incident (see below), in which more than 60 ethnic Albanian refugees were reportedly killed in an attack by USAF F-16s against what was thought to have been a VJ troop convoy. These restrictions had a far greater inhibiting influence on the effectiveness of NATO's flexible targeting efforts than the oft-cited 15,000-ft altitude floor which NATO's aircrews had been directed to observe. Unless an object of interest was clearly determined to be a valid military target, such as a VJ tank operating in the open, pilots had to get clearance for any attack from the CAOC, with General Short himself often

---

[52]Lieutenant Colonel L. T. Wight, USAF, "What a Tangled Web We Wove: An After-Action Assessment of Operation Allied Force's Command and Control Structure and Processes," unpublished paper, no date, p. 12. Colonel Wight was a member of the C-5 Strategy Cell at the CAOC.

[53]Ibid.

making the decision after checking second sources like real-time UAV video feed. Because of the delays created by these and similar hurdles, orbiting NATO aircraft often ran low on fuel before being cleared to drop their weapons and accordingly were forced to leave the area in search of a tanker.[54]

Last, and perhaps as decisive as any single other factor, VJ forces aggressively avoided making themselves easy targets for NATO air attacks. Indeed, digging in and hunkering down for defensive attrition warfare had lain at the heart of Yugoslav operational doctrine ever since the days of partisan operations against the Wehrmacht in World War II. Whenever General Clark would say, "You've got to get them in their assembly areas," the reply typically was: "These guys aren't assembling!"[55] RAF Harrier GR. Mk 7 pilots operating in kill boxes over Kosovo reported that "there was nothing moving around at all during the daytime," adding that when Clark "got up and said knocking out five tanks was a good day for NATO, he [was] telling it straight. On some days we couldn't find any tanks."[56] Even with the aid of binoculars, the ground below often seemed devoid of life to NATO aircrews orbiting overhead at 15,000 ft. This was the predictable result of trying to engage an enemy who had no need to shoot, move, or expose his position, thanks to the absence of a credible NATO ground threat.

To be sure, there were some notable bright spots in NATO's air effort against VJ forces in Kosovo. To cite one example, in those rare instances in which enemy armor and other targets exposed themselves to attack from the air, the upgraded AGM-65G2 Maverick air-to-ground missile generally performed very effectively. The effectiveness rate for older Mavericks was lower, but still reportedly higher than 90 percent.[57] Also, both U-2 imagery and pictures provided by the Navy's F-14 equipped with TARPS (Tactical Air Reconnaissance

---

[54]Tim Ripley, "Harriers over the Kosovo 'Kill Boxes,'" *World Air Power Journal*, Winter 1999/2000, p. 100.

[55]Brigadier General Randy Gelwix, USAF, "Oral Histories Accomplished in Conjunction with Operation Allied Force/Noble Anvil."

[56]Ripley, "Harriers over the Kosovo 'Kill Boxes.'"

[57]Robert Wall, "Maverick Fix Tested in Kosovo," *Aviation Week and Space Technology*, September 6, 1999, pp. 88–89.

Pod System) later proved useful to the CAOC in what the Cohen-Shelton after-action report to Congress called "several" instances involving the rapid retargeting of NATO aircraft to new targets.[58]

To cite another notable example, the two Marine F/A-18D squadrons that deployed to the former Warsaw Pact airfield at Taszar, Hungary, late in the air war played an active part in the effort against enemy forces in the KEZ.[59] For the first time on a large scale in combat, the F/A-18D aircrews, along with NATO pilots flying other combat aircraft types, made heavy use of night-vision goggles with compatible internal and external lighting modifications, thus enabling multi-aircraft formations and simultaneous night bomb deliveries.[60] Some F/A-18Ds also carried the internally mounted Advanced Tactical Aerial Reconnaissance System (ATARS). Still in operational evaluation as Allied Force began, the system provided digital, multispectral target images with its SAR and medium-altitude electro-optical (EO) imagery as a backup to pictures from other ISR sources, with a real-time connection to ground receiver stations. It figured prominently in both targeting and BDA activities.[61]

In a typical night F/A-18D flexible targeting mission (which might last as long as six hours, with four inflight refuelings), the C-130 ABCCC would pass to orbiting Marine fighters the grid coordinates of a VJ artillery position detected by the TPQ-36 and TPQ-37 counter-battery radars attached to the U.S. Army's Task Force Hawk in Albania. An airborne FAC in an OA-10 would then illuminate the target

---

[58]Secretary of Defense William S. Cohen and Chairman of the Joint Chiefs of Staff General Henry H. Shelton, *Kosovo/Operation Allied Force After-Action Report*, Washington, D.C., Department of Defense, Report to Congress, January 31, 2000, p. 58.

[59]The airfield itself offered an 8,200-ft runway and a tactical air navigation (TACAN) system enabling the aircraft to fly instrument approaches, but it lacked a ready communications link to the CAOC in Vicenza and also needed more fuel trucks, as well as runway arresting gear in the event of wet runways and aircraft emergencies. The latter were shipped in and quickly became a welcome presence because high-gross-weight landings in heavy rain proved to be routine.

[60]As one downside aspect worth noting in this respect, numerous aircrews later indicated that night-vision goggles often provided them with *too* much information because they were capable of picking up infrared events as far as 100 miles away.

[61]For further details, see Margaret Bone, "Kodak Moments in Kosovo," *The Hook*, Spring 2000, pp. 29–31.

location with flares and call in a two-plane section of F/A-18Ds to be available on short notice to attack it. In so doing, the OA-10 FAC, in effect, performed reconnaissance by fire. When shot at in return, the FAC would determine the source of fire to be hostile, and the F/A-18Ds would then be cleared to drop 500-lb Mk 82 bombs on it, which would generally stop the artillery fire for the rest of the night.[62] It was said that the greatest frustration for *all* NATO aircrews flying combat missions was to be orbiting over the KEZ night after night, for as long as six hours interspersed with multiple inflight refuelings, only to be called in at long last by an airborne FAC and cleared to attack a reported VJ tank that was no longer there.[63]

Owing in large part to such operations, at least those that produced recognizable combat results, NATO's effort to engage dispersed and hidden enemy forces in the KEZ was not a complete waste of time and assets. For one thing, VJ commanders knew all too well that as the weather began steadily improving with the onset of summer, any effort on their part to conduct large-scale operations against either the KLA or civilian ethnic Albanians would put them at extremely high risk of being attacked. Moreover, General Short reported in late May that the newly focused attacks against the VJ's 3rd Army in Kosovo were beginning to register discernible effects. He went on to predict that "if we do this for two more months, we will either kill this army in Kosovo or send it on the run."[64]

Taken as a whole, however, NATO's effort to attack enemy ground units in the KEZ was essentially a failure, the full extent of which became apparent only after the air war was over. To the very end, Short doubted that focusing exclusively, or even primarily, on elusive VJ forces in Kosovo would be enough to swing the desired outcome. He also placed little stock in claims emanating from NATO headquarters that the VJ was being progressively weakened by the air attacks. On that latter point, he observed that the only things that mattered were

---

[62]Tissue, "21 Minutes to Belgrade," pp. 38–40.

[63]Conversation with Major General P. J. M. Godderij, deputy commander in chief, Royal Netherlands Air Force, Scheveningen, the Netherlands, June 7, 2000.

[64]William Drozdiak, "Air War Commander Says Kosovo Victory Near," *Washington Post*, May 24, 1999.

that army's ability to move and its willingness to fight, and that both of those remained decidedly intact.[65]

In the first detailed official rundown of the air war's accomplishments as Allied Force approached its midpoint, the limited effects of NATO's bombing attempts against enemy forces in Kosovo were underscored by the frank admission that the VJ still retained 80 to 90 percent of its tanks.[66] Later, on May 19, NATO spokesman Major General Walter Jertz claimed more optimistically that one-third of all VJ tanks and artillery in Kosovo had been destroyed.[67] As the bombing effort drew to a close, NATO was similarly claiming that it had taken out more than one-quarter of the VJ's tanks and APCs deployed in Kosovo. Britain's chief of the defense staff, General Sir Charles Guthrie, further reported that more than 30 percent of the VJ's artillery and mortar pieces had been destroyed by NATO attackers.[68]

In its final tally as Operation Allied Force ended, the U.S. Defense Department settled on 700 out of 1,500 tanks, APCs, and artillery pieces destroyed altogether in Kosovo.[69] More specifically, General Shelton announced in an early postwar briefing that NATO attacks had destroyed "around 120 tanks, about 220 armored personnel carriers, and up to 450 artillery and mortar pieces." However, nothing like a matching number of hulks was found by allied inspectors after Allied Force ended. During their withdrawal, VJ troops took hundreds of tanks, artillery pieces, and APCs out of Kosovo. They also seemed spirited and defiant rather than beaten.[70] The VJ's com-

---

[65]William M. Arkin, "Limited Warfare in Kosovo Not Working," *Seattle Times*, May 22, 1999.

[66]Paul Richter, "Milosevic War Machine Has a Lot of Fight Left," *Los Angeles Times*, April 29, 1999.

[67]Robert Hewson, "Allied Force, Part II: Overwhelming Air Power," *World Air Power Journal*, Winter 1999/2000, p. 113.

[68]Michael Evans, "Serb Army Talks of Peace as Armor Takes a Pounding," *London Times*, June 2, 1999.

[69]Rowan Scarborough, "Pentagon Intends to Issue Final Count of Serbian Losses," *Washington Times*, July 9, 1999.

[70]Over the course of the 11-day Serb withdrawal, NATO observers counted 220 tanks, 300 APCs, and 308 artillery pieces being loaded onto trucks and transporters, along with hundreds of other vehicles and assorted military equipment. Steven Lee Myers, "Damage to Serb Military Less Than Expected," *New York Times*, June 28, 1999.

mander in chief, General Dragoljub Ojdanic, claimed after the war that only 524 Yugoslav soldiers had been killed, in marked contrast to NATO's estimate of thousands.[71]

After the dust settled in early June, a preliminary NATO postmortem concluded that the air war had had almost no effect on VJ operations in Kosovo. In an after-action briefing to senior Pentagon officials, the commander of Joint Task Force Noble Anvil, Admiral James Ellis, confirmed that NATO air operations were effective against VJ armor only after the KLA launched its offensive, forcing defending VJ troops to uncover and mass their armor and mechanized forces.[72] NATO initially claimed after the air war ended that it had disabled 150 of the estimated 400 VJ tanks in Kosovo. General Clark later scaled back that number to 110, after having determined that many tanks assumed to have been destroyed had, in fact, been decoys that the VJ had skillfully fielded in large numbers.[73]

Not only did the Serbs make successful use of tank decoys made out of tetra-pak milk carton material, they also positioned wood-burning stoves with their chimneys angled to make them look like artillery pieces. In some cases, water receptacles were found in the decoys, cleverly placed there to heat up under the sun to help replicate the infrared signature of a vehicle or hot artillery tube.[74] One source spoke of cockpit display videotapes showing targets with every appearance of being tanks collapsing instantly upon being hit. In addition, the Serbs made heavy and frequently effective use of smoke generators to protect targets against LGBs. After the air war ended,

---

[71]"Yugoslav Army Lost 524 Soldiers, Top General Says," *International Herald Tribune*, July 22, 1999.

[72]Briefing by Admiral James O. Ellis, USN, commander in chief, U.S. Naval Forces, Europe, and commander, Allied Forces Southern Europe and Joint Task Force Noble Anvil, no date given.

[73]Joseph Fitchett, "NATO Misjudged Bombing Damage," *International Herald Tribune*, June 23, 1999. General Jumper dismissed criticisms from some that expensive U.S. precision munitions had been wasted on decoys. Declaring that U.S. forces had had "plenty of bombs for decoys," he noted that what appeared to be legitimate targets were immediately attacked so that aircrews would not loiter over target areas trying to distinguish real targets from decoys and exposing themselves needlessly to enemy fire. *Aviation Week and Space Technology*, September 20, 1999, p. 25.

[74]Paul Richter, "U.S. Study of War on Yugoslavia Aimed at Boosting Performance," *Los Angeles Times*, July 10, 1999.

site-survey teams that went in on the ground in Kosovo and interviewed witnesses discovered that VJ forces had buried many of their missile launchers, covered fuel trucks with rugs, and disguised tanks as haystacks and armored vehicles as trees.

The subsequent, and putatively definitive, after-action report on Allied Force submitted to Congress by Secretary Cohen and General Shelton in the summer of 1999 claimed valid strikes on 93 enemy tanks, 153 APCs, 339 other military vehicles, and 389 artillery and mortar pieces.[75] Those downwardly revised estimates came on the heels of the findings by a munitions effectiveness assessment (MEA) team of 67 operators and intelligence experts, made up mostly of USAF officers, who went into Kosovo at Clark's behest to comb the country, both by helicopter and on foot, in an on-site survey of all actual DMPIs attacked. The team's specific mission was to perform an assessment of attacks undertaken against mobile targets in the Presevo Valley region of Kosovo by cross-referencing on-scene observations and conversations with witnesses on the ground against available cockpit display videotapes, imagery intelligence, signals intelligence, human intelligence, and interviews with airborne FACs who had been operating near the target area at the time of the attacks.[76]

The team's initial conclusion from that assessment was that "only a handful" of enemy tanks, APCs, and artillery pieces could be determined to have been catastrophically damaged by air attacks.[77] Although the team succeeded in investigating some 60 percent of NATO's claimed hits on mobile targets in the KEZ, it confirmed only 14 tanks, 18 APCs, and 20 artillery pieces as destroyed for sure. A later assessment conducted by USAFE's office of studies and analy-

---

[75]Cohen and Shelton, *After-Action Report*, pp. 84–85.

[76]As the team's concept of operations clearly stipulated, the mission objective was to "determine Allied Force munition effectiveness by selective examination of fixed and mobile target sets within Kosovo [and to] evaluate and record physical and functional target damage and precise weapons impact locations and characteristics, with emphasis on precision and near-precision air-dropped munitions." The concept of operations further stipulated that validation of NATO's air campaign, target set, BDA, and rationale for specific target selection were "beyond the scope of this survey." Documentation provided to the author by Hq USAFE/SA, May 2, 2001.

[77]Tim Butcher and Patrick Bishop, "NATO Admits Air Campaign Failed," *London Daily Telegraph*, July 22, 1999.

sis, using the team's findings as one important input, reported 93 tanks and 153 APCs as having been struck altogether, the same numbers noted above that were cited later by Secretary Cohen and General Shelton. Many of those claimed hits, however, were validated by only a single source of evidence, such as a cockpit display videotape or an infrared event detected by DSP satellites.[78] In the later aftermath of Allied Force, on-site surveys of bomb damage effects by KFOR observers and other inspectors further confirmed that NATO's attacks against VJ forces had accomplished far less than had initially been assumed, notably including at Mount Pastrik.[79]

These seeming discrepancies led some air war critics to charge that NATO and the U.S. Defense Department were engaging in a blatant cover-up of allied air power's poor performance against VJ forces in Kosovo to avoid being embarrassed by the paltry numbers the inspection team had produced. That criticism turned out, however, to have been overblown for two reasons. First, the cover-up charge was misdirected, in that it was based entirely on a leaked draft report by USAFE's inspection team that went to Kosovo earlier in the summer of 1999. That draft report, dated August 3, 1999, and titled "Operation Allied Force: Munitions Effectiveness Assessment, Vol. II: Mobile Targets," documented information collected in Kosovo and elsewhere by the MEA working group tasked with looking into mobile enemy targets. That effort was undertaken not to account for successful strikes, but rather to determine what equipment remained at the attacked sites. The freshest of the attacked sites visited was four weeks old, and some were only visited for the first time three months after the attacks.

All told, the USAFE team came across 14 tank carcasses and the hulks of 12 self-propelled artillery vehicles, which could have looked like tanks from the air and been reported as such in post-strike pilot mission reports. That added up to 26 confirmable "tanks" suffering sufficiently catastrophic damage from NATO air attacks to be written off and abandoned by departing VJ forces. Cross-referencing pilot reports with corroborating evidence from other sources, the USAFE

---

[78]John Barry, "The Kosovo Cover-Up," *Newsweek*, May 15, 2000, p. 23.

[79]Richard J. Newman, "The Bombs That Failed in Kosovo," *U.S. News and World Report*, September 20, 1999.

studies and analysis staff later documented presumed successful strikes on 93 tanks, 153 APCs, and 389 artillery pieces. It further documented another 60 instances of attacks on tanks that were believed to have been successful but that could not be validated because of the stringent criteria it had been given by SACEUR. As explained in SACEUR's subsequent strike assessment briefing at NATO headquarters, 26 tanks could be categorized as "confirmed catastrophic kills," based on physical information actually gathered on the ground in Kosovo. The remainder of the 93 reported tank kills were categorized as "assessed strikes," which meant, in effect, that there were indications suggesting that a weapon may have hit a valid target.[80]

Air warfare professionals, notably including the USAF chief of staff, General Michael Ryan, have readily acknowledged since the end of Allied Force that the problems encountered by the operation's flexible targeting effort outlined above reflected real challenges for the effective application of air power posed by such impediments as trees, mountains, poor weather, and an enemy ground force permit-

---

[80]Stephen P. Aubin, "*Newsweek* and the 14 Tanks," *Air Force Magazine*, July 2000, pp. 59–61. As USAFE's director of studies and analysis, Brigadier General John Corley, who directed that assessment, explained afterward during a Pentagon press briefing, "if a pilot claimed that he had attacked a tank at a given [location], we would go to that location and . . . begin to survey that exact site. If what we had was . . . multiple sources to confirm what had been claimed, then we would put that into a successful strike category. Let me give you an example. If we went to one of those desired mean points of impact and we found a bomb crater and we found shrapnel and oil down in the bottom of that bomb crater, then we would take a digitized photo of that crater and we would note that there would be earth scarring, as if some very heavy piece of equipment had been dragged from that bomb crater out to a road. Then we would compare that with both before and after imagery. You might have, for example, a [satellite] image showing a tank in a tree line. You may go and take a look at the cockpit video which shows that tank at that exact set of coordinates with a munition impacting it. . . . You may then go back and discover a piece of U-2 film afterward showing a damaged tank. You may then find out that an airborne forward air controller who had flown specifically over this area day in and day out would report that approximately two to three days later, whatever had been there was now gone from that location. We further wound up with some information whereby we saw bomb-damaged and destroyed equipment loaded on board flatbed trucks being taken out of Kosovo, headed back north into Serbia. So as you begin to look at all those sources of information, those multiple layers worth . . . in concert, and if we had multiple pieces of evidentiary information, we would confirm a successful strike. And that was the difference between the 26 and the 93. If we could not confirm with multiple sources, we did not claim a successful strike." News briefing, Office of the Assistant Secretary of Defense (Public Affairs), the Pentagon, Washington, D.C., May 8, 2000.

ted the luxury of dispersing and hiding rather than concentrating to maneuver to accomplish its mission.[81] The Cohen-Shelton report to Congress frankly admitted that the problems encountered with flexible targeting of VJ forces in Kosovo pointed up continued shortfalls in the nation's ability to meet "the difficult challenge of rapidly targeting enemy forces and systems that can move and hide frequently."[82] On that discomfiting point, U.S. and NATO defense officials had nothing whatever to hide and covered nothing up.

Second, and perhaps more important, although it was clearly essential for NATO to maintain constant pressure on VJ and MUP forces deployed in Kosovo and to bend every reasonable effort to suppress their freedom to operate at will against the ethnic Albanians, the majority of the combat sorties that SACEUR insisted be devoted to finding and attacking enemy forces in the KEZ arguably entailed a waste of munitions and other valuable assets. That perspective was pithily expressed by the vice chairman of the Joint Chiefs of Staff, USAF General Joseph Ralston, who later went on to replace Clark as SACEUR: "The tank, which was an irrelevant item in the context of ethnic cleansing, became the symbol for Serb ground forces. How many tanks did you kill today? All of a sudden, this became the measure of merit that had nothing to do with reality."[83] When General Jumper, on being pressed later by reporters for an honest account of how many tanks NATO had actually destroyed, replied simply "enough," he was telling the truth. The marginality of the tank issue to what really mattered in Allied Force was perhaps most convincingly explained by Brigadier General Daniel Leaf, commander of the 31st Air Expeditionary Wing at Aviano, when he declared in the immediate wake of the cease-fire that "counting tanks is irrelevant. The fact is they withdrew, and while they took tanks with them, they returned to a country whose military infrastructure has been ruined.

---

[81]Indeed, in its interim report on the Kosovo air effort, the USAF expressly conceded that "shortfalls remain . . . in the USAF's ability to locate and attack moving armor and other ground forces in poor weather. The Air Force needs to continue to develop and improve its ability to do this." *The Air War Over Serbia: Aerospace Power in Operation Allied Force*, Washington, D.C., Hq United States Air Force, April 1, 2000, p. 53.

[82]Cohen and Shelton, *After-Action Report*, p. 56.

[83]Dana Priest, "Tension Grew with Divide in Strategy," *Washington Post*, September 21, 1999.

They're not going to be doing anything with those forces for a long time."[84]

True enough, a demonstrable record of effective performance by the attacks against VJ tanks may well have been regarded at the time as being of crucial importance toward vindicating SACEUR's stress on attacks against dispersed and hidden enemy forces in Kosovo. Yet viewed in hindsight, the number of tanks taken out in the air war was, and remains, an issue of only scant pertinence to the operation's ultimate outcome. Not only that, getting into the tank-counting business in the first place made for a largely self-inflicted wound by the Department of Defense, SACEUR, and NATO. In the end, all the to-ing and fro-ing over how many enemy tanks were taken out by NATO was mainly of academic interest, since air operations in the KEZ were, by all indications, not a determining factor affecting Milosevic's ultimate decision to capitulate.[85] The KLA had been eliminated entirely as a tactical consideration by superior VJ strength. Moreover, notwithstanding more than two months of continual NATO bombing, the VJ lost few personnel to hostile fire, retained its command and control and resupply apparatus throughout the air effort, and continued to conduct ethnic cleansing forays until the last day of the air war, even though it did put itself at risk whenever its units exposed themselves to attack from the air. At bottom, NATO's failure to perform better than it did against enemy ground units in the KEZ was as much a result of the strategy chosen by its leaders as

---

[84]Ignatieff, *Virtual War*, p. 106.

[85]This is not to suggest that one should draw any particular comfort from the apparent fact that NATO's failure to take out more than a token number of VJ tanks was largely irrelevant to the overall outcome of Allied Force. For one thing, had NATO been able to render the VJ's Kosovo corps ineffective during the air war's initial month, Milosevic may well have capitulated earlier, to the relief of both NATO and the Kosovar Albanians. Second, and more important, the mission of finding, identifying, and destroying dispersed and concealed enemy tanks is not going to go away, and the U.S. Air Force will likely be asked again in some future contingency to attack fielded enemy forces under comparably challenging circumstances. Civilians in senior leadership positions who recall the more optimistic early claims on behalf of the air war's accomplishments in this respect will naturally expect air power to perform effectively. Fortunately, despite charges from some that the Air Force sought to play down its difficulties in this regard in the early aftermath of Allied Force, its leadership has frankly owned up to those difficulties and has initiated measures aimed at improving its capability. I am grateful to my RAND colleague Bruce Pirnie for directing my attention to this point.

it was of any inherent deficiencies in the air weapon. By ruling out before the fact even a ground threat, let alone any serious prospect of an early ground invasion, the Clinton administration and NATO ensured that air power would be stressed to the fullest when it came to attempts to engage fielded enemy forces.

STRAY WEAPONS AND THE LOSS OF INNOCENTS

Pressures to avoid civilian casualties and unintended damage to nonmilitary structures were greater in Allied Force than in any previous campaign involving U.S. forces. Nevertheless, despite rules of engagement characterized by USAF Major General Charles Wald as being "as strict as I've seen in my 27 years in the military," there were more than 30 reported instances throughout the air war of unintended damage caused by errant NATO munitions or mistakes in targeting, including a dozen highly publicized incidents in which civilians were accidentally killed.[86] The first serious loss of civilian lives occurred on April 12, when an electro-optically guided AGM-130 released by an F-15E struck a targeted rail bridge over the Jusna Morava river in Kosovo on the Belgrade-Skopje line 300 km southeast of Belgrade just as a passenger train full of noncombatants, in a tragic moment of fateful timing, happened to be crossing it.[87] Belgrade later reported that more than 55 civilians had been killed in that incident. Two days later, in the worst case of collateral damage

---

[86]Joel Havemann, "Convoy Deaths May Undermine Moral Authority," *Los Angeles Times*, April 15, 1999.

[87]Indeed, the train entered the AGM-130's field of regard so close to the moment of weapon impact that the F-15E weapon systems officer (WSO) who was controlling the guiding weapon noted that he had not even seen it until the videotape of his cockpit display was played back during the subsequent mission debriefing. As a measure of the extent to which F-15E aircrews, like all others, were disciplined to honor the strictest collateral-damage avoidance rules, there were numerous instances in which the WSO dragged the selected impact point of a guiding AGM-130 off the designated aim point to an open area at the last moment because the target looked through the weapon's EO seeker head like a house or some other potential opportunity for collateral damage. In a similar illustration of such discipline, one videotape of an AGM-130 attack on an enemy fuel storage tank as the weapon neared impact showed the targeted tank to be empty while others around it were full. Nevertheless, despite the WSO's natural temptation, the guiding weapon was not slewed at the last moment toward a more lucrative target because the empty fuel tank happened to be the one to which the approved DMPI had been assigned. Conversation with USAF F-15E aircrews, 492nd Fighter Squadron, RAF Lakenheath, England, April 27, 2001.

to have occurred at any time throughout the operation, attacks against presumed enemy military vehicles at two sites in southwestern Kosovo near the town of Djakovica were said to have killed numerous ethnic Albanian refugees when USAF F-16 pilots mistook civilian vehicles for a convoy.[88]

These and similar possible target identification errors resulted, in at least a few instances, from constraints imposed by the requirement that NATO aircrews remain above 15,000 ft to avoid the most lethal enemy infrared SAM and AAA threat envelopes, which made visual discrimination between military and civilian traffic difficult at best. Discriminate attacks against moving military vehicles amid a virtual sea of civilian refugees typically bordered on being an impossible mission when pilots orbiting at medium altitudes could not determine for sure whether a convoy consisted of military trucks, military vehicles carrying refugees, or civilian vehicles. General Wald, the deputy director of strategic planning on the Joint Staff and the commander at Aviano during Operation Deliberate Force in 1995, conceded that "the job is about as hard as it's going to get for targeting."[89]

Another contributing factor was the occasional tendency of allied aircrews to maneuver their aircraft in such a way as to put clouds within the targeting pod's field of view between the aircraft and the target, thus blocking the laser beam illuminating the target and depriving the weapon of guidance. On April 6, near the end of the second week, the first LGB went astray in that manner, hitting an apartment building in the small town of Aleksinac 100 miles southeast of Belgrade and reportedly killing at least seven civilians and injuring dozens more. The intended target had been an artillery brigade headquarters, but the bomb's steering toward its desired mean point of impact was disrupted by clouds that deflected the laser beam after weapon release.

In the case of the Djakovica incident noted above, there were initial reports that Yugoslav aircraft had intentionally attacked the civilian

---

[88]Rowan Scarborough, "As Strikes Mount, So Do Errors," *Washington Times*, May 11, 1999.

[89]Robert Wall, "NATO Shifts Tactics to Attack Ground Forces," *Aviation Week and Space Technology*, April 12, 1999, p. 23.

tractors and wagons near Prizren. Those reports ultimately proved groundless, although Pentagon officials did confirm that the Yugoslav air force was still operating low-flying Galeb ground-attack jets and attack helicopters.[90] In all events, the alleged occurrence of an inadvertent bombing attack on noncombatant civilians took place at midday, despite the greatest operational discipline on the part of the involved USAF pilots. The F-16 strike force leader, who was operating as an airborne forward air controller (FAC-A), determined the initial convoy to be made up of uniformly sized, colored, and spaced military vehicles whose occupants seemed engaged in systematic house-burning. Extensive radio discussion then ensued between the FAC-A and the ABCCC stressing the need to avoid inadvertently harming any Kosovar refugees. The ABCCC, backstopped by an orbiting UAV, confirmed the convoy to be a valid military target and marshaled as many fighters against it as were available in the immediate target area.

During the course of the precision attacks with 500-lb GBU-12 LGBs that then ensued, it was reported as "possible" that some of the vehicles may have been civilian tractors, at which point the FAC-A immediately called all fighters off "high and dry" (clear of the target area with their armament switches deselected), and the ABCCC, in turn, requested reverification of the targets as hostile. At that point, nearby OA-10s were called in so that their pilots might reconnoiter the situation and provide such reverification with onboard nine-power space-stabilized binoculars. One OA-10 pilot reported observing definite military vehicles but also multicolored and possibly civilian vehicles, whereupon the FAC-A terminated all further attacks. Afterward, Serb news reports claimed that 80 civilians had been killed, although the persistent ambiguities were such that NATO only conceded that it "may have attacked" civilian vehicles. Some reports suggested that the civilians involved had been machine-gunned rather than bombed, and eyewitnesses on the ground reported the use of human shields in the convoys and nearby Serb mortar fire at the same time the convoy was being attacked by the F-16s. The commander of the 31st Air Expeditionary Wing whose F-16s were involved in the tragedy, Brigadier General Leaf, later told

---

[90]Michael Dobbs and Karl Vick, "Air Strikes Kill Scores of Refugees," *Washington Post*, April 15, 1999.

reporters that the incident involved "a very complicated scenario, and we will never be able to establish all the details." He further stated that he could not explain the bodies of the civilians that had been shown on Serbian television and conceded only, in light of the ambiguous evidence, that there "may have been" unintended civilian fatalities.[91]

The extraordinary media attention that was given to events like these attested to what can happen when incurring zero noncombatant casualties becomes not just the goal of strategy but also the expectation. Thanks to unrealistic efforts to treat the normal friction of war as avoidable human error, every occurrence of unintended collateral damage became overinflated as front-page news and treated as a blemish on air power's presumed ability to be consistently precise. Indeed, the added constraints imposed on NATO aircrews as a result of such occasional tragic occurrences indicated the degree to which modern air power has become a victim of its own success. During the Gulf War, cockpit video images of LGBs homing with seemingly unerring accuracy down the air shafts of enemy bunkers were spellbinding to most observers. Yet because of that same seemingly unerring accuracy, such performance has since come to be expected by both political leaders and the public alike. Once zero collateral damage becomes accepted as a measure of strategy success, not only air power but *all* forms of force employment get set up to be judged by all but unreachably high standards. Inevitably, any collateral damage then caused during the course of a campaign becomes grist for domestic critics and the enemy's propaganda mill. Anthony Cordesman rightly noted how characterizations of modern precision bombing as "surgical" overlook the fact that patients still die on the operating table from time to time.[92] Nevertheless, a nontrivial number of proposed sorties in Operation Allied Force were either canceled outright or aborted at the last minute before any weapons were released because their targets (wryly characterized by some USAFE staffers as "morally hardened") could not be positively identified or

---

[91]Videotaped press statement by Brigadier General Daniel Leaf, USAF, Brussels, Belgium, NATO Office of Information and Press, April 19, 1999.

[92]Anthony H. Cordesman, "The Lessons and Non-Lessons of the Air and Missile War in Kosovo," unpublished draft, Center for Strategic and International Studies, Washington, D.C., July 20, 1999.

because of the perceived risk of causing collateral damage. At best, that made for a necessarily constrained and therefore inescapably inefficient air operation compared to the standard set earlier in Desert Storm.

A bevy of criticism arose from some quarters after the bombing ended alleging that many of the 500 or more Yugoslav and Kosovar Albanian civilians who lost their lives to collateral damage incidents had died needlessly as a direct result of NATO attack aircraft having been kept above 15,000 ft in the interest of minimizing the likelihood of losing friendly lives. Critics further charged that operating at that altitude had somehow been risk-free, cowardly, and even immoral on the part of NATO's aircrews.[93] In league with other detractors of the way the air war was conducted, strategist Edward Luttwak, for example, characterized 15,000 ft as a "not-optimal" but "ultra-safe" altitude from which allied pilots might carry out "perfectly safe bombing."[94]

In point of fact, 15,000–20,000 ft was precisely the "optimal" altitude block from which to conduct LGB attacks—not only to keep the attacking aircraft clear of short-range air defenses in the immediate target area but, more important, to give the LGB time to acquire the target and assume a stabilized glide. Contrary to the suggestions of critics, operating at medium altitude provides no protection whatever against radar-guided SAMs. It merely puts attacking aircraft outside the lethal envelope of "trash fire" threats (small arms, AAA, and infrared SAMs). These threats are impossible to detect in a timely way and offer little or no warning of imminent danger; as a result, they cannot be countered very effectively. Indeed, operating at medium altitude actually *increases* the risk of being engaged by unnegated enemy radar-guided SAMs because the aircraft can no longer take advantage of terrain-masking opportunities. The more important point, however, is that when medium-altitude attack tac-

---

[93]Typical of such baseless charges was the reference by one pundit to the "low altitudes at which tactical attacks work," yet where "pilots risk getting killed" (William Pfaff, "After NATO's Lies About Kosovo, It's Time to Come Clean," *International Herald Tribune*, May 11, 2000) and the allegation by another that "avoiding risk to pilots multiplied the risk to civilians exponentially" (James Carroll, "The Truth About NATO's Air War," *Boston Globe*, June 20, 2000).

[94]Edward N. Luttwak, "Give War a Chance," *Foreign Affairs*, July/August 1999, p. 40.

tics are employed, the timeline for target acquisition and weapons guidance is substantially longer, thus improving the chance of achieving a hit.

Even assuming the absence of undetectable "trash fire" threats, it is by no means a foregone conclusion that had allied aircrews routinely descended to lower altitudes in an effort to identify their targets more positively, the incidence of unintended collateral damage occurrences would have been that much lower. To begin with, VJ and MUP troops were highly accomplished at camouflage and hiding, and they made frequent use of the civilian populace as human shields. Moreover, in Kosovo, where most of the inadvertent civilian fatalities occurred, the mandated altitude floor was not invariably 15,000 ft as the critics implied. On the contrary, once operations against dispersed and hidden VJ forces in Kosovo began in earnest in mid-April, FACs were cleared down to 5,000 ft as necessary to make positive target identifications, and strike aircraft could descend to as low as 8,000 ft for a nonprecision dive-bomb delivery.

Even at those lower altitudes, however, positive identifications tended to be difficult, although in one case, as noted above, USAF OA-10 pilots using nine-power space-stabilized binoculars managed to observe civilians intermingled with a VJ truck convoy after one vehicle had already been hit, as a result of which the ongoing attack was instantly terminated.[95] As a rule, however, routinely going lower and accepting the increased risk of losing an aircraft in the hope of doing better target discrimination would not, in all likelihood, have produced the desired result. True enough, flying even as low as 100 ft above ground level might have enabled NATO pilots to distinguish civilian from military traffic in a few fleeting moments, if that traffic happened to lie almost directly underneath the aircraft's flight path. Yet operating that close to the ground at normal fighter airspeeds (500 nautical miles per hour or more) in defended airspace would have offered zero perspective and zero precision-attack capability. It also would have increased the chance of NATO aircraft losses to enemy "trash fire" and just possibly brought about the overall failure

---

[95]"NATO Jets May Have Erred in Convoy Attack, General Says," *Aerospace Daily*, April 20, 1999, p. 102.

rather than success of Allied Force as a result. Moreover, hidden targets would still have remained hidden.

The point of the foregoing is that for the kinds of circumstances that repeatedly occasioned the accidental loss of civilian life in Allied Force, the United States, to say nothing of its NATO allies, has yet to develop fail-safe target discrimination capabilities and tactics for use either above *or* below 15,000 ft. As a result, it has had little choice but to rely on draconian rules of engagement (ROE), which are designed to hedge on the side of caution yet are anything but foolproof. In one case during Allied Force in which the ROE worked as intended, a USAF pilot was directed not to attack a confirmed SA-6 launcher because it was parked immediately adjacent to a civilian structure in a village. There were other reported instances in which precision munitions in the process of guiding were deliberately steered away from targets at the last minute to avoid harming civilians who had not been seen in the target area until after weapon release.[96] In the most egregious instance in which the ROE regime appears to have failed, however, namely, the tragedy involving the convoy along the Djakovica road in Kosovo, the FAC who was coordinating the attack had been given a positive identification by the ABCCC that was completely consistent with the prevailing ROE. Upon observing that the vehicles were uniformly colored and evenly spaced, the FAC declared the convoy to be a valid target. He had also been given ABCCC approval to clear the fighters under his control to drop at will after one F-16 orbiting overhead had drawn fire from one of the convoy's vehicles.[97]

---

[96]John A. Tirpak, "The State of Precision Engagement," *Air Force Magazine*, March 2000, p. 26.

[97]It further bears stressing in this regard that most cases of unintended damage resulting in civilian deaths occurred inside targeted buildings, which were prespecified in the ATO and against which NATO aircrews were not free to exercise real-time discretion. Other such cases were occasioned by munitions failures such as faulty cluster-bomb fuses or laser target designators that were disrupted by smoke or clouds while a weapon was guiding. Neither had anything to do with weapon-release altitude. The only clear case of noncombatant fatalities that can be even indirectly ascribed to altitude was the April 14 Djakovica convoy incident, during which the attack was immediately called off once the target identification error was discovered.

The solution to such challenges lies not in more relaxed operating restrictions but rather in the development of better tactics, techniques, procedures, and equipment—perhaps beginning with a more aggressive and effective use of offboard platforms like UAVs to perform combat identification and to provide cueing for engaged shooters.[98] Unfortunately, the sensor-to-shooter links that have been refined to a high art over the years for the air-to-air arena, such as the E-3 AWACS and the joint tactical information distribution system (JTIDS) carried by some F-15s, remain far less developed for ground-attack operations when it comes to situation characterization and target identification.[99] In the absence of such capabilities, flying lower in Allied Force not only would not have solved the target identification problem, it would also have rendered weapons deliveries less accurate and, as a result, probably compounded the collateral damage problem rather than ameliorating it. As matters stood, although regrettable tragedies did occur because of occasional misdirected weapons, the munitions and tactics used by NATO in Operation Allied Force made the air effort a record-setter when it came to achieving its declared goals with a minimum of collateral damage for an operation of that magnitude. Indeed, given the high volume of ordnance that was expended over the course of the 78-day air war, it is most remarkable—even astonishing—that the incidence of unintended civilian fatalities was not higher.

---

[98]Email from Lieutenant Colonel James Tubbs, AF/XPXQ, to Colonel James Callard, AF/XPXS, February 11, 2000. Lieutenant Colonel Tubbs was the operations officer of the 510th Fighter Squadron flying F-16CGs out of Aviano Air Base during Operation Allied Force.

[99]Although, as in Desert Storm, AWACS generally provided a superb threat picture to allied pilots operating in hostile airspace, at least one specific instance of friction was reported by a USAF F-15C pilot who downed a Yugoslav MiG-29 during a day defensive counterair mission on March 26. The pilot complained that the supporting AWACS controller "did not have any inkling [that] someone was flying on the other side of the border, although he was real good at calling out every friendly *west* of us" (email communication to the author, June 4, 1999). The F-15 pilot further charged that the supporting AWACS was still unaware of the MiG-29's presence even after initial moves had commenced. The intercepting pilot accordingly assessed the assumed threat aircraft to be hostile by origin, since there were no NATO offensive counterair missions airborne at the time. Only after the engagement was fully joined and the F-15 pilot had visually confirmed his target to be a MiG-29 did the AWACS controller finally report two possible hostile contacts in lead-trail formation.

THE CHINESE EMBASSY BOMBING

By far the most consequential instance of unintended bomb damage in Allied Force occurred on May 7, when three JDAMs intended for the headquarters of a Yugoslav arms agency were dropped instead with unerring accuracy by a B-2 on the Chinese embassy in Belgrade. That colossal blunder was reminiscent of the ill-fated attack on the Al Firdos bunker by an F-117 during Desert Storm, which accidentally killed more than a hundred Iraqi women and children who, unbeknown to U.S. target planners, had been sleeping inside in the false belief that it offered them shelter. The inadvertent bombing of the Chinese embassy, which killed four occupants who happened to be in the targeted portion and sent 26 more embassy staffers to the hospital, became the latest of more than a dozen strikes in Allied Force that had gone awry by that time. Not only did the bombing cause a huge international uproar, it dramatized yet again how seemingly "tactical" errors can have immensely disproportionate strategic consequences. Among other things, the event triggered a diplomatic crisis of the first order between Washington and Beijing, disrupted moves to negotiate an end to the Kosovo conflict, and prompted a politically directed halt to any further bombing of targets in Belgrade for two weeks thereafter.[100]

At least two failures seem to have accounted for the inadvertent bombing. First, CIA officials who nominated the intended target wrongly deduced where it was located in Belgrade. Second, those same officials were unaware that the actual targeted building was the Chinese embassy, which had been moved there from another site four years before. During Desert Storm, target planners almost always had knowledge of all off-limits buildings in and around Baghdad, including foreign embassies, and they put red circles around those buildings on planning maps to ensure that they would not be inadvertently struck. Gulf War planners were also more proactive in updating the no-strike list, to include having U.S. officials contact

---

[100]The error was also reminiscent of earlier damage to the French embassy in Tripoli, Libya, in 1986 during the joint U.S. Air Force–U.S. Navy Operation El Dorado Canyon against Libya's ruler, Moammar Khaddafi, caused when the bomb fragmentation pattern from a preceding F-111 forced the trailing pilot to shift course, inadvertently sending his bombs into the embassy. That, however, was an operational error occasioned by the heat of battle, not a planning error committed by target nominators.

foreign governments directly whenever there was any doubt about the location of their embassies.[101] In this case, although the target development process most definitely included the creation and continual updating of a "no-strike" list of facilities, locations, and assorted other entities that was duly vetted throughout the intelligence community, U.S. officials admitted afterward that they had relied on an outdated map of Belgrade. Some laid the blame on a budget-cutting decision by the Clinton administration in 1996 to fold the CIA's National Photographic Interpretation Center (NPIC) into the Defense Department's National Imagery and Mapping Agency (NIMA), which had prompted many of NPIC's most experienced analysts to quit in protest.

In the immediate aftermath of the blunder, Secretary Cohen said: "Clearly, faulty information led to a mistake in the initial targeting of this facility. In addition, the extensive process in place used to select and validate targets did not correct this original error."[102] Cohen added that the bombing had resulted not from a mechanical or human mistake but from "an institutional error."[103] It was later determined that the error had occurred in considerable part because of the intense pressure that was being applied at the time by General Clark for planners to come up with 2,000 suggested targets in Yugoslavia, prompted by the scramble for targets that had commenced once the air war's first few disappointing nights made it clear that Milosevic was not about to fold quickly as had originally been hoped. It was in this forced atmosphere of trying to find and justify 2,000 plausible targets at any cost that the CIA's Counter-Proliferation Division, which had no particular expertise with respect either to Yugoslavia or to targeting, was led to submit the CIA's first target nomination in Allied Force.

As it turned out, U.S. intelligence had the correct street address for the intended target, which was a Yugoslav weapons-producing agency called the Federal Directorate of Supply and Procurement.

---

[101]David A. Fulghum and Robert Wall, "Intel Mistakes Trigger Chinese Embassy Bombing," *Aviation Week and Space Technology*, May 17, 1999, p. 55.

[102]Eric Schmitt, "Aim, Not Arms, at the Root of Mistaken Strike on Embassy," *New York Times*, May 10, 1999.

[103]Paul Richter and Doyle McManus, "Pentagon to Tighten Targeting Procedures," *Los Angeles Times*, May 11, 1999.

Yet when overhead imagery was examined to match up the address with the intended target, responsible individuals at CIA selected the wrong building. The actual target turned out to have been on the same street, only a block away to the south. The map used had been created in 1992 and updated in 1997. It did not, however, show the Chinese embassy at its current location, to which it had moved in 1996. No one in the planning loop had thought to check the match-up of the target address with its presumed location, because no one had any reason to believe that there might be a problem in the making. One midlevel CIA analyst who was familiar with the intended target reportedly "was concerned, raised some questions, and they did not get resolved." Doubts about the target's validity also were aired at the working level at USEUCOM, but those concerns were never passed up to more senior levels before the strike.[104] Afterward, in a classic case of closing the barn door after the horse had escaped, NATO officials cited a new "iron-clad requirement" that targets be reviewed by people who had first-hand knowledge of them.[105] Yet despite that belated measure, on the first day after NATO's bombing of Belgrade resumed two weeks later, attacking aircraft inadvertently damaged the residences of the Swedish, Spanish, and Norwegian ambassadors, the Libyan embassy, and a hospital in which four civilians were killed.[106]

Perhaps predictably when viewed in hindsight, more than a few people around the world came to conclude in the early wake of the Chinese embassy bombing that notwithstanding the U.S. government's insistent claims to the contrary, the bombing had, in fact, been not only far from accidental, but planned with calculated intent from the very start. Much of the apparent strength of this conspiracy theory stemmed from the fact that the three JDAMs that were dropped by the B-2 had, all too conveniently, landed squarely on that part of the embassy that housed the office of the defense attaché and the embassy's intelligence cell, the latter of which was widely believed in

---

[104]Vernon Loeb and Steven Mufson, "CIA Analyst Raised Alert on China's Embassy," *Washington Post*, June 24, 1999.

[105]Eric Schmitt, "Pentagon Admits Its Maps of Belgrade Are Out of Date," *New York Times*, May 11, 1999, and Bradley Graham, "U.S. Analysts Misread, Relied on Outdated Maps," *Washington Post*, May 11, 1999.

[106]Steven Pearlstein, "NATO Bomb Said to Hit Belgrade Hospital," *Washington Post*, May 21, 1999.

informed circles to be the single largest Chinese collection center in all of Europe.[107]

One can readily understand how that curious coincidence might have helped energize Chinese allegations, which continue to this day, that the bombing of the embassy was intentional. Yet as much as one might wish to savor the thought that U.S. planners may have been just clever enough to contrive to take out a Chinese SIGINT site that was suspected of providing aid and comfort to the enemy while maintaining a reliable basis for plausible denial, it defies credibility to believe that those responsible for implementing Allied Force, at whatever level such putative machinations may have occurred, attacked the offending part of the embassy with premeditation. Although truth is indeed stranger than fiction on occasion, *no* coalition of democratic partners—least of all one led by an official Washington that, since Watergate, has become famously reputed for leaking like a sieve at even the slightest hint of high-level impropriety—could have pulled off such a stratagem without it being exposed. Ivo Daalder and Michael O'Hanlon perhaps best clinched this point when they wrote that the strongest proof of the groundlessness of the conspiracy theory was that "the attack's predictable damage—not only to U.S.-PRC relations but even to NATO solidarity—was far too great to justify the military benefit of silencing any Chinese military or intelligence assistance to Serbia that could theoretically have been provided from that building."[108]

TASK FORCE HAWK

As noted earlier in Chapter Three, within days after Operation Allied Force commenced, General Clark asked the Army to deploy a contingent of its AH-64 Apache attack helicopters to the combat zone to provide a better close-in capability against enemy tanks and APCs than that offered by fixed-wing fighters, which remained restricted to operating at medium altitudes. Clark initially had hoped to deploy this force to Macedonia, where the roads and airfields were better

---

[107]Steven Lee Myers, "Chinese Embassy Bombing: A Wide Net of Blame," *New York Times,* April 17, 2000.

[108]Ivo H. Daalder and Michael E. O'Hanlon, *Winning Ugly: NATO's War to Save Kosovo,* Washington, D.C., The Brookings Institution, 2000, p. 147.

and the terrain less challenging. The Macedonian government, however, declined to grant permission because it was already swamped by the flood of Kosovar refugees, so Clark sought Albania instead as the best available alternative.[109] Within four hours, NATO had approved Clark's request. It took more than a week, however, for the U.S. and Albanian governments to endorse the deployment. That approval finally came on Day 12 of Allied Force. The U.S. Defense Department at first indicated that it would take up to 10 days to deploy the package. In the end, it took 17 days just to field the first battalion of Apaches, which arrived in Albania on April 21.

At first glance, the idea of using Apaches to reinforce NATO's fixed-wing aircraft seemed entirely appropriate, considering that the AH-64 had been acquired by the Army expressly to engage and destroy enemy armor. As Pentagon spokesman Kenneth Bacon put it in announcing the deployment, they would offer NATO "the type of tank-killing capability that the bad weather has denied us . . . the capability to get up close and personal to the [VJ] units in Kosovo."[110] In a normal weapons load, the Apache mounts up to 16 Hellfire antitank missiles, 76 folding-fin antipersonnel rockets, and 1,200 rounds of 30mm armor-piercing ammunition. With that armament, it gained deserved distinction by destroying more than 500 Iraqi armored vehicles during Operation Desert Storm. In Desert Storm, the Apaches had deployed as an organic component of two fully fielded U.S. Army corps. But in this case, the Army was being asked by SACEUR to cobble together an ad hoc task force designed to operate essentially on its own, without the backstopping support of a fielded U.S. ground combat presence in the theater. The Army is not configured to undertake such ad-hoc deployments, and its units do not train for them. Instead, an Apache battalion normally deploys only as part of a larger Army division or corps, with all of the latter's organically attached elements.

---

[109]Another reported problem with the Macedonia basing option was the fact that it would have been a violation of the Dayton accords to station any offensive forces within the territorial confines of the former Yugoslavia. Albania was thus the only realistic alternative.

[110]Bradley Graham and Dana Priest, "Allies to Begin Flying Refugees Abroad," *Washington Post*, April 5, 1999.

Accordingly, the Army was driven by its own standard operating procedures to supplement the two Apache battalions with an additional heavy contingent of ground forces, air defenses, military engineers, and headquarters overhead. As the core of this larger force complement, now designated Task Force (TF) Hawk, the Apaches were drawn from the Army's 11th Aviation Brigade stationed at Illesheim, Germany. The deployment package included, however, not only the two battalions of AH-64s, but also 26 UH-60L Blackhawk and CH-47D Chinook helicopters from the 12th Aviation Regiment at Wiesbaden, Germany. Additional assets whose deployment was deemed essential for supporting the Apaches included a light infantry company; a multiple-launch rocket system (MLRS) platoon with three MLRS vehicles; a high-mobility multipurpose wheeled vehicle (HMMWV, or "humvee") antitank company equipped with 38 armed utility vehicles; a military intelligence platoon; a military police platoon; and a combat service support team. The Army further determined a need for its Apaches to be accompanied by a mechanized infantry company equipped with 14 Bradley AFVs; an armor company with 15 M1A2 Abrams main battle tanks; a howitzer battery with eight 155mm artillery pieces; a construction engineer company; a short-range air defense battery with eight more Bradley AFVs armed with Stinger infrared SAMs; a smoke generator platoon; a brigade headquarters complement; and diverse other elements. In all, to backstop the deployment of 24 attack helicopters to Albania, TF Hawk ended up being accompanied by a support train of no fewer than 5,350 Army personnel.

To be sure, there was a legitimate force-protection rationale behind this accompanying train of equipment and personnel. Unlike the Marines, who deployed 24 F/A-18D fighters to Hungary only a few weeks thereafter and had them flying combat missions within days with nothing even approaching TF Hawk's overhead and support baggage, Army planners had to be concerned about the inherent risks of deploying a comparable number of Apaches on terrain that was not that of a NATO ally, that lacked any semblance of a friendly ground force presence, and that could easily have invited a VJ cross-border attack in the absence of a U.S. ground force sufficient to render an attack an unacceptable gamble for VJ commanders.[111]

As one might have expected with so much additional equipment and personnel, however, the Apache deployment soon encountered the predictable consequences of the Army's decision. It was at first estimated that 200 USAF C-17 transport sorties would be needed to airlift the assorted support elements with which the Apaches had been burdened. (The Tirana airport lacked the required taxiway and ramp specifications to accommodate the more capacious C-5.) In the end, it took more than 500 C-17 sorties, moving some 22,000 short tons in all, to transfer TF Hawk in its entirety to Albania. Commenting later on the deployment, one Army officer complained that the Army is "still organized to fight in the Fulda Gap." Even the outgoing Army chief of staff, General Dennis Reimer, admitted in an internal memo to senior Army staff officers once the deployment package had finally been assembled in theater that the manifold problems encountered by TF Hawk had underscored a "need for more adaptive force packaging methodology."[112]

In all events, the Apaches with their attached equipment and personnel arrived in Albania in late April. No sooner had the Army declared all but one of the aircraft ready for combat on April 26 when, only hours later, one crashed at the Tirana airfield in full view of reporters who had been authorized to televise the flight. (The 24th Apache had developed hydraulic trouble en route and remained on the ground in Italy.) Neither crewmember was injured, but the accident was an inauspicious start for the widely touted deployment. Less than two weeks later, on May 5, a second accident occurred, this time killing both crewmembers during a night training mission some 46 miles north of Tirana. The aircraft was carrying a full load of

---

[111]That said, it bears noting that the threat of Serbian forces coming across the Albanian border did not appear to be a matter of great concern to anyone in the Allied Force command hierarchy *before* the arrival of TF Hawk, even though there were U.S. troops already on the ground in Albania as a part of JTF Shining Hope, the Albanian refugee relief effort, who were not provided with any comparable force-protection package.

[112]Elaine M. Grossman, "Army's Cold War Orientation Slowed Apache Deployment to Balkans," *Inside the Pentagon*, May 6, 1999, p. 6. Notably, the C-17 demonstrated for the first time the ability to air-deliver a significant Army force of M1 tanks, M2 AFVs, MLRSs, howitzers, and engineering equipment.

weapons and extra fuel. A subsequent investigation concluded that the first accident had been caused by the pilot's having mistakenly landed short of his intended touchdown point.[113] The second was attributed to an apparent failure of the tail rotor because the aircraft had been observed to enter a rapid uncontrolled spiral during the last moments before its impact with the ground.

As of May 31, the cost of the TF Hawk deployment had reached $254 million, much of that constituting the expense for the hundreds of C-17 sorties that had been needed to haul all the equipment from Germany to Albania, plus the additional costs of building base camps and port services and conducting mission rehearsals.[114] Yet despite SACEUR's intentions to the contrary, the Apaches flew not a single combat mission during the entire remainder of Operation Allied Force. The reason given afterward by the JCS chairman, General Shelton, was that Serb air defenses in Kosovo, although noticeably degraded by early May, remained effective enough to warrant keeping the Apaches out of action until SEAD operations had "reduced the risk to the very minimum."[115]

In a final coda to the Army's plagued TF Hawk experience, Shelton conceded in later testimony to the Senate Armed Services Committee that "the anticipated benefit of employing the Apaches against dispersed forces in a high-threat environment did not outweigh the risk to our pilots."[116] Shelton added that by the time the deployment had reached the point where the Apaches were ready to engage in combat, VJ ground formations were no longer massed but had become dispersed and well hidden. Moreover, he went on to note, the weather had improved, enabling Air Force A-10s and other fixed-wing aircraft to hunt down dispersed and hidden enemy forces while

---

[113]Paul Richter and Lisa Getter, "Mechanical Error, Pilot Error Led to Apache Crashes," *Los Angeles Times*, May 13, 1999.

[114]Ron Lorenzo, "Apache Deployment Has Cost Quarter Billion So Far," *Defense Week*, June 7, 1999, p. 6.

[115]Molly Moore and Bradley Graham, "NATO Plans for Peace, Not Ground Invasion," *Washington Post*, May 17, 1999.

[116]Sheila Foote, "Shelton: Risk Was the Key in Decision Not to Use Apaches," *Defense Daily*, September 10, 1999, p. 2.

incurring less risk from enemy infrared SAMs, AAA, and small-arms fire than the Apaches would have faced.[117]

Beyond the problems created for the deployment by the Army's decision to bring along so much additional overhead, there was a breakdown in joint doctrine for the combat use of the helicopters that was disturbingly evocative of the earlier competition for ownership and control of coalition air assets that had continually poisoned the relationship between the joint force air component commander (JFACC) and the Army's corps commanders during Desert Storm.[118] The issue stemmed in this case from the fact that the Army has traditionally regarded its attack helicopters not as part of a larger air power equation with a theater-wide focus, but rather as an organic maneuver element fielded to help support the ground maneuver needs of a division or corps. Apache crews typically rely on their own ground units to select and designate their targets. Yet in the case of Allied Force, with no Army ground combat presence in theater to speak of, they would either have had to self-designate their targets or else rely on Air Force forward air controllers flying at higher altitudes to designate for them. The idea of using Apaches as a strike asset in this manner independently of U.S. ground forces was simply not recognized by prevailing Army doctrine. On the contrary, as prescribed in Army Field Manual FM 1-112, *Attack Helicopter Operations,* an AH-64 battalion "never fights alone. . . . Attacks may be conducted out of physical contact with other friendly forces," but they must be "synchronized with their scheme of maneuver." FM 1-112 expressly characterizes deep-attack missions of the sort envisaged by Clark as "high-risk, high-payoff operations that must be exercised with the utmost care."[119]

---

[117]True enough, the terrain and weather presented by Kosovo were more challenging than the open and featureless Iraqi desert, where the Apaches had performed so effectively against enemy armor in Desert Storm. Yet the biggest concern in the minds of many U.S. leaders was the specter of a replay of the 1993 "Bloody Sunday" horror in Mogadishu, Somalia, with dead Army Rangers and crewmembers from downed Blackhawk helicopters being dragged through the streets on live television worldwide.

[118]David Atkinson and Hunter Keeter, "Apache Role in Kosovo Illustrates Cracks in Joint Doctrine," *Defense Daily,* May 26, 1999, p. 6.

[119]Quoted in Elaine M. Grossman, "As Apaches Near Combat, White House Seeks Diplomatic Solution," *Inside the Pentagon,* May 6, 1999, p. 7.

In light of this, the Army's V Corps commander, Lieutenant General John Hendrix, was willing to have the Apaches included in the USEUCOM Air Tasking Order (ATO), but demurred on having them incorporated as well into the separate NATO ATO, notwithstanding General Short's insistence that such inclusion would be essential in any situation in which the attack helicopters were ever committed to actual combat. Apart from that, however, Short never sought operational control of the Apaches or attempted to task them. He also offered to provide TF Hawk as much operational support (including EA-6B jamming support) as possible, and even went so far as to propose to subordinate himself and his CAOC to Hendrix, who as V Corps commander was also the ultimate commander of TF Hawk, as a supporting (as opposed to supported) combat element.[120]

In the end, an agreement was reached that included the Apaches with all other ATO missions yet left to Hendrix's discretion much essential detail on mission timing and tactics. A window was provided in the ATO such that the Apaches would be time-deconflicted from friendly bombs falling from above and also assured of some fixed-wing air support. However, the agreement reached in the end was so vague that it allowed each service to claim that it maintained tactical control over the Apaches in the event they were ever committed to combat. For their part, Army officers insisted that fire support for the AH-64s would come *only* from MLRS and Army tactical missile systems (ATACMS) positioned on the Albanian side of the border. That doctrinal stance was enough all by itself to ensure that the Apaches would never see combat, considering that the massive MLRS and ATACMS fires envisaged for any AH-64 operations would have rained literally multiple thousands of CBU submunitions all over Kosovo in an indiscriminate attempt to suppress enemy AAA and IR SAMs, a tactic that was out of the question from the very start, given NATO's determination to avoid any significant incidence of noncombatant casualties. In contrast, Air Force planners maintained that excluding the Apaches from CAOC control would increase their level of risk by depriving them of support from such key battlespace awareness assets as Joint STARS, Rivet Joint, Compass Call, and the EA-6B. As a USAF officer attached to Hendrix's deep operations coordination cell

---

[120]Telephone conversation with Lieutenant General Michael Short, USAF (Ret.), August 22, 2001.

(DOCC) reportedly put it, "they do not know, nor do they want to know, the detailed integration required to get the Prowler to jam the priority threats, provide acquisition jamming on the correct azimuth, etc. . . . The benefits of integrating with platforms like Compass Call, Rivet Joint and others are off their radar scope."[121]

After Allied Force ended, the assistant chief of staff for operations at Supreme Headquarters Allied Power Europe (SHAPE), USAF Major General John Dallager, touched the heart of the overriding interests and equities at stake here when he stated, during a briefing at a NATO Reaction Force Air Staff conference on JFACC issues: "Clearly the JFACC's authority must not infringe upon operational C2 [command and control] relationships within and between national or service commands and other functional commands. But to ensure deconfliction of simultaneous missions and to minimize the risk of fratricide, all air operations within the [joint operating arena] must be closely coordinated by the JFACC through the ATO . . . process. This last point may be difficult to swallow for land and maritime commanders, but if air history teaches us anything, it is that air, the truly joint activity, needs to be coordinated centrally if we are to make efficient use of scarce resources and if we are to avoid blue-on-blue."[122]

---

[121]Elaine M. Grossman, "Army Commander in Albania Resists Joint Control over Apache Missions," *Inside the Pentagon*, May 20, 1999, p. 9. In his memoirs, Clark later scored this article for "personally attacking Jay Hendrix and claiming, among other accusations, that he would not allow the Apache sorties to appear on Short's Air Tasking Order." Clark made no attempt to refute that accusation, however, but merely dismissed it as the complaint of a "disgruntled Air Force officer" whose "misunderstanding, communicated without perspective to friends in other units, suddenly surfaced to make news weeks after it had been written, after the problems it addressed, if real then, had been corrected." General Wesley K. Clark, *Waging Modern War: Bosnia, Kosovo, and the Future of Combat*, New York, Public Affairs, 2001, p. 320.

[122]Major General John Dallager, USAF, "NATO JFACC Doctrine," briefing at a conference on "The NATO Joint Force Air Component Commander Concept in Light of the Kosovo Air Campaign," Headquarters NATO Reaction Force Air Staff, Kalkar, Germany, December 1–3, 1999. It might be noted in passing here that another Army–Air Force difference of view that had an even greater operational impact than the joint doctrinal disagreement discussed above (because all involved had to live through its consequences) was the disconnect between the two services at Tirana as to who was in charge of the airfield and force protection, a disconnect that, according to one senior USAF planner who was involved, created "some real problems." Comments on an earlier draft by Brigadier General Robert Bishop, Hq USAF/XOO, April 17, 2001.

Interestingly, the Army leadership in the Pentagon seemed far more disposed than General Hendrix, at least in principle, to assign operational control of the Apaches to the CAOC. The incoming Army vice chief of staff, Lieutenant General Jack Keane, frankly commented at an industry symposium that "it boggles my mind, but we still have senior leaders, people who wear stars . . . that don't recognize that if you're going to fly Apaches at a distance and range, it's got to be on the [air tasking order]." General Keane added that the Apaches had to be under the operational control of the JFACC in the Army's "self-interest" because that arrangement offered a more effective way of employing them in this particular instance: "The JFACC should determine what the Apache's targets are as a result of the entire responsibility he has in conducting that air campaign." He further noted that the JFACC had the comparative advantage of being able to retask combat assets based on real-time intelligence, something that the Army could take advantage of as well if it could get itself out of "the business of being myopic about ground operations." In closing, he acknowledged that in the Army, "we've got this nagging fear that somehow, if we turn over our organization to somebody in another uniform, that that organization is somehow going to suffer as a result of that. And I just fundamentally disagree with that."[123]

In yet further testimony to the ill-fated nature of the Army's TF Hawk experience, an internal Army memorandum written after Allied Force ended acknowledged that the aircrews sent with the Apaches had been both undertrained and underequipped for their intended mission. In a report to the incoming chief of staff, General Eric Shinseki, then–Brigadier General Richard Cody, the Army's director of operations, resources, and mobilization, warned that because of those shortcomings, "we are placing them and their unit at risk when we have to ramp up for a real world crisis." Cody, who earlier had planned and executed the Army's highly successful Apache operations during the Gulf War, noted that more than 65 of the assigned aviators in TF Hawk had less than 500 hours of flight experience in the Apache and that none were qualified to fly missions requiring night-vision goggles. He further noted that the radios in the deployed Apaches had insufficient range for conducting deep operations and that the crews were, in the absence of night-vision goggles,

---

[123]Ibid.

dependent solely on their forward-looking infrared (FLIR) sensors. Given the rugged terrain, unpredictable weather, and poorly marked power lines that crisscrossed Kosovo, relying on FLIR alone, he suggested, "was not a good option." Moreover, he added, in order for the Apaches to have flown the required distances and crossed the high mountains of Kosovo, Hellfire missiles would have had to be removed from one of their two wing mounts to free up a station for auxiliary fuel tanks. As for the MANPADS threat, Cody remarked that "the current suite of ASE [aircraft survivability equipment] was not reliable enough and sometimes ineffective."[124]

The TF Hawk experience underscored how little the U.S. Army, by its own leadership's candid admission, had done since Desert Storm to increase its capacity to get to an emergent theater of operations rapidly and with sufficient forces to offer a credible combat presence. Shortly after the Gulf War, the Army's leadership for a time entertained the thought of reorganizing the service so that it might become more agile by abandoning its structure of 10 combat divisions and opting instead for 25 "mobile combat groups" of around 5,000 troops each. Ultimately, however, the Army backed away from that proposed reform, doing itself out of any ability to deploy a strong armored force rapidly and retaining the unpalatable alternatives of airlifting several thousand lightly armed infantrymen to a theater of conflict within days or shipping a contingent of 70-ton M1A2 Abrams main battle tanks over the course of several months.[125]

On his second day in office as the Army's new chief of staff, General Shinseki acknowledged that the Army had been poorly prepared to move its Apaches and support overhead to Albania. Part of the problem, he noted fairly, was that the only available deployment site that made any operational sense had poor rail connections, a shallow port, and a limited airfield capacity that could not accommodate the Air Force's C-5 heavy airlifter. However, he admitted that the Army

---

[124]George C. Wilson, "Memo Says Apaches, Pilots Were Not Ready," *European Stars and Stripes*, June 20, 1999.

[125]Thomas E. Ricks, "Why the U.S. Army Is Ill-Equipped to Move Troops Quickly into Kosovo," *Wall Street Journal*, April 16, 1999. The most fully developed and widely cited articulation of this proposed Army reorganization, which failed to take root, may be found in Colonel Douglas A. Macgregor, USA, *Breaking the Phalanx: A New Design for Landpower in the 21st Century*, Westport, Connecticut, Praeger, 1997.

was nevertheless overdue to develop and act on a plan to make its heavy forces more mobile and its lighter forces more lethal.[126] In what may have presaged a major shift in Army force development policy for the years ahead, he declared: "Our heavy forces are too heavy and our light forces lack staying power. Heavy forces must be more strategically deployable and more agile with a smaller logistical footprint, and light forces must be more lethal, survivable, and tactically mobile. Achieving this paradigm will require innovative thinking about structure, modernization efforts, and spending."[127]

One positive role played by TF Hawk after the KLA's counteroffensive began registering effects in late May was the service provided by the former's counterbattery radars in helping NATO fixed-wing pilots pinpoint and deliver munitions against enemy artillery positions. Its TPQ-36 and TPQ–37 firefinder radars were positioned atop the hills adjacent to Tirana to spot Serb artillery fire and backtrack the airborne shells to their point of origin. Army EH-60 helicopters and RC-12 Guardrail electronic intelligence aircraft were further able to establish the location of VJ command posts whenever the latter transmitted. Although TF Hawk's Apaches and other combat assets never saw action, its ISR assets exerted a significant influence on the air effort at one of its most crucial moments. The KLA's counteroffensive had forced the VJ to mass its forces and maneuver, to communicate by radio, and to fire artillery and mortars to protect itself. In response, the sensors of TF Hawk, operating in conjunction with the Army's Hunter UAVs, spotted VJ targets and passed that information on to those in the command loop who could bring air-delivered ordnance to bear in a timely manner. "The result," said a retired Army three-star general, "was that NATO air power was finally able to target precisely and hit the Serb army in the field. The Kosovars acted as the anvil and TF Hawk as the eyes and ears of the blacksmith so that the hammer of air power could be effective."[128] Echoing this conclusion, USAFE's commander, General Jumper, con-

---

[126]Eric Schmitt, "New Army Chief Seeks More Agility and Power," *New York Times,* June 24, 1999.

[127]"Shinseki Hints at Restructuring, Aggressive Changes for the Army," *Inside the Army,* June 28, 1999, p. 1.

[128]Lieutenant General Theodore G. Stroup, Jr., USA (Ret.), "Task Force Hawk: Beyond Expectations," *Army Magazine,* August 1999.

firmed that the counterbattery radars of TF Hawk had played "a very big part" in allied targeting during the final stages of Allied Force.[129]

Another bright spot in the otherwise troubled TF Hawk experience was the USAF air mobility system's superb performance in opening up the Rinas air base in Albania and flowing forces and relief supplies into it. The combined efforts of USAFE's Air Mobility Operations Command Center (AMOCC), the Allied Force Air Mobility Division, USAFE's 86th Contingency Response Group at Ramstein Air Base, Germany, and multiple supporting Air Mobility Command entities resulted in a stand-out success amid the generally dismal story of TF Hawk's immobility and the Army's persistent go-it-alone approach to command relations and putting the Apaches into the ATO. Simply put, the C-17 made the TF Hawk movement possible. (See Figure 6.3 for the sharp spike in C-17-delivered short tonnage connected with TF Hawk from the second week of April through the first week of May.) No other aircraft could have done the job—yet another testimonial to the direct-delivery concept that shaped the aircraft's design and got it through one of the most hard-fought acquisition battles in the USAF's history. Thanks to the C-17 acquisition, TF Hawk (despite its near-fatal growing pains) got in, and many thousand Albanian refugees survived—two signal accomplishments of what the commander of the U.S. Army in Europe, General Montgomery Meigs, later called one of the most successful airlift operations in history.[130]

SHORTCOMINGS IN INTELLIGENCE CYCLE TIME

Commanders and other air operators throughout the course of Allied Force found themselves repeatedly frustrated by the amount of time it often took to cycle critical information about enemy pop-up

---

[129]Response to a question at an Air Force Association Eaker Institute colloquy, "Operation Allied Force: Strategy, Execution, Implications," held at the Ronald Reagan International Trade Center, Washington, D.C., August 16, 1999.

[130]Comments on an earlier draft by Brigadier General Robert Bishop, Hq USAF/XOO, April 12, 2001, and Colonel Robert Owen, Hq AMC, May 10, 2001. See also General Charles T. Robertson, Jr., USAF, commander in chief, U.S. Transportation Command, and commander, Air Mobility Command, "Air War Over Serbia: A Mobility Perspective," briefing charts, 2000, Hq USAFE/SA library.

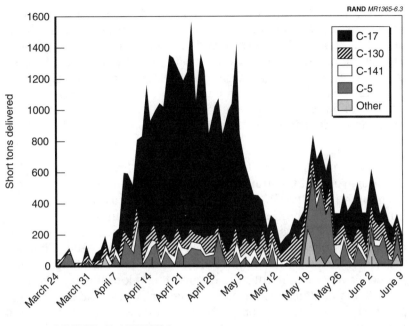

SOURCE: Hq USAFE/SA.

Figure 6.3—Short Tonnage Delivered by USAF Airlift

targets of opportunity from sensors to shooters who were positioned to engage them effectively. Although the requisite architecture was in place throughout most of the air war once a flexible targeting cell had been established by the end of the first month, it lacked a sufficiently high-volume data link with enough channels to quickly get the information where it needed to go.

To be sure, there were occasional instances of major success stories. For instance, the U-2 demonstrated its ability to be retasked in real time to image a reported SA-6 site, data-link the resulting imagery via satellite back to its home base at Beale AFB, California, within minutes for an assessment of the target's coordinates, and have the results transmitted back to the cockpit of an F-15E just as its pilot was turning inbound toward the target to fire an AGM-130.[131] In another such case, on Day 4 a Navy TLAM on short notice successfully attacked a "target of opportunity" believed to have been a pop-up MiG-29 detected on the runway at Batajnica by real-time imagery from a U-2.[132] Although those examples were not representative, they previewed the sort of fusion toward which the U.S. ISR system is heading and represented what USAF Lieutenant General Marvin Esmond later described as "the first-ever distributed ISR architecture."[133]

More typically, however, target images from Predator UAVs flying over Kosovo would be transmitted to the CAOC in real time, only to encounter difficulty being forwarded from there to operating units in time for them to be tactically useful. In addition, the Joint STARS crew complement was found to be too small to accommodate many of the data processing and reporting demands it was asked to handle. The aircraft was said to require either more battle managers integrated closely enough into the commander's loop for targets to be identified and attacked in near-real time, or wider-band data links to ground stations, where a larger number of mission specialists could do the analysis and handling.[134]

Yet a third bottleneck identified was the classified worldwide Internet link called SIPRNET (Secure Internet Protocol Router NETwork), upon which USEUCOM's Joint Analysis Center (JAC) at RAF Molesworth, England, relied heavily. As a rule, intelligence sources would forward proposed target materials to Molesworth for validation, with the JAC staff tasking additional intelligence collection as deemed necessary. That process would have been all but impossible

---

[131]The AGM-130 is a rocket-boosted variant of the electro-optical and infrared guided GBU-15 2,000-lb PGM featuring midcourse GPS guidance updates. At the start of the air war, 200 of these weapons had been fielded, and those used were pulled from Air Combat Command's Weapons System Evaluation Program (WSEP), leaving no munitions for training. William M. Arkin, "Kosovo Report Short on Weapons Performance Details," *Defense Daily*, February 10, 2000, p. 2.

[132]Ibid.

[133]Lieutenant General Marvin R. Esmond, testimony to the Military Procurement Subcommittee, House Armed Services Committee, Washington, D.C., October 19, 1999.

[134]David A. Fulghum, "Lessons Learned May Be Flawed," *Aviation Week and Space Technology*, June 14, 1999, p. 205.

without the aid of the Internet, which made for vastly more rapid worldwide information availability than did the former hard-copy practices. Frequently, however, because of the absence of institutionalized procedures, the use of SIPRNET made for confusion and difficulty in finding some target materials on short notice. In addition, real-time target information would be withheld from U.S. allies as U.S. officials argued over who should be allowed to see what. Finally, NIMA was frequently slow to deliver overhead photography of proposed targets and of targets already attacked, which in turn slowed the battle-damage assessment process and the decision as to whether to retarget a previously attacked site. One informed source commented that ISR fusion worked better in Allied Force than it did during Desert Storm, but that it still rated, at best, only a grade of C-plus in light of what remained to be done. In contrast, what generally worked well was the "reach-back" procedure first pioneered in Desert Storm, in which commanders and planners in the forward theater used secure communications lines to tap into information sources in the intelligence community in Washington and elsewhere.[135]

AIRSPACE AND TRAFFIC FLOW MANAGEMENT

A major concern for Allied Force mission planners entailed the coordination of air operations with so many allied aircraft transiting the relatively dense and compact airspace between Italy and the Balkans. Among other things, the CAOC coordinated operations by some 200 NATO tanker aircraft operating out of eight countries to support strikers flying from 15 bases in Germany, France, Italy, Hungary, Spain, the United Kingdom, and the United States.[136] There were numerous reported instances of near-midair collisions caused by marginal weather and an insufficiency of battle management information relayed by AWACS to friendly aircraft operating in and near the combat zone. Mission planners at the CAOC sought to deconflict allied aircraft by parceling out the most impacted airspace so that only a given number of friendly aircraft would be operating inside

---

[135]Rowan Scarborough, "Kosovo Target Data Stalled in Transit," *Washington Times*, July 28, 1999.

[136]Tim Ripley, "Tanker Operations," *World Air Power Journal*, Winter 1999/2000, p. 121.

any block at a given time. The danger of midair collisions was of particular concern in designated engagement zones, or "kill boxes," in the KEZ, with only a few allied aircraft being permitted to operate within a given box at any time for that reason. Both the E-3 AWACS and the EC-130 ABCCC carried copies of the daily ATO, which allowed them to keep track of scheduled flight operations and remind allied aircrews of pertinent details as necessary. Another problem caused by the unusually congested airspace over and near Yugoslavia entailed linking some combat aircraft with their assigned tankers, particularly the German Tornado ECR variants and the EA-6B, which lacked air-to-air radars and had to be vectored to their tankers by AWACS.[137]

In an important contribution to easing the air traffic nightmare that threatened to ensue over the Adriatic and in the adjacent airspace as the air effort unfolded, Italian air traffic authorities lent their expertise to the CAOC's air traffic control cell in order to make key staffers there more familiar with Italian airspace structure and regulations. They also dispatched a representative to the military cell of the regional civilian air traffic control (ATC) center to smooth out potential difficulties in controlling the heavy flow of ATO sorties going in and out of the area of responsibility (AOR). Measures taken to manage that flow and to deconflict it from civil traffic included closing the airspace over parts of the Adriatic, establishing a no-fly zone encompassing the airports of Bari and Brindisi, suppressing all or parts of some airways, establishing a special corridor to permit the transit of Italian airspace by air traffic entering from outside the AOR, providing a system of safe operating routes to allow the departure and return of combat aircraft loaded with weapons operating from Italian air bases, and establishing six emergency weapons jettison areas in international waters and six active inflight refueling zones over the Adriatic 24 hours a day.

Not surprisingly, the Italian ATC system experienced considerable difficulty in handling this large volume of daily traffic. To begin with, because of the air war's length and the shortage of available controllers, ATC found it a major challenge to maintain round-the-clock control of all the active and alternate military airfields that were in-

---

[137]Wall, "Airspace Control Challenges Allies."

volved in air operations. Second, Eurocontrol experienced problems managing civil aviation flight plans, given the density of military traffic, and was not always able to maintain the impermeability of the posted no-fly zone over the Adriatic. Third, ATC was frequently unable to track military aircraft operating from the several aircraft carriers that were deployed in the Adriatic and, for that reason, faced serious deconfliction problems with civil traffic flying along the southern air routes toward Greece and Turkey. Fourth, communication problems were often encountered between and among the various agencies engaged in air traffic flow management, such as airfield control towers, approach and departure control centers, military regional control, air defense radars, and AWACS. Finally, there was far too little time available to debug, test, and properly validate these highly jury-rigged arrangements. Although the system worked in the end with no catastrophic or otherwise untoward incidents, numerous aircrews reported that the aerial traffic jams of ingressing and egressing NATO aircraft transiting the AOR throughout Allied Force often appeared more dangerous than the threat presented by Serbia's SAMs and AAA.[138]

As it unfolded and expanded in scope and intensity, Operation Allied Force became the largest civilian emergency ever confronted by the airlines, although it produced little major traffic dislocation in the end. Before the cold war ended, there had been only two options from which to choose—either a peacetime operating mode, with the military taking only a small portion of the available airspace and time for training, or a wartime mode, with no civil operations whatever and unrestricted military flying. This time, as NATO's top official on civil airspace put it, the coalition was "waging what we may plainly call war in a localized area of Europe, while throughout the rest of the continent it was business as usual."[139] The situation required air traffic controllers to reroute as many as 8,000 airliners a day on some occasions. One concern was that inconveniencing civilians at peak summer travel time would erode public support and cause a back-

[138]Colonel E. Baldazzi, Italian Air Force, "Host Nation Support for the Kosovo Air Campaign," briefing at a conference on "The NATO Joint Force Air Component Commander Concept in Light of the Kosovo Air Campaign," Headquarters NATO Reaction Force Air Staff, Kalkar, Germany, December 1–3, 1999.

[139]Joseph Fitchett, "For NATO, Keeping Peak Air Traffic on the Go Was a Critical Goal," *International Herald Tribune*, March 31, 2000.

lash against the effort. Another was to avoid any replay of the downing of an Iranian airliner, which the cruiser USS *Vincennes* mistook for an Iranian F-14 over the Persian Gulf in 1988. That latter concern led to a double-checking of identification procedures for electronically identifying aircraft operating in and near the combat zone. Toward the end of the air war, NATO finally succeeded in easing the airspace congestion problem at least marginally, when it in effect opened a second front by initiating Marine F/A-18D operations out of Hungary and USAF fighter operations out of Turkey.

DEFICIENCIES WITH RESPECT TO SPACE

Fortunately, U.S. space superiority was not challenged during Operation Allied Force. Against the remote yet distinct possibility that Milosevic and his erstwhile supporters in Moscow might somehow have sought to do so, however, the enemy's space order of battle, rudimentary though it may have been, was never seriously examined. Nor was the vulnerability of U.S. space systems sufficiently assessed and hedged against using the needed countermeasures. Other space-related problems were also highlighted by the Allied Force experience. With respect to ISR, intelligence collectors and combat aircrews both had repeated difficulty finding mobile targets. Adverse weather and enemy camouflage, concealment, and deception measures presented additional complications, with the result that the "kill chain" was too long by a discomfiting margin. Relatedly, space-based weather support suffered. For example, there was no continuous weather coverage of the theater of operations, so some scheduled strike missions may have been needlessly canceled because available weather information was not current. Battlespace characterization also suffered because of a lack of enough space-derived imagery of the right kinds.[140]

As for other deficiencies in the availability of on-orbit assets, some satellites that had been tasked primarily against the Middle East and Pacific basin were recommitted to the Balkans, leaving important ar-

---

[140]"Space Support to Operation Allied Force: Preliminary Lessons Learned," briefing to the author by Colonel Robert Bivins, director of operations, U.S. Air Force Space Warfare Center, Schriever AFB, Colorado, February 25, 2000.

eas of interest uncovered in other theaters.[141] Moreover, the United States was shown to continue to lack a real-time targeting capability and to suffer significant problems with respect to real-time distribution, all of which pointed to the still-unresolved challenge of getting the right information to the right people at the right time. To be sure, information cycle time was compressed significantly in comparison to earlier aerospace operations, as attested by one case in which a single TLAM was targeted and launched early during Allied Force against a MiG-29 that had suddenly been detected in the open at a Serbian air base. However, there was no mechanism available for providing shooters in near-real time with radar imagery and other intelligence gathered by the multitude of collection platforms and surveillance systems that were available and functioning. Joint STARS is slated to receive an upgrade that will permit it to transmit a map through a satellite uplink directly into a fighter cockpit, but that capability is not yet in place.[142] Also, U.S. space-based intelligence assets, including NRO's classified ELINT and SIGINT satellites, DSCS, and other systems, were shown not to have improved greatly since Desert Storm. As one U.S. intelligence official noted, "three to four hours is the best we can do" from target identification to weapons delivery.[143] The good news in all this is that many needed fixes were discovered to lie in the realm of essentially cost-free improvements in techniques, tactics, and procedures rather than in more expensive hardware solutions.

Finally, the Allied Force experience indicated that considerable room remains for further progress in bringing operators to a fuller appreciation of what space systems now have to offer. The director of NRO, Keith Hall, commented after the air war ended that although allied operators turned in an effective performance, they made some important aspects of the operation harder for themselves than they needed to be. Stressing that professional military education and officer specialization training at all levels in the four U.S. services still do

---

[141]Bill Gertz and Rowan Scarborough, "Dangerous Drawdown," *Washington Times*, April 30, 1999.

[142]"Space Support to Operation Allied Force: Preliminary Lessons Learned," briefing by Colonel Robert Bivins, February 25, 2000.

[143]Roy Bender, "Allies Still Lack Real-Time Retargeting," *Jane's Defense Weekly*, April 7, 1999.

not offer enough needed first-hand exposure to space systems and their capabilities, he went on to say: "I impress upon [the service chiefs] the need to organize, train, and equip to use this stuff if they're going to rely on it, and not just call up the NRO and say, 'Can you do this for us?' when we're engaged in an operation. . . . We're dealing with a situation where people are not trained, it hasn't been practiced in peacetime, and you have to scramble. . . . If they're going to rely on it, they're going to have to do their part of it."[144]

Air Force space professionals would undoubtedly concur that shortcomings in the use of available space assets identified during Allied Force highlighted a continuing need for more space involvement in peacetime exercises, on the sensible premise followed as gospel for years by fighter pilots that you should "train like you expect to fight." That means a need for advanced space education and training of a highly specific and focused nature—not just greater "space awareness"—for operators at all levels, from the most senior command echelons all the way down to shooters working within tactical confines. It also means a need for better development and documentation of space operational support capabilities and options in theater contingency plans worldwide. Acknowledging this and more after the air war was over, the commander in chief of U.S. Space Command, Air Force General Richard Myers, remarked frankly that in terms of using space assets, the Kosovo operation was "probably the best we've done—surely superior to Desert Storm from everything we can learn. But there's still a long way to go before space is really integrated with the rest of the campaign."[145]

INTEROPERABILITY PROBLEMS

One of the most surprising aspects of the Allied Force experience was what it revealed about the extent of the discontinuity that had been allowed to develop between U.S air power and that of most other NATO allies who participated.[146] One concern had to do with inade-

---

[144]John Donnelly, "NRO Chief: Services Ill-Prepared to Work with Spy Satellites," *Defense Week*, July 12, 1999, p. 2.

[145]Quoted in *The Air War Over Serbia*, p. 53.

[146]For a fuller treatment of the allied contribution to the air war and the interoperability problems that became manifest as a result of it, see John E. Peters, Stuart John-

quacies in the equipment operated by the allies. To begin with, there was a pronounced dearth of interoperability with respect to rapid and secure communications. Only at Aviano were there some old STU-2 secure telephones that allowed the U.S. participants to transfer classified information quickly to allied units. (The STU-3 secure phone system used by U.S. forces was not available to the allies.) Other classified communications required passing a hard copy of the information by hand, repeating one of the worst command and control deficiencies that had been exposed earlier in Desert Storm, when the ATO had to be flown every day to each of the Navy's six participating aircraft carriers because the latter were not equipped to receive it electronically.

In addition, many NATO European fighters lacked Have Quick–type frequency-hopping UHF radios and KY-58–like radios allowing encrypted communications. As a result, U.S. command and control aircraft were often forced to make transmissions in the clear to those fighters about targets and aircraft positions, enabling the enemy to listen in and gain valuable tactical intelligence.[147] Also, in at least one case, British Harrier GR. Mk 7 pilots were said to have observed suspected refugees in a convoy but were unable to communicate that information to the ABCCC or to USAF F-16s operating in the same area.[148] For their part, U.S. aircraft equipped with JTIDS frequently were not allowed to rely on that asset, but were instead obliged to use voice communications to ensure adequate situation awareness for all players, notably allied participants not equipped to receive JTIDS signals.[149]

---

son, Nora Bensahel, Timothy Liston, and Traci Williams, *European Contributions to Operation Allied Force: Implications for Transatlantic Cooperation*, Santa Monica, California, RAND, MR-1391-AF, 2001.

[147]Since allied aircraft could not receive Have Quick radio transmissions and since enemy forces made no effort to jam allied UHF communications, which Have Quick was expressly developed to counter, the Have Quick capability was not used by U.S. combat aircrews during Allied Force.

[148]"NATO Jets May Have Erred in Convoy Attack, General Says," p. 102.

[149]David A. Fulghum and Robert Wall, "Data Link, EW Problems Pinpointed by Pentagon," *Aviation Week and Space Technology*, September 6, 1999, pp. 87–88. The JTIDS offers aircrews a planform view of their tactical situation, as well as a capability for real-time exchange of digital information between aircraft on relative positions, weapons availability, and fuel states, among other things. It further shows the position of all aircraft in a formation, as well as the location of enemy aircraft and ground threats. Fighters can receive this information passively, without highlighting them-

Second, among all participating allied air forces, only U.S., British, Canadian, French, Spanish, and Dutch combat aircraft had the ability to deliver LGBs without offboard target designation assistance. General Short frankly admitted that he could not risk sending the aircraft of many allied countries into harm's way because of concern for the safety of their pilots and for the civilian casualties that might be caused by inaccurately aimed weapons. Largely for that reason, around 80 percent of all strike sorties flown in Allied Force were carried out by U.S. aircraft.

Additional problems making the job of AWACS operators difficult included the absence of a robust alliance-wide IFF (identification friend or foe) system, the lack of a capability to detect which SAM systems were targeting allied aircraft, and the small number of non-U.S. aircraft able to laser-designate targets, all of which inhibited the usefulness of many allied assets. Some aspects of the discrepancy between U.S. and allied capability were a result of the fact that the European nations typically spend only half the annual U.S. percentage of defense expenditure on military procurement and a third of the annual U.S. percentage on research and development.[150] Others merely reflected allied decisions to invest in different types of equipment. Largely because of that asymmetry, however, the United States provided almost all of the aerial intelligence employed in Allied Force and selected virtually every target attacked in Operation Allied Force. Commenting on these and other interoperability problems, General Naumann expressed concern that the growing technology gap between the United States and its allies could eventually lead to their inability to fight together or even communicate in the same battlespace.[151]

To be sure, not all participating allied air forces suffered equally pronounced problems with respect to capability and versatility. The Royal Netherlands Air Force, for example, not only kept its F-16s up to date but also provided some aerial refueling capability. The Dutch

---

selves through radio voice communications. See William B. Scott, "JTIDS Provides F-15Cs 'God's Eye View,'" *Aviation Week and Space Technology*, April 29, 1996, p. 63.

[150]John D. Morrocco, "Kosovo Reveals NATO Interoperability Woes," *Aviation Week and Space Technology*, August 9, 1999, p. 32.

[151]Barton Gellman and William Drozdiak, "Conflict Halts Momentum for Broader Agenda," *Washington Post*, June 6, 1999.

and the Belgians operated a total of 28 Block 15 F-16A/B midlife update (MLU) aircraft as a single detachment at Amendola AB, Italy, incorporating modifications that made the aircraft, to all intents and purposes, Block 50-equivalents. A Dutch F-16 downed a Serb MiG-29 with an AIM-120 AMRAAM during the opening night of the air war, and another used its LANTIRN targeting pod to identify and successfully attack a MiG-29 on the ground while ignoring several decoys that were parked directly adjacent to it. According to the principal Dutch airman assigned to the CAOC, the Royal Netherlands Air Force (RNLAF) was "not 100-percent interoperable but close" and was characterized by senior U.S. airmen as being "most definitely on the A-Team."[152]

Moreover, German and Italian Tornados contributed valuable SEAD capabilities, firing some 37 percent of all HARM shots taken during Allied Force. Seven of the nine allies contributing aircraft that dropped bombs in the air war operated PGM-capable aircraft, which at least made them effective in precision attacks in clear weather against fixed targets. USAF Block 40 F-16CGs equipped with low-altitude navigation and targeting infrared for night (LANTIRN) targeting pods and using cooperative strike tactics designated targets for numerous allied aircraft, including the Italian AMX, which were capable of dropping LGBs but lacked any onboard self-designation capability.

With the USAF now out of the manned tactical reconnaissance business altogether and the Navy's TARPS-equipped F-14s providing the only remaining U.S. operational capability of that nature, three of the five remaining French Mirage IVP supersonic bombers, since converted to the reconnaissance role, added valuable support by being flown daily when the weather permitted, accounting in the end for 20 percent of the Allied Force reconnaissance missions. Operating out of Solenzara, Italy, they flew at 40,000–50,000 ft at a speed of Mach 2.05, typically entering the war zone over Belgrade and exiting over Kosovo, covering some 20 targets on each flight in around 15 minutes. Returning traditional wet-film photographs to Solenzara, they eventually developed a routine whereby high-quality images anno-

---

[152]Conversation with Major General P. J. M. Godderij, deputy commander in chief, RNLAF, Scheveningen, the Netherlands, June 7, 2000.

tated with target information would be digitized for transmission to the CAOC and to French headquarters in Paris.[153]

Finally, two decades of multinational training at Red Flag and elsewhere paid off handsomely in Allied Force. There were no midair collisions or other near-catastrophic aerial incidents resulting from allies operating from their own private playbooks.

THE WAGES OF U.S. OVERCOMMITMENT

The demands placed by Allied Force on U.S. equipment and personnel underscored the extent to which the U.S. defense posture has been stretched dangerously thin by the post–cold war force drawdown and concurrent quadrupling of deployment commitments worldwide. During the initial post–cold war decade of the 1990s, the U.S. active-duty force in all services shrank by 800,000 personnel to 1.4 million, a reduction of more than one-third. The Army was cut from 18 to 10 active divisions, the Navy diminished in size from 567 ships to just over 230, and the Air Force lost half of its 24 fighter wings. Yet during that same period, the U.S. armed forces were tasked with 48 major deployment missions overseas, in contrast with only 15 between the time of the U.S. exit from Vietnam and the collapse of the Soviet Union nearly two decades later.[154]

The first practical effect of this drawdown manifested during Allied Force was the unexpectedly high rate at which scarce and expensive consumables were being expended to meet the air war's demands. After only the first week, the Air Force found itself running low on CALCMs, with the initial stock of 150 down to fewer than 100.[155] The Air Force had had preexisting plans in hand to convert 92 additional nuclear-configured ALCMs to CALCMs, but that process was expected to take more than a year. JDAM was still being tested at the time it was committed to combat. As of April 20, less than a month into Allied Force, there were only 609 JDAM kits remaining in

---

[153]Chris Pocock, "Mirage IV Reconnaissance Missions," *World Air Power Journal,* Winter 1999/2000, p. 111.

[154]Rowan Scarborough, "Record Deployments Take Toll on Military," *Washington Times,* March 28, 2000.

[155]Hewson, "Operation Allied Force," p. 21.

stock.[156] The burdens placed by the air war's demands on materiel of all kinds prompted a rising groundswell of military complaints that the results of seven years of underfunding were finally making their impact fully felt.[157]

On that point, a memorandum from Air Combat Command (ACC) to the Air Staff in late March frankly admitted that "our operational units are suffering, with few serviceable engines [and] depleted wartime spare kits."[158] ACC's commander, General Hawley, reported a month later that five weeks of bombing had left U.S. munitions stocks, notably CALCM and JDAM, in critically short supply, adding that "it's going to be really touch-and-go as to whether we'll go Winchester [the pilot's term for running out of ammunition] on JDAMs." Hawley warned that should a more serious crisis erupt elsewhere, ACC would be "hard-pressed to give them everything that they would probably ask for. There would be some compromises made."[159] The later resort to an increased use of dumb bombs in Allied Force was driven in part by the steady depletion of stocks of precision munitions of all kinds.

Seeking an explanation for this increased stress on the U.S. defense establishment across the board, General Hawley laid the blame squarely on the nation's military overcommitment: "I would argue that we cannot continue to accumulate contingencies. At some point you've got to figure out how to get out of something." Hawley added that because of a fourfold spike in the number of deployments in the 1990s at the same time the force was undergoing a reduction by half, "we are going to be in desperate need, in my command, of a significant retrenchment in commitments for a significant period of time. I think we have a real problem facing us three, four, five

---

[156]The principal deputy assistant secretary of the Air Force for acquisition at the time, then–Lieutenant General Gregory Martin, acknowledged that the shortage of JDAMs was the result of a conscious choice made five years ago to emphasize other procurement needs. David A. Fulghum, "Bomb Shortage Was No Mistake," *Aviation Week and Space Technology*, May 17, 1999, p. 55.

[157]See Rowan Scarborough, "Smaller U.S. Military Is Spread Thin," *Washington Times*, March 31, 1999.

[158]Ibid.

[159]Bradley Graham, "General Says U.S. Readiness Is Ailing," *Washington Post*, April 30, 1999.

months down the road in the readiness of the stateside units."[160] Earlier during Allied Force, even before SACEUR's twofold force increase request was approved, Hawley cautioned that because of the existing strain on the system, "if we deploy the additional forces that are under consideration, those strains will become more evident," causing a "significant decline in the mission-capable rates" of the remaining forces to as low as 50 percent or less for some aircraft types.[161]

A second indication of the extent to which the U.S. military had come to find itself strapped as a result of the force drawdown was the sharply increased personnel tempo that was set in motion by the air effort. In all, some 40 percent of the active-duty U.S. Air Force was committed to Operation Allied Force and to the concurrent Operations Northern and Southern Watch over Iraq. That was roughly the same percentage of Air Force personnel that had been committed during Operation Desert Storm, when the total force was much larger. Among other things, as noted earlier in Chapter Three, the heightened personnel tempo obliged President Clinton to approve a Presidential Selected Reserve Call-Up authorizing a summons of up to 33,102 selected reservists to active duty.[162] It further prompted the Air Force chief of staff, General Michael Ryan, to insist that the USAF needed a recovery time no less than that routinely granted to the Navy every time one of its carriers returns from a deployment. Ryan flatly declared that "we are not a two-MTW [major theater war] Air Force in a lot of areas, and one of them is airlift." That shortfall made for one of many reasons why the Air Force later insisted that it needs 90 days to reconstitute its forces between MTWs.[163]

Earlier, as Allied Force entered its second month, Ryan told reporters that "the U.S. Air Force is in a major theater war." (He later amended that remark to indicate that he had meant to say that the Air Force's commitment level included Operations Northern and Southern

---

[160]Ibid.

[161]John A. Tirpak, "The First Six Weeks," *Air Force Magazine*, June 1999, p. 27.

[162]"U.S. Mobilizes Guard, Reserve for Balkan Duty," *Air Force Magazine*, June 1999, p. 16.

[163]Vince Crawley, "Air Force Needs 90 Days Between Wars, Chief Says," *Defense Week*, August 9, 1999, p. 12.

Watch over Iraq.)[164] In the eight years since Desert Storm, deployment demands on Air Force assets had never before exceeded the level of two AEFs of around 175 aircraft each. NATO's air war for Kosovo, however, demanded four AEF-equivalents' worth of USAF assets. Then-acting Secretary of the Air Force F. Whitten Peters declared that as a result, the AEF concept would need to be reexamined.[165]

Third, the demands of Allied Force placed a severe strain on such low density/high demand (LD/HD) aircraft as Joint STARS, AWACS, the U-2, the B-2, the F-16CJ, and the EA-6B.[166] So many of these scarce assets were committed to the air effort that day-to-day training in home units suffered major shortfalls as a result. The most acute strains were felt in the areas of surveillance, SEAD, and combat search and rescue. Almost every Block 50 F-16CJ in line service was committed to support SEAD operations, necessitating a virtual halt to mission employment training in the United States. (Figure 6.4 shows the overall USAF commitment to Allied Force, broken down by aircraft type.)

Similarly, Vice Admiral Daniel Murphy, the commander of the 6th Fleet, which provided the U.S. naval forces that were operating in the Adriatic, reported that there was an insufficiency of EA-6B jammers and they, along with their aircrews, were being worn out by the air war's demands.[167] Almost half of the initial batch of 11 EA-6Bs used to spearhead the air operation had been drawn from assets previously committed to Operation Northern Watch at Incirlik Air Base, Turkey. Navy and Marine spokesmen declined to admit that their EA-6Bs were being stressed to the danger point, but they did concede that they were being run ragged trying to marshal enough aircraft out

---

[164]Tirpak, "The First Six Weeks," p. 27.

[165]John T. Correll, "Assumptions Fall in Kosovo," *Air Force Magazine*, June 1999, p. 4.

[166]Characteristics of LD/HD include single-unit asset, limited numbers of aircraft and pilots, and likely tasking in more than one theater. Joint Vision 2010, the "revolution in military affairs," improved sensor to shooter links, and decisive attack operations all depend on more support to LD/HD assets. They transcend individual service and weapon system boundaries.

[167]Dale Eisman, "Kosovo Lesson: Navy Says It Needs More High-Tech Tools," *Norfolk Virginian-Pilot*, June 10, 1999.

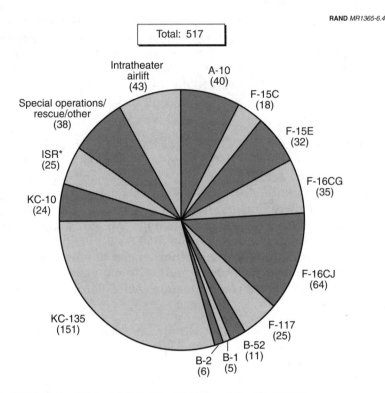

RAND *MR1365-6.4*

*ISR includes RQ-1, E-3, E-8, RC-135, U-2, and EC-130 ABCCC.

SOURCE: AWOS Fact Sheet.

Figure 6.4—USAF Aircraft Types Employed

of the total inventory of 124 to support the launching of Allied Force.[168]

An even greater demand was imposed on the Air Force's various ISR platforms, which left none available for day-to-day continuation training once the needs of Allied Force were superimposed on preexisting commitments. During the time in question, the Air Force had

---

[168]Greg Seigle, "Prowler Jammers Used to Aid NATO Air Assault," *Jane's Defense Weekly,* March 31, 1999.

only four operational E-8 Joint STARS aircraft, two of which were committed to Allied Force (it has since acquired a fifth). As a result, the Joint STARS community found itself so stripped of its most skilled personnel that there was no instructor cadre left to work with new crewmembers who were undergoing conversion training. The low Joint STARS availability rate made for a typical Allied Force E-8 mission length of more than 17 hours, with the longest missions lasting 21 hours. It took two or more inflight refuelings and backup pilots and crews to sustain each mission.[169] Some Joint STARS aircraft were flown at more than three times their normal use rates, creating a major maintenance and depot backlog that would take months to clear up. In all, U.S. LD/HD assets were stretched to their limit with tasking demands whose reverberations will continue to be felt for years in the areas of platforms, systems, reliability, parts, personnel, retention, and replacement costs. On this point, Admiral Ellis cautioned that the trend line is working in precisely the wrong direction—the demand for these assets in the future will only grow and they should be viewed as national assets requiring joint funding, irrespective of service, as the highest priority.[170]

Finally, Operation Allied Force exposed the extent to which U.S. forces are being stretched to the limit to support real-world peacekeeping and peacemaking commitments on a routine basis, while also meeting the demands of engaging successfully in two simultaneous or near-successive major theater wars. In the prevailing defense lexicon, Kosovo was supposed to be only a "smaller-scale contingency." Yet the number of U.S. aircraft committed to Allied Force quickly approached the level of a major theater war and exposed shortcomings in the availability of needed assets in all services. For example, the diversion of the USS *Theodore Roosevelt* from the Mediterranean to the Adriatic to support the air effort deprived U.S. Central Command of a vital operational asset. Likewise, the later redeployment of the USS *Kitty Hawk* from the Pacific to the Persian

---

[169]Edmund L. Andrews, "Aboard Advanced Radar Flight, U.S. Watches Combat Zone," *New York Times*, June 14, 1999.

[170]Briefing by Admiral James O. Ellis, USN, commander in chief, U.S. Naval Forces, Europe, and commander, Allied Forces Southern Europe and Joint Task Force Noble Anvil, "The View from the Top," 1999.

Gulf deprived U.S. Pacific Command of a carrier in the western Pacific for the first time since the end of World War II.

The Air Force was similarly forced to juggle scarce assets to handle the overlapping demands imposed by Kosovo, Iraq, and Korea. It positively scrambled to find enough tankers to support NATO mission needs in Allied Force. Ironically, both Kosovo and Iraq, in and of themselves, represented lesser contingencies whose accommodation was not supposed to impede the U.S. military's ability to handle two major theater wars. Yet the burdens of both began to raise serious doubts as to whether the two-MTW construct, at least at its current funding level, was realistic for U.S. needs. For example, when USEUCOM redeployed 10 F-15s and 3 EA-6Bs from Incirlik to support Clark's requirements for Allied Force, it was forced to suspend its air patrols over northern Iraq immediately. Air patrols to enforce the no-fly zone over southern Iraq were continued, but at a slower operational tempo. The net result was U.S. aircraft being flown two to three times more often than in normal peacetime operations.[171]

One example of the negative effects on combat readiness that surfaced during Allied Force was the frequent and widespread complaint by unit personnel in all services that their combat performance suffered because their lack of prior training opportunities with live weapons adversely affected their precision-weapons employment techniques and procedures in actual combat. Indeed, the majority of American bomb-droppers had never dropped a live LGB in training. That shortfall in combat proficiency was partly a reflection of limited range space, but it was also the result of under-resourcing of combat units in the training-munitions category. Numerous misses in Allied Force occurred because aircrews did not understand target-area effects such as thermal bloom, smoke, and dust, which cannot be duplicated in peacetime training without live weapon drops. By one informed account, civilians were injured in Pristina and Surdulica as a direct result of smoke and IR bloom effects. Targets were also missed when aircrews discovered several surprising effects in the LANTIRN system when using the combat laser in the presence of clouds. The training laser (which is eye-safe)

---

[171] Elizabeth Becker, "Needed on Several Fronts, U.S. Jet Force Is Strained," *New York Times*, April 6, 1999.

fires at a much lower power and rate, with the result that the noted effects were not discovered until they were actually seen in combat— usually in the middle of a drop.[172] Bowing to the inevitable, General Shelton finally acknowledged the cumulative impact of these multiple untoward trends when he admitted to Congress at the beginning of May 1999 that there was "anecdotal and now mea- surable evidence . . . that our current readiness is fraying and that the long-term health of the total force is in jeopardy."[173]

---

[172]Comments on an earlier draft by Hq USAF/XOXS, July 9, 1999.

[173]Kate O'Beirne, "Defenseless: The Military's Hollow Ring," *National Review*, May 3, 1999, p. 18.

Chapter Seven

LAPSES IN STRATEGY AND IMPLEMENTATION

In the predictable rush to identify "lessons learned" that followed in the wake of the air war's successful outcome, senior administration officials hastened to acclaim Operation Allied Force as "history's most successful air campaign."[1] Yet NATO leaders on both sides of the Atlantic had little to congratulate themselves about when it came to the manner in which the air war was planned and carried out. On the contrary, there was a dominant sense among both participants and observers that the desultory onset of Allied Force and its later slowness to register effects reflected some fundamental failures of allied leadership and strategy choice.

Indeed, the six years that preceded Allied Force saw a clear regression in the use of air power after the latter's casebook performance in Desert Storm. With the singular exception of Operation Deliberate Force in 1995, a trend toward what came to be called "cruise missile diplomacy" had instead become the prevailing U.S. pattern, owing to the ability of cruise missiles to deliver a punitive message without risking the lives of any U.S. aircrews. The origins of this pattern went back to June 1993, when President Clinton first ordered the firing of several TLAMs in the dead of night against an empty governmental building in Baghdad in symbolic reprisal for confirmed evidence that Saddam Hussein had underwritten an assassination attempt against former President George Bush.

---

[1]Paul Richter, "U.S. Study of War on Yugoslavia Aimed at Boosting Performance," *Los Angeles Times*, July 10, 1999.

That trend was next reflected in the administration's unwillingness or inability to use air power decisively in dealing with Bosnian Serb atrocities throughout the two years before Operation Deliberate Force, and in the costly, yet apparently ineffectual, TLAM strikes launched later by the administration against presumed assets of the terrorist Osama bin Laden in Sudan and Afghanistan.[2] It culminated in the three-day Operation Desert Fox, a mini-air operation that was executed against Iraq, to no significant consequence, at the very height of President Clinton's impeachment trial in December 1998. Less than a year earlier, a more serious campaign plan called Operation Desert Thunder, set in motion shortly after Iraq had expelled the UN's arms inspectors in January 1998, was aborted by President Clinton literally at the last minute, as allied strike aircraft were taxiing for takeoff, in response to the extraction by UN Secretary General Kofi Annan of an eleventh-hour, later unfulfilled, promise from Saddam Hussein to permit UN inspections.[3] In all of these cases, the declared emphasis was merely on "degrading" or "damaging," rather than destroying, enemy assets, so that the operation could be terminated at any moment in a manner allowing success to be declared.

That may have been the administration's going-in hope for Operation Allied Force as well. Not long after the effort began, however, senior U.S. military leaders began voicing off-the-record misgivings over the slow pace of the air operation, its restricted target base, and its rules of engagement that all but proscribed any serious application of air power. One Air Force general spoke of officers in Europe who had characterized the air war to date as "a disgrace," adding that "senior military officers think that the tempo is so disgustingly slow it

---

[2]In fairness to the Clinton administration, it must be said that bombing the Bosnian Serbs unilaterally was not a realistic option for the United States as long as three NATO allies (France, the Netherlands, and the United Kingdom) had troops on the ground who would have been helpless against Serb reprisals had U.S. air strikes taken place. It was only after the UN Protection Force (UNPROFOR) pulled back into defensible positions so that the Serbs could not take its troops hostage that Operation Deliberate Force became politically feasible. Weakness on the ground can often negate strength in the air.

[3]For an informed, if also sharply judgmental, account of this history, see Joshua Muravchik, "The Road to Kosovo, *Commentary*, June 1999, pp. 17–23. See also Lieutenant Colonel Paul K. White, USAF, *Crises After the Storm: An Appraisal of U.S. Air Operations in Iraq Since the Persian Gulf War*, Military Research Papers No. 2, Washington, D.C., Washington Institute for Near East Policy, 1999.

makes us look inept."[4]   Another, harking back to the initial concept of operations developed for Desert Storm, complained: "This is not Instant Thunder, it's more like Constant Drizzle."[5]   Yet a third Air Force general, reflecting the consensus of most airmen, commented that "the hammer is working just fine.   But when the blueprints have to undergo revision each day by 19 separate architects before it is determined where to drive the nail, one has to wonder what the final product is going to look like."[6]

Indeed, the highly politicized and sometimes seemingly random targeting process was so cumbersome that Clark himself would discover from time to time that he was stymied by the system as action time neared.[7]   The frequent hesitancy and indecision on the part of NATO's political leaders, and the resultant fits and starts which that indecision inflicted on the daily target allocation machinery, ended up producing what some uniformed critics later faulted as "ad hoc targeting": Air strikes were demanded on the same day that they had been approved, missions that had not yet been approved were assigned to the JFACC, and those same missions were later removed from the list at the last minute if they had not been approved by NATO's civilian authorities.   The resulting confusion led the commander in chief of Allied Forces in Southern Europe, Admiral James Ellis, to complain: "We don't like this kind of process where something could be left on [the ATO] by omission."[8]   The burdensome rules and restrictions that dominated the target approval process, moreover, contributed to a defensive and reactive mind-set among target planners and mission coordinators at the working level, who

---

[4]Rowan Scarborough, "U.S. Pilots Call NATO Targeting a 'Disgrace,'" *Washington Times,* April 1, 1999.

[5]John D. Morrocco, David Fulghum, and Robert Wall, "Weather, Weapons Dearth Slow NATO Strikes," *Aviation Week and Space Technology,* April 5, 1999, p. 26.

[6]William M. Arkin, "Inside the Air Force, Officers Are Frustrated About the Air War," *Washington Post,* April 25, 1999.

[7]To illustrate, Clark recalled after the cease-fire that he would often have to call Solana at the last minute with an urgent request like: "You've got to help me with target 183. I need 183." Michael Ignatieff, "The Virtual Commander: How NATO Invented a New Kind of War," *The New Yorker,* August 2, 1999, p. 34.

[8]Ibid.

were said by some to be locked into a resigned "we can't do it" position rather than amenable to a more creative "let's try it" attitude.[9]

To be sure, it was not as though NATO's uniformed professionals had been railroaded into an operation against Milosevic without having given it prior consideration. On the contrary, serious and detailed options planning for an air operation of some sort against Yugoslavia had begun at USAFE headquarters as far back as June 1998—planning that was never ultimately made use of for political reasons. Nevertheless, it became clear, shortly after the bombing effort began, that the relatively seamless performance by the coalition in Desert Storm was not to be replicated in Allied Force. Instead, what unfolded was a highly dissatisfying application of air power that showed not only the predictable fits and starts of trying to prosecute a war through an alliance of 19 members bound by a unanimity rule, but also some failures even within the operation's U.S. component to make the most of what air power had to offer within the prevailing constraints of alliance warfare.

ALLIED MISCALCULATIONS AND FALSE HOPES

To begin with, despite the ultimate success of Allied Force, a misjudgment of near-blunder proportions came close to saddling the United States and NATO with a costly and embarrassing failure: NATO's leaders did not appreciate the historical and cultural importance of Kosovo to the Serbs and the consequent criticality of Kosovo to Milosevic's continued political livelihood. Fortunately for the allies, their faulty assessment was not a show-stopper, although it easily could have been had Milosevic refrained from launching his ethnic cleansing campaign and instead merely hunkered down in a defensive crouch to wait out the bombing in a contest of wills with NATO. Once he elected to raise the stakes by proceeding with Operation Horseshoe, however, NATO's determination to prevail at all cost deprived his strategy of any foundation it may previously have had.

---

[9]Roundtable discussion with Hq USAFE/XP, USAFE/DO, and USAFE/IN staff, Ramstein AB, Germany, May 2, 2001.

One reason for NATO's overconfidence that air power alone would suffice in forcing Milosevic to yield on Kosovo was almost surely a misreading of the earlier Bosnian war and the role of Operation Deliberate Force in producing the Dayton accords of 1995. As has been widely noted since Allied Force ended, Bosnia was a part of the former Yugoslav Federation where Milosevic generally got what he wanted and to which he was not particularly deeply attached. In the negotiations that eventually yielded the Dayton accords, Milosevic succeeded in keeping Kosovo unburdened by their strictures at the price of abandoning Sarajevo to the Muslims, in a direct and outright betrayal of his Bosnian Serb compatriots, because there was no significant Serb minority living there.

In contrast, Kosovo was generally acknowledged to be of profound historical importance for Serbia. Among other things, it contained Kosovo Polje, the site where the Ottoman Turks defeated the Serb kings in 1389. As journalist Michael Ignatieff has pointed out, "it was here that the Kosovar lands passed under Turkish Ottoman control for more than five centuries; it was here that the Serbian dream of reconquering Kosovo one day was born, a dream not realized until just before World War I. And it was here, in 1989, that Milosevic held his infamous rally of 250,000 supporters which launched his campaign for a Greater Serbia."[10] With that depth of commitment, it was all but inconceivable that Milosevic would be talked out of Kosovo by allied diplomacy, even if supported by a threat of NATO bombing which he was inclined, for good reason, not to take seriously.[11]

Expounding further on the erroneousness of assuming that Operation Allied Force would produce the same relatively quick and easy results that the earlier Operation Deliberate Force had produced in the Bosnian crisis of 1995, Adam Roberts noted that "the mythologizing of [that earlier] campaign ignored one inconvenient fact: that it followed a period of sharp Serb military reverses on the ground,

---

[10]Michael Ignatieff, *Virtual War: Kosovo and Beyond*, New York, Henry Holt and Company, Inc., 2000, p. 24.

[11]As one observer wrote of Operation Allied Force afterward, "so low was NATO's credibility with Milosevic that the threat of war and even war itself were not enough to convince him that he had anything to fear." Christopher Cviic, "A Victory All the Same," *Survival*, Summer 2000, p. 178.

including the mass expulsion of the Serbs from the Croatian Krajina. Also, the 1995 bombing was not against Serbia proper, and thus did not arouse the same nationalist response as would the bombing in 1999. The real lesson of those 1995 events might be a very different one: that if NATO wants to have some effect, including through air power, it needs to have allies among the local belligerents and a credible land-force component to its strategy."[12] A false assumption that air power alone had produced the Dayton accords may thus have contributed further to NATO's miscalculation that Milosevic could be induced to give up in Kosovo after merely a few days of to-ken bombing.[13] Aleksa Djilas, son of the Yugoslav cold-war dissident Milovan Djilas and an able intellectual in his own right, attested from first-hand knowledge that the West had "badly underestimated the Serbian attachment to Kosovo."[14] In light of that, rather than ask why it took so long for NATO's bombing to coerce Milosevic to back down, a more appropriate question might be why he yielded as quickly as he did.

PROBLEMS AT THE COALITION LEVEL

In their joint statement to the Senate Armed Services Committee af-ter the war ended, Secretary Cohen and General Shelton rightly

---

[12]Adam Roberts, "NATO's 'Humanitarian War' over Kosovo," *Survival,* Autumn 1999, pp. 110–111.

[13]This point bears emphasizing. It was not just that Serbia's stakes in Kosovo were much higher than in Bosnia. The two cases diverged additionally in three fundamen-tal ways, each of which should logically have led the United States and NATO to adopt a more robust and considered strategy in the Kosovo war. First, the 1995 NATO air campaign was linked to a major ground effort by Croatian and Bosnian forces coming in from the north and west and by some 10,000 NATO troops who had been deployed weeks prior to the onset of the bombing. In 1999, in contrast, the ground element was expressly ruled out at the highest levels. Second, the objective of Deliberate Force was limited (ending the siege of Sarajevo) and achievable through a phased, coercive bombing campaign, whereas the goals of Allied Force were ambiguous (including forcing Milosevic back to the bargaining table) and more difficult to achieve through air power alone. Finally, even before the onset of the 1995 bombing, Milosevic had told U.S. negotiators that he was interested in forging a deal to end the war in Bosnia on terms acceptable to the international community. That was anything but the case on the eve of Allied Force. I thank Ivo Daalder of the Brookings Institution for calling my attention to these differences.

[14]Michael Dobbs, "'Europe's Last Dictator' Digs In," *Washington Post,* April 26, 1999.

insisted that Operation Allied Force "could not have been conducted without the NATO alliance and without the infrastructure, transit and basing access, host-nation force contributions, and most important, political and diplomatic support provided by the allies and other members of the coalition."[15] Yet the conduct of the air war as an allied effort, however unavoidable it may have been, came at the cost of a flawed strategy that was further hobbled by the manifold inefficiencies that were part and parcel of conducting combat operations by committee.

Those inefficiencies did not take long to manifest themselves. During the air war's first week, NATO officials reported that up to half of the proposed strike missions had been aborted due to weather and "other considerations," the latter, in many cases, being the refusal of some allies to approve certain target requests.[16] Indeed, the unanimity principle made for a rules-of-engagement regime that often precluded the efficient use of air power. Beyond that, there was an understandable lack of U.S. trust in some allies where the most important sensitivities were concerned. The Pentagon withheld from the allies mission specifics for literally hundreds of sorties that entailed the use of F-117s, B-2s, and cruise missiles, to ensure strict U.S. control over those U.S.-only assets and to maintain a firewall against leaks from any allies who might compromise those operations.[17]

In addition to the natural friction created by NATO's committee approach to target approval, the initial reluctance of its political leaders to countenance a more aggressive air campaign produced a resounding failure to capitalize on air power's potential for taking down entire systems of enemy capability simultaneously. In his first interview after Allied Force had begun six weeks earlier, the air component commander, USAF Lieutenant General Michael Short, was frank in airing his sense of being constrained by the political limits imposed by NATO, pointing out that the graduated campaign was

---

[15]Secretary of Defense William S. Cohen and General Henry H. Shelton, "Joint Statement on the Kosovo After-Action Review," testimony before the Senate Armed Services Committee, Washington, D.C., October 14, 1999.

[16]Thomas W. Lippman and Bradley Graham, "Yugoslavs Fire on U.S. Troops; 3 Missing," *Washington Post*, April 1, 1999.

[17]Bob Deans, "Pentagon Mum About Air Mission," *European Stars and Stripes*, April 27, 1999.

counter to all of his professional instincts.[18] Short further admitted that he was less an architect of the campaign than its implementor. He was particularly critical of NATO's unwillingness to threaten a ground invasion from the start, noting that that failure was making it doubly difficult for NATO pilots to identify their targets because of the freedom it had given VJ forces to disperse and hide their tanks and other vehicles.

Finally, Operation Allied Force was hampered by an inefficient target planning process. Because NATO had initially expected that the bombing would last only a few days, it failed to establish a smoothly running mechanism for target development and review until late April. The process involved numerous planners in the Pentagon and elsewhere in the United States, at SHAPE in Belgium, at USEUCOM headquarters in Stuttgart, Germany, and at the CAOC in Vicenza, Italy, with each participant logging on daily to the earlier-noted secure digitized military computer network called SIPRNET.

Daily target production began at the U.S. Joint Analysis Center at RAF Molesworth, England, where analysts collated and transmitted the latest all-source intelligence, including overhead imagery from satellites and from Air Force Predator, Navy Pioneer, and Army Hunter UAVs. Because the United States commanded the largest number of intelligence assets both in the theater and worldwide by a substantial margin, it proposed most of the targets eventually hit, although other allies made target nominations as well.[19] With the requisite information in hand, target planners at SHAPE and USEUCOM would then begin assembling target folders, conducting assessments of a proposed target's military worth, and taking careful looks at the likelihood of collateral damage. In addition, lawyers would vet each proposed target for military significance and for conformity to the law of armed conflict as reflected in the Geneva Conventions.

Once ready for review and forwarding up the chain of command for approval, these target nominations would then go to the Joint Target

---

[18]Michael R. Gordon, "Allied Air Chief Stresses Hitting Belgrade Sites," *New York Times*, May 13, 1999.

[19]General Wesley Clark, USA, testimony to the Senate Armed Services Committee, Washington, D.C., July 1, 1999.

Coordination Board for final vetting. That board's recommendations would then go to Admiral James Ellis, commander of Joint Task Force Noble Anvil and commander in chief, Allied Force Southern Europe (CINCSOUTH), and his staff in Naples, who would review all target nominations and forward his recommendations to General Clark, who in turn would personally review each target to ensure that it fit the overall guidelines authorized by the NAC.[20]

Approved targets would then go back to Admiral Ellis, who would task both the USAF's 32nd Air Operations Group at Ramstein Air Base, Germany, and the 6th Fleet command ship deployed in the Mediterranean to develop target folders. The 32nd AOG would assign multiple aim points per nominated target set and multiple weaponeering solutions for a broad spectrum of air-delivered munitions. The 6th Fleet planning staff would do the same for TLAM targets.[21] As one might expect, this exceptionally time-consuming process greatly limited the number of potential targets that could be struck at any given time. Moreover, even after these multiple hurdles had been crossed, an approved target could still be countermanded or withheld by U.S. or NATO political authorities.[22]

---

[20]John A. Tirpak, "The First Six Weeks," *Air Force Magazine*, June 1999, pp. 27–29.

[21]Dana Priest, "Target Selection Was Long Process," *Washington Post*, September 20, 1999.

[22]Comments on an earlier draft by Hq USAFE/SA, April 6, 2001. As a rule, the 19 individual allies did not deliberate over every new target added to the list. True enough, the NAC—that is, all 19 members, from the United States to Luxembourg—had to agree to move from one phase in the air war to the next. On January 30, 1999, for example, the NAC authorized NATO's secretary general to commence Phase I (attacking the IADS and some command and control targets) whenever diplomatic efforts had been deemed exhausted (as it turned out, on March 24, when Solana finally ordered Clark to begin the bombing). The NAC also approved moving to Phase II on March 27, thereby allowing NATO to strike against military targets north of the 44th parallel. Although it never approved Phase III, which entailed strikes against military targets throughout the former Yugoslavia, the NAC gave de facto approval to entering this phase on March 30. From that point on, aside from Britain, France, and the United States, no NATO country ever reviewed, let alone approved or vetoed, any individual weapon aim point. France insisted on reviewing targets in Montenegro; Britain, France, and the United States all demanded the right to review any target that had high political significance or was located in or near civilian areas where the risks of collateral damage were significant. But the remainder of the allies only got to vote on proposed new target categories. Moreover, targets struck by U.S. aircraft operating outside NATO but within USEUCOM were not subject to outside review unless they met these two criteria.

Further compounding the unavoidable inefficiency of this multistage and circuitous process, two parallel but separate mechanisms for mission planning and air tasking were used (see Figure 7.1). As noted earlier, any U.S.-specific systems involving special sensitivities, such as the B-2, F-117, and cruise missiles, were allocated by USEUCOM rather than by NATO, and the CAOC maintained separate targeting teams for USEUCOM and NATO strike planning. This dual ATO arrangement meant increased burdens on the planning system to execute workarounds in cases where automated mission planning systems could not support the dual process, as well as added complications in airspace control planning created by the presence of low-observable aircraft, the limited use of IFF systems in some cases, and the absence of a single, integrated air picture for all participants. Although the use of stealthy aircraft in this dual-ATO arrangement was dealt with by time and space deconfliction, it nonetheless made for problems for allies who were not made privy to those operations, yet who needed information about them in the interest of their own situation awareness and force protection.[23] Commenting on the friction that was inevitably occasioned by this cumbersome system, General Short recalled in hindsight that he was constantly having to tell allied leaders to "trust me" regarding what U.S. assets would be doing and that he would have preferred to find a way of ensuring that the daily allied air operations schedule reflected those U.S. systems in some usable way. As it was, their absence led on occasion to some significant force deconfliction problems, such as U.S. aircraft suddenly showing up on NATO AWACS displays when and where they were not expected.[24]

---

[23]This problem will only get worse as the low-observable F-22 and Joint Strike Fighter begin coming on line in significant numbers toward the end of this decade. Should the United States intend to use these third-generation stealth aircraft in a coalition context, as seems to be most likely, a dual ATO arrangement of the type used in Allied Force will not work. New standardized tactics, techniques, and procedures will need to be perfected and employed regularly in routine allied and combined peacetime training. I am grateful to my RAND colleagues James Schneider, Myron Hura, and Gary McLeod for this important insight.

[24]John A. Tirpak, "Short's View of the Air Campaign," *Air Force Magazine*, September 1999.

RAND *MR1365-7.1*

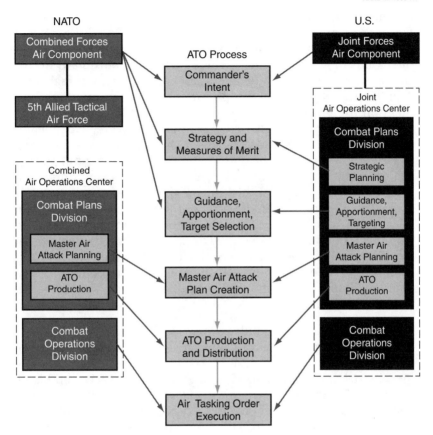

Figure 7.1—Operation Allied Force Planning and Implementation

PROBLEMS AT THE U.S. LEVEL

It was not only the alliance-induced friction that made the air war inefficient. As Allied Force unfolded, it became increasingly clear that even the U.S. military component was divided in a high-level struggle over the most appropriate targeting strategy—a struggle reminiscent of the feuding that had occurred nine years earlier between the Army's corps commanders and the JFACC, USAF Lieutenant General Charles Horner, over the ownership and control of air operations in Desert Storm.[25] There was visible tension in this regard between General Clark and his air commander, General Short, over the heated issue of target priorities: Aggressive micromanagement on the former's part was eventually met by understandably frustrated and increasingly transparent passive-aggressive rebellion against it on the latter's. As Clark later characterized this difference of view in his memoirs, he considered the achievement of success against Serbian ground troops in the KEZ to be the air effort's "top priority," unlike "some of [his] American commanders [who] subscribed to a more doctrinaire view of the conflict," one which, he added, was "the classic view of the American air power adherents who saw air power as strategically decisive, without recourse to the dirty business of ground combat," in contrast to the view of "Army leaders, who want the Air Force to make a difference on the ground." Short, no doubt, would offer his own no-less-principled view of that characterization.[26]

Once the initial hope that Milosevic would fold within a few days after the bombing commenced was proven groundless, NATO was forced into a scramble to develop an alternative strategy. The immediate result was an internecine battle between Clark and his Air Force subordinate over where the air attacks should be directed. Short had naturally chafed from the very beginning at the slowness of Operation Allied Force to gather momentum—three successive

---

[25]For the pertinent details of that controversy, see Benjamin S. Lambeth, *The Transformation of American Air Power*, Ithaca, New York, Cornell University Press, 2000, pp. 130–138.

[26]General Wesley K. Clark, *Waging Modern War: Bosnia, Kosovo, and the Future of Combat*, New York, Public Affairs, 2001, pp. 241, 243–244. As for charges of "alleged micromanagement," Clark said only that he many times "found [himself] working further down into the details than [he] would have preferred, in an effort to generate the attack effectiveness against the ground forces that [he] knew we needed." Ibid., p. 245. Short's countervailing take on all this is presented in candid detail in Lieutenant General Michael C. Short, USAF (Ret.), "An Airman's Lessons from Kosovo," in John Andreas Olsen, ed., *From Maneuver Warfare to Kosovo*, Trondheim, Norway, Royal Norwegian Air Force Academy, 2001, pp. 257–288.

nights had been required just to get through the 51 targets that had been approved up to that point, most of them air defense-related and only a few located anywhere in or near Belgrade.[27] In light of the absence of an allied ground threat to flush out Serbia's dispersed and hidden forces in Kosovo, Short insisted that a more effective use of allied air power would be to pay little heed to those forces and to concentrate instead on infrastructure targets in and near downtown Belgrade and other cities, including key electrical power plants and government ministries.

Indeed, by the account of numerous observers who either participated in or later watched the videotapes of the 94 top-level video teleconferences (VTCs) conducted throughout Allied Force, a typical exchange between Clark and Short during the air war's early days would have Clark ask: "Are we bombing those ground forces yet, Mike?" To which Short would typically offer a noncommital response. Even in the case of fixed infrastructure targets, Clark reportedly would venture deep into the most minute details of the target list. "Let's turn to target number 311," Clark would say, by this account "opening his binder as other participants flipped to the proper page, as if they were holding hymnals." He would then raise questions about a target's relevance, expostulate on allied sensitivities, or abort attacks already in progress. He would also, by this account, sometimes gainsay his own intelligence experts and targeteers by looking at a particular DMPI placement and asking "Isn't that an apartment building?" or "Can't we move that [DMPI] over 100 feet?" At which point Short would be seen "slumping back in his chair, folding his arms in disgust, and mentally checking out." General Jumper would then weigh in out of earshot of the others, and a compromise arrangement would typically be worked out. By this informed account, it was never clear to participants whether Clark, through such ex cathedra interventions, was genuinely responding to political pressure from above or was engaged in a divide-and-rule game by playing on putative "constraints" to his advantage and

---

[27] Of these initial approved targets, 35 were IADS-related, seven entailed VJ and MUP facilities, seven involved command and control nodes, and two were industrial. Comments on an earlier draft by Hq USAFE/HO, May 10, 2001.

gathering diverse inputs and opinions until he heard the one he wanted to hear.[28]

As the commander of U.S. naval forces participating in Allied Force, Vice Admiral Daniel Murphy, recalled after the air war ended, "there was a fundamental difference of opinion at the outset between General Clark, who was applying a ground commander's perspective . . . and General Short as to the value of going after fielded forces." Short believed that it made little sense to waste valuable munitions, sorties, and time going after the VJ's 3rd Army in Kosovo "if we don't have an army in the field [or] unless we have defined the opposing army in the field as a center of gravity."[29] He later commented that he thought going after that elusive army entailed a "high level-of-effort, high-risk, low-payoff option" because there was no friendly ground presence poised nearby "to make them predictable."[30] Nevertheless, Clark's view as to where the target priority emphasis should lie prevailed throughout most of the air war. Not only did Clark insist on attacking dispersed and hidden VJ ground forces as the first priority—indisputably his prerogative as the theater CINC—he reportedly micromanaged the day-to-day execution of Allied Force, at times even choosing the particular type of weapon to be used against a given target.[31]

---

[28]William M. Arkin, "How Sausage Is Made," *Washington Post*, July 17, 2000. Clark himself later affirmed in a backhanded way that he regarded General Short more as a subordinate to be managed than as a source of trusted counsel on air employment matters, and that he looked instead to Short's immediate Air Force superior, General Jumper, for the latter: "My real window on the operation was going to be provided by the senior American airman in Europe, John Jumper. Although he wasn't in the NATO chain of command for this operation, as the senior American airman he was my adviser and had all the technology and communications to keep a real-time read on the operations. As Mike Short's commander in the American chain of command, he also had a certain amount of influence in an advisory capacity." Clark, *Waging Modern War*, p. 195.

[29]Tirpak, "Short's View of the Air Campaign."

[30]Interview with Lieutenant General Michael Short, USAF, PBS *Frontline*, "War in Europe," February 22, 2000. Short also later indicated his belief that the use of VTCs "improperly allowed senior leadership to reach down to levels they did not need to be involved in."

[31]In one reported exchange during a daily video teleconference, Clark insisted that NATO air power remain committed against enemy fielded forces in Kosovo, and Short countered that such missions were a waste of assets and should be supplanted by missions against downtown Belgrade. Noting that U.S. aircraft were about to attack the Serbian special police headquarters in Belgrade, Short said: "This is the jewel in

In fairness to the record, Clark was in the decidedly unenviable position of having multiple masters tugging at him from different directions, including the civilian ambassadors to NATO who made up the NAC; NATO's Secretary General Solana, who was responsible for political control over NATO military operations; and the diverse cast of players in Washington, notably the president, Secretary Cohen, General Shelton, and the service chiefs with their independent interests. In the presence of these often conflicting influences, Clark's overarching responsibility as SACEUR was to ensure that coalition warfare worked and that the allies remained in step until they produced a successful outcome. To his credit, keeping the other 18 allies on board to the very end was an immense and remarkable accomplishment. As Columbia University political scientist Richard Betts later pointed out in this respect, Clark's command "was compromised by more conflicting pressures—political, diplomatic, military, and legal—than any other in history. Given these constraints, keeping the enterprise from flying apart was no mean feat."[32]

That said, Clark had the option all along of leaving the day-to-day operational responsibilities of planning and implementing the air effort to his JTF commander, Admiral Ellis, as the principal subordinate warfighting CINC. That is what U.S. Army General George Joulwan had done as SACEUR in 1995 with Admiral Leighton Smith during Operation Deliberate Force, so he could devote his full time, attention, and energy to his paramount duties as a diplomat in uniform. Instead, Clark elected not only to shoulder his diplomatic burdens as NATO's supreme commander, but also to conduct the air war himself from Brussels, in the process bypassing not only Admiral Ellis but also his air component commander, General Short, in making air apportionment decisions. Whereas General H. Norman Schwarzkopf, on the eve of Desert Storm, had become wholly persuaded by his trusted JFACC, then–Lieutenant General Horner, of the merits of the chosen air campaign strategy, Clark would not be moved by Short from his less trusting insistence that the VJ's 3rd

---

the crown." To which Clark replied: "To me, the jewel in the crown is when those B-52s rumble across Kosovo." Short: "You and I have known for weeks that we have different jewelers." Clark: "My jeweler outranks yours." Dana Priest, "Tension Grew with Divide in Strategy," *Washington Post*, September 21, 1999.

[32] Richard K. Betts, "Compromised Command: Inside NATO's First War," *Foreign Affairs*, July/August, 2001, p. 126.

Army in Kosovo, rather than vital equities closer to Milosevic in and around Belgrade, constituted the principal enemy target set.[33]

THE DESULTORY ONSET OF THE AIR WAR

Notwithstanding their narrow intent and the admitted constraints that impeded them, the initial strikes of Allied Force, by their measured nature, stood in marked contrast to the massed and highly orchestrated hammer-blows that were delivered with such paralyzing effect by coalition air power against Iraq from the earliest moments of Operation Desert Storm. On the home front, criticism of NATO's seeming timidity was both instant and searing. The morning after the operation's opening night, Senator John McCain, a former Navy attack pilot and Vietnam POW, complained that "these bombs are not going to do the job. . . . It's almost pathetic. You're going to solidify the determination of the Serbs to resist a peace agreement. You'd have to drop the bridges and turn off the lights in Belgrade to have even a remote chance of changing Milosevic's mind. What you'll get is all the old Vietnam stuff, bombing pauses, escalation, negotiations, trouble."[34] In a similar vein, NATO's tentativeness and preemptive forswearing of a ground option led the respected London *Economist* to declare that the West had "stumbled into one of its riskiest ventures" since World War II and to predict that if the bombing eventually succeeded, it would "owe as much to luck as to precision."[35]

---

[33]During a 10th-anniversary retrospective featuring Schwarzkopf's principal deputies in Desert Storm, Horner was emphatic on the crucial importance of the ability of those key deputies to work together harmoniously in producing the war's successful outcome: "The one thing you need to understand if you're going to understand Desert Storm is that the relationship among the four people at this table—[Admiral Stanley] Arthur, [General Walter] Boomer, [Lieutenant General John] Yeosock, and me—was highly unusual. Such a relationship probably has never existed before, and it probably won't exist in the future. The trust and respect we had for one another was unbelievable. This was a function of personality as much as a desire to get the job done. Unless you understand our relationships, then you really won't understand what went on in Desert Storm, all the good and bad—and there was plenty of each." "Ten Years After," *Proceedings*, January 2001, p. 65.

[34]R. W. Apple, Jr., "With Decision to Attack, a New Set of U.S. Goals," *New York Times*, March 25, 1999.

[35]"Stumbling into War," *The Economist*, March 27, 1999, p. 17.

In response to such charges, NATO's spokesman at the time, RAF Air Commodore David Wilby, gamely said of the enemy as Allied Force entered its second week: "He's hurting. We know that he's running short of fuel. We're starting to hit him very hard on the ground. You will start to see the resolve starting to crack very quickly."[36] However, USAF officers were complaining bitterly about the restrictive rules of engagement from the first days of combat operations. Similarly, RAF pilots flying combat missions out of Italy scored the insipid air effort as "nancying around" and bordering on cowardice.[37] General Short later commented that the frustration felt by airmen was "under control" because the alliance was not losing aircraft and airmen. He added, however, that had losses begun to occur on a repetitive basis, the alliance would have had to rethink the guidance its leaders were handing down on strategy and rules of engagement.[38]

Indeed, so counter to military common sense was the strategy selected by NATO that Short became convinced early on that strike planning was all "just planning for diplomatic threat," that his air planners were "just going through the motions to some degree," and that "we're probably never going to drop a bomb." Short added that he and his planners had determined that there were somewhere between 250 and 300 "valid, solid military targets" in the area for the sort of campaign effort that airmen ideally would like to conduct, but that he was told: "You're only going to be allowed to bomb two, maybe three nights. That's all Washington can stand, that's all some members of the alliance can stand, that's why you've only got 90 targets, this will all be over in three nights." At that, Short frankly conceded that he assumed a prior deal had been struck with Milosevic, whereby Milosevic had told NATO, in effect, that he could not accept NATO's terms and keep his job unless NATO bombed him and inflicted some degree of at least symbolic damage.[39] That meant, or so Short thought, a token NATO bombing effort against the approved set of 90 targets, 51 of which were IADS targets selected for force

---

[36]James Gerstenzang and Elizabeth Shogren, "Serb TV Airs Footage of 3 Captured U.S. Soldiers," *Los Angeles Times*, April 1, 1999.

[37]Jonathan Foreman, "The Casualty Myth," *National Review*, May 3, 1999, p. 40.

[38]Short, interview on PBS *Frontline*.

[39]Ibid.

protection—both south and north of the 44th parallel—and some in Montenegro, after which Milosevic would dutifully show the white flag.

Short later declined even to give Allied Force the courtesy of calling it a "campaign," saying that it was not an operation aimed at achieving clear-cut strategy goals with dispatch, but rather something more in the nature of "random bombing of military targets."[40] It was one thing, Short said, to go after enemy tanks and APCs in the Iraqi desert the way the coalition did with such success in Desert Storm before the ground offensive began. In that instance, everything behind the forward edge of the battle area was enemy territory, where one could attack targets at will without concern for collateral damage or the potential for killing refugees. In the contrasting case of Kosovo, he said, "we felt that the risk was enormous, and we felt that we were going to spend a lot of assets to get minimum return. It was going to take a lot of sorties to kill a tank, and there was enormous risk of hitting the wrong target because we knew refugees would be moving around in this ethnic cleansing environment." Short's preference was to "go after the head of the snake," as he put it. In an illustration of what he meant, he suggested that ten combat sorties against Belgrade would all hit their targets and achieve a desired effect, whereas "if I send those same ten sorties into Kosovo, perhaps we'll find a tank, perhaps not, [and] if we don't, we send the ten sorties to what in my business we call a 'dump target,' which is a suspected assembly area or a barracks from which the enemy has fled two weeks ago, and we'll blow up empty buildings. So the bombs will hit something but the impact on ethnic cleansing is zero."

For their part, NATO's civilian leaders could not even bring themselves to face the fact that they were engaged, to all intents and purposes, in an ongoing war. Three weeks into Allied Force, Secretary Cohen declared before the Senate Armed Services Committee: "We're certainly engaged in hostilities. We're engaged in combat. Whether that measures up to, quote, a classic definition of war, I'm not prepared to say."[41] Such diffidence on the administration's part was ostensibly intended to reflect due executive-branch obeisance to

---

[40]Ibid.

[41]"Verbatim Special: The Balkan War," *Air Force Magazine*, June 1999, p. 50.

the war declaration powers of Congress. Indeed, one report noted that the White House had expressly ordered all U.S. government agencies and departments not to refer to ongoing operations as a war out of concern that by so doing, they might bring the administration into a confrontation with Congress over war declaration powers.[42] Yet the stance also reflected an ingrained administration discomfort over coming to full grips with what its leaders had signed up for in Operation Allied Force. That discomfort was most palpably telegraphed in President Clinton's statement on March 26 that the standoff was "not a conventional thing, where one side's going to win and one side's going to lose."[43]

True enough, there was no pronounced groundswell of American popular support for the Kosovo air war as there had been for the 1991 Gulf War, thanks largely in the latter case to the obvious economic interests at stake in the Gulf, the blatant cross-border aggression that characterized Saddam Hussein's invasion, and President Bush's sustained efforts during the preceding five months to mobilize such support. At the end of the first week, a *Washington Post* and ABC News poll found that only 51 percent of the American people approved of the way President Clinton was handling the Kosovo crisis, with 55 percent supporting NATO's air war against Serbia.[44] In contrast, 79 percent of the American populace had supported the air offensive against Iraq at the start of Operation Desert Storm.[45]

One can reasonably ask whether NATO's initial assumptions about public opinion on the issue of casualties underestimated the degree of popular support that could have been mobilized for a more robust and effective strategy by a more proactive and committed U.S. leadership. The chairman of the respected Louis Harris and Associates polling firm rejected easy suggestions that the American people would inevitably oppose the commitment of ground troops or any other determined use of force. "When the U.S. achieves victory in a

---

[42]Bill Gertz and Rowan Scarborough, "No War," *Washington Times*, April 16, 1999.

[43]"Verbatim Special: The Balkan War," p. 51.

[44]Charles Babington, "Clinton Sticks with Strikes as Poll Shows 51 Percent in U.S. Approve," *Washington Post*, March 30, 1999.

[45]Richard Benedetto, "Support Not as High as for Other Strikes," *USA Today*, April 2, 1999.

just cause," he pointed out, "the public applauds the use of force. When it loses—worse still, when America is defeated or runs away (as in Somalia or Vietnam)—the public reasonably says the use of the military was a mistake." Citing the precedent of Desert Storm, he recalled how during the days immediately preceding the outbreak of hostilities, no poll found a majority of Americans in favor of prompt military action. Yet immediately after the air campaign had begun and was deemed to have gotten off to a good start, surveys found that between 68 and 84 percent of those polled approved. Similarly, up to the day before the Desert Storm ground push commenced, a typical poll taken by the *New York Times* and CBS found that the public preferred a continuation of the air war by 79 percent, with only 11 percent favoring the start of ground operations. A few days after the ground push began, however, a full 75 percent of those polled believed it had been "right to start the ground war," as opposed to only 19 percent who opposed it.[46]

In contrast to the celebratory reaction and commemorative parades down Wall Street and Constitution Avenue that predominated in the heady aftermath of Operation Desert Storm, one reason for the subdued response of the American rank and file to the successful conclusion of Allied Force may have been that popular expectations were so low—limited, at bottom, to the simplest hope that the United States might somehow extricate itself from the morass it had entered with its reputation as a superpower still intact. Up to the day that Milosevic finally caved in, even the most ardent air power proponents were gloomily eyeing the prospect of an open-ended bombing campaign. They were also coming to accept the growing likelihood of having to send in allied ground troops to bring the nation's involvement to a decisive end. Immediately after the ceasefire, a *USA Today*/CNN/Gallup poll reported that 53 percent of Americans did not consider the outcome to be a victory for the United States, as opposed to only 40 percent of respondents who did. The poll further reported 46 percent as believing that worldwide respect for the United States had declined as a result of U.S. actions in the crisis, as opposed to 44 percent who thought that it had grown.[47]

---

[46]Humphrey Taylor, "Win in Kosovo and the Public Will Approve," *Wall Street Journal*, June 3, 1999.

[47]James Cox, "Poll: Mission Isn't Seen as U.S. Victory," *USA Today*, June 15, 1999.

THE FAILURE TO EMPLOY A COHERENT PLAN

As noted earlier, everything having to do with arrangements already in place when Allied Force began was driven by the assumption that the operation would entail, at most, a two- to three-day series of air strikes directed at approximately 50 targets. Numerous earlier planning exercises had generated air attack options that varied in length from two to roughly ten days. None, however, came close to approaching anything as protracted as the 78 days that the air effort ultimately required. In February 1999, SACEUR directed that all existing attack plans be interwoven and that two to three days be assumed as the likely length of expected operations. Taking into account SACEUR's guidance ("I'm only going to give you 48 hours"), the lack of stomach either in the United States or in Europe for a serious combat operation, and the past history of post–Desert Storm air power application in mere token doses by the Clinton administration, virtually no one in the planning loop questioned the short length of the expected operations.

Once NATO's hope proved hollow, a frenetic rush ensued at SHAPE to come up with additional target nominations that could be more quickly and easily approved by NATO's political authorities. At the end of the air war's first week, Clark had only 100 approved targets.[48] With the bombing effort going nowhere, he accordingly went to the NAC and received blanket approval to go after certain broad classes of targets, including air defenses, command and control, fielded forces, and resupply sources, at his own discretion. Other broad target sets and individual targets of a more politically sensitive nature, however, still had to be submitted for review by the United States, Britain, and France.

Having thus been cleared to go after most military targets at will, Clark pressed his staff to identify 5,000 candidates. His target planners quickly convinced him that 5,000 legitimate aim points were not to be found in all of Serbia, whereupon Clark declared a new goal of coming up with 2,000 target candidates, a goal later derided by some

---

[48]Ignatieff, *Virtual War*, p. 99.

planners as "T2K."[49] That goal soon led to the targeting of objects that had no connection whatever to Yugoslavia's military capability, what William Arkin later characterized as a "mechanical process of meticulous selection with little true military justification."[50] Sometimes the target selection criterion entailed little more than the fact that an assigned DMPI was located safely away from civilian homes. That resulted in an approach to force employment that was "neither calibrated nor intelligible," but instead spawned "a succession of unfocused and unconvincing air excursions—experiments in communication by detonation."[51] It was only at that point that coalition planners began a serious and methodical target development process, in which prospective targets were categorized into four ascending tiers of collateral damage sensitivity.

Even then, there was little by way of a consistently applied strategy behind the target development process. As one U.S. officer reporting to an assignment at the CAOC midway into the operation noted afterward, he was told upon arrival: "I know you won't believe this, but we don't have a plan." He learned that NATO aircrews could only attack those targets that came out of the target approval process and could never, at any time, attack an entire target set systematically in pursuit of paralysis. Target allocations, he said, were driven by rules of engagement of the moment, which, in turn, were set primarily on the basis of judgments regarding what the political traffic would bear domestically and within the alliance. Whenever an untoward event occurred that had a negative impact on public opinion, the ROE would seem to tighten almost reflexively. As a case in point, he noted, target planners were directed by the "highest levels" to cease using CBUs after Milosevic's press staff had persuaded CNN to do a story on the CBU "terror weapon" that was being employed by

---

[49]Elaine M. Grossman, "U.S. Military Debates Link Between Kosovo Air War, Stated Objectives," *Inside the Pentagon*, April 20, 2000, p. 7. According to one Allied Force participant, Clark would press his operators down the line to propose target candidates. They would reply, "Give us the targets and we will take them out," to which Clark countered: "You don't get it. *You* develop the targets." Quoted in Ignatieff, *Virtual War*, p. 99. Clark himself later justified 2,000 as "a large round number, large enough to get us past the daily struggle over the number of targets approved for that day." Clark, *Waging Modern War*, p. 250.

[50]William M. Arkin, "Smart Bombs, Dumb Targeting?" *Bulletin of the Atomic Scientists*, May/June 2000.

[51]Ibid.

NATO.[52] In the words of another officer, "nobody ever said, 'no fooling, what we want to accomplish in this country is X.'" As a result, NATO started "throwing bombs around, hoping that objectives would materialize." Said still another, "the targets we selected—because we had no objectives—were based on nothing other than that they had been approved. So we slung lead on targets [but] we couldn't say, 'the objectives are X, so we blew up Y.'"[53]

Indeed, although the methodology of effects-based targeting had long since been elevated to a high art, most of the attack planning throughout Allied Force was not driven by desired effects but rather entailed simply parceling out sortie and munitions allocations by target category in boilerplate fashion, without much consideration given to how neutralizing a target might contribute to advancing the operation's objectives. A typical example involved attacking refineries, factories, and bridges in ones and twos over time rather than as interconnected components of a larger entity whose simultaneous destruction might instantly undermine Yugoslavia's capacity to function effectively. To be sure, some bridges were dropped not to curtail the flow of traffic *over* the bridges, but rather to halt the flow of commodities that flowed along the river *under* the bridges, or to cut fiber-optic cables and other conduits that ran *through* the bridges. To that extent, effects-based targeting could be said to have been successfully applied. For the most part, however, owing to the absence of any systematic effects-based target analysis and strategy execution, NATO military chiefs had an unnecessarily hard time convincing NATO's civilian leaders of the importance of many targets. General Jumper scored this failure when he stressed the importance of effects-based targeting and faulted what often happened instead, namely, what he called "campaign-by-target-list management," whereby planners simply took a list of approved targets and managed them on a day-to-day basis.[54]

---

[52]Personal communication to the author, August 23, 1999.

[53]Grossman, "U.S. Military Debates Link Between Kosovo Air War, Stated Objectives," p. 8.

[54]Comments at an Air Force Association Eaker Institute colloquy, "Operation Allied Force: Strategy, Execution, Implications," held at the Ronald Reagan International Trade Center, Washington, D.C., August 16, 1999. When asked about effects-based targeting applications in Allied Force, the former commander of the Joint Warfare Analysis Center, which provides senior warfighters with the principal analytical

On the plus side, the methodology used in *individual* target planning, now a bona fide science in its own right, had evolved to a point where target analysts could predict, for any given weapon type and impact angle, how far the blast effects would extend, how far shards of glass could be expected to fly, and even at what distance they would retain enough force to penetrate skin. The use of this methodology in arriving at a precisely determined weapon yield, aim-point placement, and weapon heading and impact angle to minimize unwanted collateral damage often proved decisive in persuading NATO's civilian leaders to approve attacks on many of the most politically sensitive targets. The four-tier collateral damage predictive model that had been developed toward that end was validated time and again in strike operations against sensitive targets in built-up areas. Not only did it permit targeting successes against electrical power, POL, lines of communication, and other objects of interest in the very heart of downtown Belgrade, it also allowed for the planned *preservation* of systems, such as road links within Kosovo for later use by KFOR peacekeeping troops.

Nevertheless, the scramble to form a targeting cell and establish smoother planning procedures in the CAOC spotlighted gross inefficiencies in the air tasking arrangement. That led General Jumper to suggest afterward that the Air Force needed to start thinking of the air operations center "as a weapons system" and giving it the same seriousness of thought that is now given to weapon systems, recognizing that "our product in war is dead targets, and our product in peace is all that goes into generating the warrior proficiency that kills those targets in wartime"—including proficiency at planning and managing an air campaign.[55]

After the dust of Operation Allied Force had settled, the since-retired commandant of the U.S. Marine Corps, General Charles Krulak,

---

support for such targeting, remarked, "the campaign was more like random acts of violence than true effects-based targeting. The legal restrictions and political constraints in the target approval process were inexplicably given as excuses not to do effects-based targeting. Achieving the desired effects while minimizing the undesired effects, particularly under the restrictions and constraints that were placed on SACEUR, is precisely why effects-based targeting should have been applied. Anything else is just high-tech vandalism." Conversation with Captain C. J. Heatley, USN (Ret.), Arlington, Virginia, June 21, 2000.

[55]John A. Tirpak, "Kosovo Retrospective," *Air Force Magazine*, April 2000, p. 31.

commented from firsthand involvement that "we did not have a real strategy."[56] Likewise, General Short remarked, in what was surely an understatement for him, that the bombing effort had produced its objectives "to some extent by happenstance rather than by design."[57] There were later intimations that a hidden agenda of both the Clinton administration and General Clark had been not just a reversal of the ethnic cleansing in Kosovo, but nothing less than the removal of Milosevic from power and the democratization of Yugoslavia. On that point, one NATO official later described Clark as having said, "you must understand that the objective is to take Yugoslavia away from Mr. Milosevic, so we can democratize it and modernize it. That's our objective."[58] But it was never communicated to subordinate staffs or made a declared goal of Allied Force.[59]

Given the unseemly rush for targets that ensued at SHAPE and elsewhere for more than a month after NATO's initial assumptions proved groundless, it seemed more than a bit disingenuous for administration officials to have claimed afterward that although they had "hoped" that military action would end the Serb abuses in Kosovo quickly, "we knew that it was equally possible that it would not and that a sustained campaign might be necessary to stop the killing and reverse the expulsions" and that "we were prepared to do what it took to win."[60] In what bore every hallmark of a post-hoc attempt at historical revisionism, one official professed that "people in Washington" knew that there would be a need to attack infrastructure targets once it became clear that a three- to four-day bombing effort would not compel Milosevic to settle, but because the allies, especially the French, were "not on board" initially, NATO could not

---

[56]Grossman, "U.S. Military Debates Link Between Kosovo Air War, Stated Objectives," p. 6.

[57]Tirpak, "Kosovo Retrospective," p. 33.

[58]Quoted in Grossman, "U.S. Military Debates Link Between Kosovo Air War, Stated Objectives," p. 7.

[59]General Krulak later remarked that even had it been an unstated goal, it was a "nonstarter," because it would never have gained the backing of NATO.

[60]James B. Steinberg, "A Perfect Polemic: Blind to Reality on Kosovo," *Foreign Affairs*, November/December 1999, p. 131.

start attacking Phase III targets until it had consensus about the bombing.[61] Two critics of administration policy countered convincingly that such claims by the administration that it had been prepared all along for the possible need for a prolonged air campaign were flatly belied by "the hasty improvisation that marked the bombing effort."[62] True enough, General Clark was said on strong authority never to have suggested that just a few days of bombing would suffice to do the job, even though he did limit his planners to a short-duration operations plan out of a conviction that the alliance's political leaders would not sit still for anything longer.[63] But the presumptions of both NATO and the most senior officials of the Clinton administration were well reflected in U.S. interagency reports in January and February 1999, which argued confidently that "after enough of a defense to sustain his honor and assuage his backers, [Milosevic] will quickly sue for peace."[64]

---

[61]This official further claimed that Clinton had never intended to take the ground option off the table but "downplayed" it at first on the grounds that any public mention of it could have prompted a bruising debate in Congress and premature pressures to invoke the War Powers Act. He added that by April, the administration felt compelled to change that perception when it had become clear that important audiences had concluded that the president had flatly ruled out any ground option. That attempt to shift perceptions, he said, included asking Solana to initiate a review of the forces that would be required and encouraging Clark to accelerate planning for a ground invasion, making no effort to keep this quiet. The official admitted that there was no way a ground invasion could have been imminent when Milosevic capitulated on June 3, but that any decision to proceed with an invasion most definitely would have had to be made by mid-June so that the logistical provisions needed to support a ground offensive could be completed before the onset of winter. Interview by RAND staff, Washington, D.C., July 11, 2000.

[62]Christopher Layne and Benjamin Schwarz, "Kosovo II: For the Record," *The National Interest*, Fall 1999, p. 12.

[63]Conversation by RAND staff with Lieutenant General Ronald Keys, USAF, director of operations, U.S. European Command, Stuttgart, Germany, March 8, 2000. Clark himself was clear on this point in his subsequently published memoirs. Although he acknowledged that "there was a spirit of hope at the political levels [going into the bombing] that Milosevic might recognize that NATO was actually going to follow through with its threat and then quickly concede in order to cut his losses," he, for his own part, suspected all along that it was "going to be a long campaign." Clark, *Waging Modern War*, pp. 177, 201.

[64]Elaine Sciolino and Ethan Bronner, "How a President, Distracted by Scandal, Entered Balkan War," *New York Times*, April 18, 1999.

THE DOWNSIDE OF ALLIANCE WARFARE

Throughout Operation Allied Force, there were targets that one or more of the key NATO countries would not approve, those that such countries would not allow to be hit by attacks launched from their soil, and those that they would not hit themselves but would allow other allies to hit. The principal NATO member-states also had differing political agendas and even differing business and financial interests, which heavily affected their reluctance or unwillingness to countenance attacks against certain targets. As a result, General Short was never able to mass forces in the execution of an integrated campaign plan in pursuit of desired strategic effects that had been carefully thought through in advance. Instead, he was left to go after approved targets largely in piecemeal fashion, in what one Allied Force participant caustically dismissed as "target-based targeting" rather than conscious effects-based targeting.

As the air war entered its second fitful week, one senior U.S. official suggested that the bombing effort was turning out to be a real-world battle laboratory, in which the allies were "learning by doing how you conduct a NATO operation, both at a political and at a military level."[65] Another later declared, less charitably: "This is coalition warfare at its worst." After Allied Force ended, yet another complained that "the NATO troops had too many political masters. The system was so cumbersome that it limited the effectiveness of some of the best technology. Joint STARS, for example, couldn't be used to direct aircraft to the targets it saw because it took too long to get approval for a strike."[66]

A senior NATO official commented that "NATO got in way over its head, stumbled through, didn't know how to get out, [and] was

---

[65]John M. Broder, "How to Lay Doubt Aside and Put the Best Face on a Bad Week in the Balkans," *New York Times,* April 1, 1999.

[66]David A. Fulghum, "Lessons Learned May Be Flawed," *Aviation Week and Space Technology,* June 14, 1999, p. 205. Even deeper than the problem of slow target approval, however, was the problem of positive target identification, given the exceptional stringency of the prevailing rules of engagement. For example, Joint STARS could not distinguish a column of refugees from a column of military vehicles loaded with enemy troops, a performance shortfall far more difficult to fix than streamlining the approval process. I am grateful to my colleague Bruce Pirnie for pointing this out.

scared to death by what was happening." This official added that the entire bombing effort had been a "searing experience" that had "left a bitter taste of tilting within governments, between governments, between NATO headquarters in Brussels and the military headquarters at Mons."[67] Reflecting the consensus arrived at by many senior U.S. military officers, both active and retired, Admiral Leighton Smith concluded that "the lesson we've learned is that coalitions aren't good ways to fight wars" and that, at a minimum, the political process in NATO needed to be streamlined so that the collective could use force in a way that made greatest military sense.[68]

In what became a particular sore spot, leaks of target information were discovered early on during Allied Force, contributing in part to the change in procedure described above to streamline the target selection process to allow commanders and planners greater freedom to bomb without consulting every NATO ally every time. In one instance of a suspected leak, two empty Interior Ministry buildings in Belgrade were struck by cruise missiles at the end of the third week. Only 24 hours previously, those buildings had been full of employees, suggesting that the enemy knew the attack was coming and when.[69]

Even before that event, the Pentagon had admitted the discovery of operational security problems, as well as its suspicions that the Serbs had gained access to at least parts of the ATO, thereby enabling them to reposition mobile SAMs in anticipation of planned attacks.[70] Allegations that France, in particular, had been kept out of the loop with respect to some target planning because of concern that the information would be passed on to Milosevic were tacitly confirmed in early April by a Clinton confidant, who remarked that "there are cir-

---

[67]Jane Perlez, "For Albright's Mission, More Problems and Risk," *New York Times*, June 7, 1999.

[68]Bradley Graham and Dana Priest, "'No Way to Fight a War': Hard Lessons of Air Power, Coalitions," *Washington Post*, June 6, 1999.

[69]Hugo Gurdon, "U.S. Admits Milosevic Spies Are Inside NATO," *London Daily Telegraph*, April 15, 1999.

[70]Roberto Suro and Thomas E. Ricks, "Pentagon: Kosovo Air War Data Leaked," *Washington Post*, March 10, 2000.

cles and circles within NATO."[71] In a post–Allied Force interview, Clark admitted that at least one ally had leaked secret targeting information to Yugoslav officials. Without naming the alleged culprit, he said that the security breach was "as clear as the nose on your face."[72]

After the air war ended, Secretary Cohen conceded in a statement to the Senate Armed Services Committee that "it was very difficult to take 19 different countries and get an effective campaign under way without some bumps in the road." Cohen added that the alliance was "slow, in some cases too slow, to achieve a consensus."[73] Citing what he called "self-inflicted wounds in asymmetric warfare," Admiral Ellis added, in his own after-action briefing to Pentagon officials, that the enemy had most definitely drawn aid and comfort from the cumbersome White House and NAC target approval process, as well as from the poor operational security the coalition operations had generated, not only on the NATO side but on the U.S. side as well.[74]

COMMAND AND CONTROL SHORTCOMINGS

The problems created by the lack of a coherent strategy in Allied Force were further aggravated by a confusing chain of command, unsuitable organizational structures, and a lack of staff integration where it was needed most. Indeed, the air war was dominated by what General Short called "about as murky a command relationship as you could possibly get."[75] Two parallel chains of command (see

---

[71]Hugo Gurdon, "France Kept in Dark by Allies," *London Daily Telegraph*, April 9, 1999.

[72]"NATO Chief: Targeting Goals Leaked to Yugoslavia," *Pacific Stars and Stripes*, August 13, 1999.

[73]Tom Raum, "Cohen: NATO Process Prolonged Air Strikes," *Philadelphia Inquirer*, July 21, 1999.

[74]Other examples of such self-inflicted wounds, in Ellis's view, were excessively high standards for limiting collateral damage, NATO's self-suspension of the use of cluster munitions, the aversion to casualties and ground combat, and the reactive as opposed to proactive public affairs posture, all of which slowed allied response time and reduced allied control over the air war's operational tempo.

[75]Quoted in Lieutenant Colonel L. T. Wight, USAF, "What a Tangled Web We Wove: An After-Action Assessment of Operation Allied Force's Command and Control Structure and Processes," unpublished paper, no date, p. 1. Colonel Wight was a member of the C-5 Strategy Cell at the CAOC.

Figure 7.2) worked simultaneously for each allied participant: The first was a NATO chain of command, which began at the North Atlantic Council, the alliance's political leadership, and went from

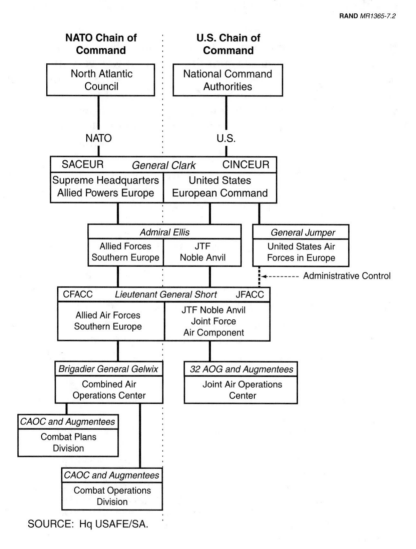

RAND *MR1365-7.2*

SOURCE: Hq USAFE/SA.

Figure 7.2—U.S. and Allied Organization for Allied Force

there to General Clark as SACEUR, through the NATO military staff at SHAPE, to the regionally involved CINCSOUTH, Admiral Ellis, and his JTF staff in Naples, and finally to General Short as commander, Allied Air Forces, Southern Europe (COMAIRSOUTH) and his staff, along with his subordinate Allied Tactical Air Forces, including 5 ATAF, which also operated the CAOC at Vicenza, Italy.

Paralleling this NATO chain of command were the individual chains of each allied member, typified by that of the United States, which began with the National Command Authorities (NCA) at the White House and Pentagon and proceeded to the regional commander in chief, General Clark, in his capacity as CINCEUR (CINC U.S. European Command) and, in turn, to the various subordinate U.S. component commands. The most important two of those subordinate commands were JTF Noble Anvil, established under the command of Admiral Ellis as CINCSOUTH, and USAFE, under the command of General Jumper, who retained operational control of some U.S. assets, specifically the B-1, B-2, B-52, F-117, E-3, KC-135, and U-2 aircraft that flew in Operation Allied Force. General Short exercised tactical control over these aircraft and was assigned operational control of all other combat aircraft assigned to the 31st Air Expeditionary Wing at Aviano Air Base, Italy.[76] Finally, a joint special operations task force maintained operational control over all aircraft dedicated to combat search and rescue missions, and the allied participants ceded operational and tactical control over their aircraft to General Short, who, in his capacity as COMAIRSOUTH, was the designated NATO operational commander and who directed all air missions flown in the NATO-releasable ATO.[77]

This dual-hatting of so many commanders and operational functions often made it hard for Allied Force participants, irrespective of level, to determine exactly who was operating in what capacity at any given time. For example, the CAOC at Vicenza, which was operated by

---

[76]Although the USAF's still-embryonic Air Expeditionary Forces were not available for participation in Operation Allied Force, the AEF concept was exercised at Aviano when the reinforced 31st Fighter Wing was designated a provisional air expeditionary wing for the air war's duration.

[77]Complicating matters even further was the added confusion created by having Task Force Hawk and JTF Shining Hope functioning as separate command entities within the joint operating area.

NATO's 5 ATAF, performed command and control functions both for NATO and for U.S.-only operations. That odd arrangement emanated from the fact that the command and control apparatus put in place for what ultimately became Operation Allied Force had initially been created for a U.S.-only operation, an apparatus that remained in place even as the air war became a NATO effort. As one informed account of this "flawed organizational structure" later observed, the JCS, the USAFE staff, and Admiral Ellis's JTF all "performed roles outside their doctrinal bounds," further confusing the execution of Allied Force and producing numerous instances of "conflicting guidance, command echelons being skipped or omitted entirely, and either a duplication of effort or functions not being performed at all, since one organization erroneously thought the other was responsible for a particular task."[78]

Amplifying further on this bizarre command arrangement, RAF Air Commodore Andrew Vallance later noted from his vantage point as chief of the NATO Reaction Forces air staff in Kalkar, Germany, that the control of an operation in NATO's southern region would normally have fallen to CINCSOUTH and his subordinate air commander (COMAIRSOUTH), Admiral Ellis and General Short, as had been the case earlier with Admiral Smith and then–USAF Lieutenant General Michael Ryan during the successful Operation Deliberate Force over Bosnia in 1995. Yet in the case of Allied Force, following the precedent set earlier by NATO's IFOR/SFOR operation in Bosnia, General Clark as SACEUR elected to take direct personal control of the air effort, effectively cutting CINCSOUTH out of the command chain, to all intents and purposes.

In contrast, the commander, Allied Air Forces, Central Europe (COMAIRCENT), a USAF four-star general, would not normally have been directly involved in a southern region operation. However, in the case of Allied Force, through his national responsibilities as commander, U.S. Air Forces in Europe (COMUSAFE), General

---

[78]Wight, "What a Tangled Web We Wove," p. 7. As a case in point, the Joint Chiefs, despite their formal status as advisers to the NCA, issued directives as though they were part of the warfighting chain of command, for instance, ruling out the use of CBUs by U.S. forces and placing certain targets on "JCS withhold." Likewise, JTF Noble Anvil was often placed in a position of providing direction and guidance to NATO operational units, even though it nominally exercised operational and tactical control over U.S. assets only.

Jumper had "a major say in how the huge USAF contribution was used."[79] Moreover, unlike General Horner in Desert Storm, who answered directly to the theater CINC, General Schwarzkopf, Short reported not to Clark but rather to Admiral Ellis, who in turn reported to Clark—a situation which, Short cautiously said, "colors the equation a bit in terms of my latitude, if you will, in this air campaign."[80] Considering all this confusion and more, concluded an informed and expert observer, operational effectiveness in Allied Force was probably achieved "in spite of the . . . command structures and processes rather than as a direct result of them."[81]

In addition, because NATO had initially anticipated that the bombing would last only a couple of days, the CAOC was woefully understaffed and unprepared for the demands that immediately fell upon it. For example, on the night the air war began, there was no assigned strategy cell, no flexible targeting cell, no established guidance, apportionment, and targeting (GAT) process, and no BDA team in place.

Even when more fully developed, the BDA process left much to be desired. It was well enough equipped, calling as required on national and theater offboard sensors such as satellites and the U-2, tactical sensors such as Predator and Hunter UAVs, and onboard sensors such as the LANTIRN targeting pod carried by the F-14D, the F-15E, and the Block 40 F-16CG. Inputs from these information sources would be forwarded to the JAC at RAF Molesworth, which wielded chief BDA authority, and other BDA-related entities such as the CAOC, national agencies, the SACEUR staff, JTF Noble Anvil, and the JFACC apparatus. However, inputs from national and theater assets could take days to register an impact because of frequent weather complications and higher-priority taskings. Moreover, because BDA

---

[79]Air Commodore A. G. B. Vallance, RAF, chief of staff, NATO Reaction Forces (Air) Staff, Kalkar, Germany, "After Kosovo: Implications of Operation Allied Force for Air Power Development," unpublished paper, p. 3. Although Clark did, by numerous eyewitness accounts, sometimes treat Jumper as though he were the air component commander by virtue of his seniority to Short, Jumper never usurped his superior rank, never insisted that Short follow his suggestions, and frequently lent a helpful hand by quietly adjudicating the more prickly VTC sessions to good effect when Clark and Short got into their differences over targeting strategy and target priorities.

[80]Michael R. Gordon, "Allied Air Chief Stresses Hitting Belgrade Sites."

[81]Wight, "What a Tangled Web We Wove," p. 1.

often required two or more independent sources to confirm a target kill, combat assessment often took longer than the time required for mission planning and retargeting. As a result, targets were often reattacked unnecessarily, which made for additional operational inefficiencies, and the air war's overall progress could not be adequately tracked and measured. For fixed targets in Serbia, BDA confirmation was generally adequate, but the results were frequently not incorporated into replanning. Daily counts of flexible targets known to have been hit in the KEZ were not kept, resulting in a large band of uncertainty with respect to estimates of kills of mobile targets. Finally, there was a recurrent problem with ISR prioritization, reflected in repeated tension between SACEUR's tasking of information sources to support BDA and the felt need at the operator level for information to support the attacking of targets.[82]

The CAOC also suffered from an inadequate airspace management system for assigning tanker tracks and for managing the nightly flow of combat and combat-support aircraft. Not until late April did the CAOC create separate flexible targeting cells for enemy IADS assets and fielded forces. Only by Day 37 was there a smoothly running target development and review mechanism in place, and only on Day 47 was the first Joint Integrated Prioritized Target List (JIPTL) produced, along with the first operational assessment briefing to Short and Clark. Until that time, the would-be Master Air Attack Plan (MAAP) team had been picking targets almost solely on the basis of what had been politically approved. That meant that for the first half of Operation Allied Force, a consistent targeting strategy not only was not attempted but was not even possible.[83]

Moreover, the generally poor intelligence preparation of the battlefield (IPB) occasioned by the faulty assumption that Milosevic would capitulate after just a few days of token bombing complicated both planning and execution. NATO's failure to anticipate and prepare adequately for a range of adverse enemy actions, such as the commingling of Kosovar Albanian civilians with Serb military convoys and the highly successful VJ and MUP camouflage, concealment, and

---

[82]Briefing to the author by Brigadier General Daniel J. Darnell, commander, 31st Fighter Wing, Aviano Air Base, Italy, June 13, 2000.

[83]Wight, "What a Tangled Web We Wove," p. 9.

deception measures, made air operations against both fixed and mobile targets far more difficult than they had been in Desert Storm. In addition, IPB in the KEZ was hindered by the absence of a land component commander in the Allied Force chain of command, which meant that some of the attendant organizations that could have helped the JFACC with this mission were also absent.[84] On top of that, the nonstandard target nomination and approval process, SACEUR's unusually heavy involvement at the micro-level of targeting, and a de facto requirement for zero friendly losses and an absolute minimum of collateral damage hindered the application of classic doctrinal solutions, limited the choices that were available, and put extra stress on systems such as UAVs and other ISR assets that always seemed to be in insufficient supply. Finally, the extended timelines created by the demands of the target approval process, as well as the multiplicity of players at senior levels who had managed to insert themselves into that process, frequently rendered operations against fleeting targets downright impossible and further attested to the poor integration of ISR management practices with the command and control functions required to respond within those timelines. Because the process was so time-consuming, it was frequently impossible to balance the competing priorities of target development and battle damage assessment.

Yet another source of friction in the orderly execution of the daily ATO was the complex overlay of institutional roadblocks and delays, the net result of which was an information-sharing arrangement described by one participant as "cumbersome. It really means we were unable to get timely intelligence to our allies, particularly the British. . . . It's not that the information is so secret. It's that we have a bureaucracy, and the way we transfer from 'U.S. Secret' to 'NATO Secret' takes a little bit of time."[85] As a rule, each allied nation had its own levels of security classification, and each of these had to be

---

[84]The problem was not just the absence of a land component per se, but that no component whatsoever undertook the task of IPB until far too late in the operation. What is required are clearer stipulations regarding whose responsibility it is to conduct IPB, as well as new approaches and processes for doing so. At present, only the land component is resourced and prepared to meet that responsibility. Comments on an earlier draft by Hq USAF/XOXS, July 11, 2001.

[85]Rowan Scarborough, "Kosovo Target Data Stalled in Transit," *Washington Times*, July 28, 1999.

downgraded in order for the information to be released to other allied participants. Frequently the computer systems that operated with these different levels were not mutually compatible, and there were instances, notably in the area of information operations, but also including B-2 and F-117 operations, in which the very nature of the activity meant that information could not be widely released.[86]

Over time, the CAOC went from badly understaffed to packed with a surfeit of personnel as a result of the rampant inefficiencies of the target planning and apportionment process. On one occasion, there were as many as 1,400 people in the small and cramped facility, producing a staffing level that bordered on gridlock.[87] Some augmentees from other USAF commands brought only limited experience with high-intensity operations, further hampering the CAOC's operational effectiveness. In a representative example of the needless inefficiencies that ensued, a PACAF colonel, say, serving as senior duty officer, would overrule something decided at a lower level with a "we don't do that in PACAF," only to have a lieutenant colonel on the permanent CAOC staff reply, uneasily, that that was the way it was done in Allied Force, for good reason.[88] In general, the abnormally large number of senior officers (lieutenant colonels and colonels) populating the CAOC limited the effectiveness of the often more expert junior officers in shaping key decisions. As a rule, the CAOC and General Short mainly performed battle management and support functions rather than operating as a master planning center and high-level command and control entity along the lines of the Air Operations Center and General Horner in Desert Storm.

Yet for all its eventually ramped-up staffing and improved organization, according to its director at the time, the CAOC remained "target

---

[86]As for information operations, one Allied Force participant commented that "due to the involvement of a few compartmented programs, the entire planning effort was classified at an unnecessarily high level, unreleasable to all but a very few U.S. planners. Unfortunately, implementing the overall plan was critical to the success of the operation, but because of the excessive classification, those charged with implementing it could not be told of the plan until it was too late."

[87]The CAOC's normal peacetime manning was around 250 assigned personnel. It had a reinforced staff of 375 on March 24, the night the air war began, which was finally ramped up to more than 1,400 as Allied Force peaked at more than 900 sorties a day.

[88]Conversation with Major General P. J. M. Godderij, deputy commander in chief, Royal Netherlands Air Force, Scheveningen, the Netherlands, June 7, 2000.

poor" throughout much of Allied Force. Because it was denied any opportunity to apply an overarching strategy in shaping the air operation's plan owing to the slowness and randomness of the target approval process, "as targets were approved, we'd go hit them. . . . We had plenty of targets [in principle to go after]—850 or 900—but no authority to hit them." Indeed, the CAOC was reportedly so lacking in available targets and BDA feedback that by Days 55–65, planners were "putting the same targets up [for approval] two and three nights in a row, hoping we could give you different DMPIs from the night before."[89]

As for the flexible targeting effort against VJ forces in the KEZ, the CAOC at first lacked any on-hand Army expertise to help develop the ground order of battle. With no land component in place, the Army's TPQ-36 and TPQ-37 counterbattery radars in Albania required a direct feed to the CAOC, yet information from them was not provided until the very end because Army doctrine had planned for those systems to be used in a different manner and the CAOC was not configured to take advantage of them. Worse yet, TF Hawk and its parent command, the U.S. Army in Europe (USAREUR), evidently elected not to provide processed intelligence data to the JFACC and JTF Noble Anvil until circumstances and senior-official intervention occurred later.[90] Eventually, Clark sent a 10-man Army team to the CAOC to provide such assistance, which aided considerably in the flexible targeting effort. By mid-May, TF Hawk finally began sending the CAOC useful real-time targeting information collected by its counterbattery radars, and a battlefield coordination element staffed with TF Hawk representatives was established in the CAOC to provide additional ground intelligence and operator input into the flexible targeting cell concerned with dispersed and hidden enemy forces in the KEZ.

---

[89]Brigadier General Randy Gelwix, USAF, "Oral Histories Accomplished in Conjunction with Operation Allied Force/Noble Anvil."

[90]During an after-action presentation by the USAREUR battlefield coordination element, Hq USAFE's AWOS study team learned that JTF Noble Anvil had prepared a memorandum of agreement for USAREUR coordination expressly stipulating that TF Hawk would provide the CAOC with processed intelligence data from the TPQ-36 and TPQ-37 counterbattery radars. In the ensuing coordination process, the USAREUR intelligence directorate reportedly excised pertinent language from the text. Comments on an earlier draft by Hq USAF/XOXS, July 11, 2001.

These ground support elements became progressively more integrated with CAOC operations over time, but their contribution was disturbingly slow in coming. In his postwar briefing to the Pentagon leadership, Admiral Ellis suggested that even though no ground operation had been planned for Allied Force, having an assigned joint-force land component commander in place from the very beginning would have gone far toward obviating these and most other related deficiencies.[91] There was also a sentiment in the CAOC toward the end of the air war that the many other units involved in the war effort, including naval air and the B-2 and F-117 communities, needed to send their most experienced operators to the CAOC where their expertise was most badly needed, even if they risked hindering the operational performance of their parent units as a result. As it was, the best use of certain systems available to the JFACC was not always made. For example, the 6th Fleet battle staff consistently felt that its Carrier Air Wing 8 deployed aboard the USS *Theodore Roosevelt* was improperly treated by the CAOC merely as just another allied fighter squadron, rather than the integrated and independent strike force with ISR and command-and-control backup it actually was. Navy planners and operators also pressed repeatedly to have the F-14 TARPS capability employed for direct mission support, whereas the CAOC persisted in using it primarily for BDA.[92]

In a widely noted operations management "first," the use of video teleconferencing communications was pioneered in Allied Force,

---

[91]Amplifying on this point a year after the air war ended, Ellis further remarked that because air power had been the only force element actively used in Allied Force, the JFACC naturally had a heavy air emphasis. Yet, he added, the planning and execution system badly needed land and maritime component commanders deep in the loop as well, so they could explain to the JFACC, as authoritative equals, what their services were able to bring to the planning table. Noting how the "J" in JFACC was all too often silent, Ellis recalled that the contributions of other services were not invariably made the best use of. For example, he said, the EA-6B, TLAM, and F-14 TARPS all brought good capabilities to the fight and the JFACC needed to know about those capabilities directly from their most senior operators. TARPS, in particular, offered excellent potential value, but the Air Force, now out of the manned tactical reconnaissance business, sometimes gave the impression of believing that if the information did not come from space, it did not have an obvious use. Ellis's overall point was that the services have not yet become sufficiently joint-minded at the operational and tactical levels, let alone the strategic level. Interview with Admiral Ellis, May 30, 2000.

[92]Conversation with Vice Admiral Daniel J. Murphy, USN, 6th Fleet commander, aboard the USS *LaSalle*, Gaeta, Italy, June 8, 2000.

with VTC sessions taking place daily at the most senior level because of the wide geographic spread of the key players. Sometimes as many as three or four VTCs were conducted in one day among the most senior principals. Admiral Ellis later characterized them as a powerful tool if properly used, owing to their ability to shorten decision cycle times dramatically, to communicate a commander's intent clearly and unambiguously, and to obviate any requirement for the leading commanders to be collocated. But he cited the propensity of VTCs to be voracious consumers of leadership and staff working hours (often involving time wasted composing flashy but unnecessary—and even at times counterproductive—briefing graphics) and poor substitutes for rigorous mission planning and written orders. Decisions made in the VTC were all too readily prone to misinterpretation as key guidance was successively handed down to lower staff levels.[93]

Indeed, in contrast to Desert Storm, the ad hoc nature of the initial planning, the absence of collocation of senior commanders, the highly distributed nature of the bombing effort, the compartmented and often overclassified planning, and an overreliance on email, VTCs, and other undocumented communication resulted in a notable lack of integration of many of the key staff elements in Allied Force. Typically the only time General Clark was able to speak to his subordinate commanders was via the daily VTC, a limitation that one observer said "made it extremely difficult for the senior leaders to develop a useful working relationship where they possessed the necessary trust and confidence to issue and execute 'mission-type' orders without the need to provide detailed tactical guidance."[94] Clark's VTC guidance was never written down or distributed in any systematic way. In the absence of such formal documentation, most cell chiefs did their best to debrief their staffs. Yet the time-pressures of combat frequently made doing that nigh impossible, with the result that "rumor guidance" tended to predominate throughout the course of Allied Force.[95]

---

[93]Briefing by Admiral James O. Ellis, USN, commander in chief, U.S. Naval Forces, Europe, and commander, Allied Forces Southern Europe and Joint Task Force Noble Anvil, "The View from the Top," 1999.

[94]Wight, "What a Tangled Web We Wove," p. 10.

[95]Ibid., p. 11.

After the war ended, criticism of the VTC approach by many senior officers was quite vocal. In a characteristic observation, the UK Ministry of Defense's director of operations in Allied Force, RAF Air Marshal Sir John Day, remarked that for all its admitted efficiencies when its use was properly disciplined, the VTC mechanism was highly conducive to "ad-hocracy" of all sorts, sometimes resulting in a lack of clarity regarding important matters of both planning and execution. For example, he observed that because of the federated nature of the operation's planning and the extensive use of VTCs involving a large number of U.S. and NATO headquarters, many agencies had full knowledge of the planning details. That generated initial confusion among the UK participants as to who precisely was running the air war, since, until it was confirmed (as suspected) that it was indeed General Short, they could obtain the same information from any headquarters that was involved in the VTC. Consistent with others who reflected on the many negatives of VTCs with the benefit of hindsight, Air Marshal Day suggested that participation in high-level VTCs should henceforth be limited exclusively to those directly in the chain of command and that the commander in chief should devote careful thought beforehand to the following: (1) the appropriate participants and viewers; (2) a prior agenda, so that essential participants would not hesitate to raise an item out of fear that an item might already be on the CINC's checklist; (3) diligent minute-taking; and (4) a summary of command decisions taken, so that the commander's intent would always be unambiguous.[96]

---

[96]Interview with Air Marshal Sir John Day, RAF Innsworth, United Kingdom, July 26, 2000. Rather more bluntly, retired USAF General Chuck Horner, the JFACC during Desert Storm, commented that had he been SACEUR during Allied Force, he would have shot every TV monitor in sight. The biggest problem with VTCs, Horner said, is that one does not know who is present and listening, even as a videotaped record of the proceeding is being made. That, he added, inclines participants to pull their punches and speak "for the record," rather than to speak their mind in a manner that only privacy can ensure. Conversation with General Horner at Farnborough, United Kingdom, July 27, 2000.

Chapter Eight

NATO'S AIR WAR IN PERSPECTIVE

Operation Allied Force was the most intense and sustained military operation to have been conducted in Europe since the end of World War II. It represented the first extended use of military force by NATO, as well as the first major combat operation conducted for humanitarian objectives against a state committing atrocities within its own borders. It was the longest U.S. combat operation to have taken place since the war in Vietnam, which ended in 1975. At a price tag of more than $3 billion all told, it was also a notably expensive one.[1] Yet in part precisely because of that investment, it turned out to have been an unprecedented exercise in the discriminate use of force on a large scale. Although there were some unfortunate and highly publicized cases in which innocent civilians were tragically killed, Secretary of Defense William Cohen was on point when he characterized Allied Force afterward as "the most precise application of air power in history."[2] In all, out of some 28,000 high-explosive munitions expended altogether over the air war's 78-day course, no more than 500 noncombatants in Serbia and Kosovo died as a direct result of errant air attacks, a new low in American wartime experience when compared to both Vietnam and Desert Storm.[3]

---

[1]Lisa Hoffman, "U.S. Taxpayers Faced with Mounting Kosovo War Costs," *Washington Times*, June 10, 1999.

[2]Bradley Graham, "Air Power 'Effective, Successful,' Cohen Says," *Washington Post*, June 11, 1999.

[3]That was the final assessment of an unofficial post–Allied Force bomb damage survey conducted in Serbia, Kosovo, and Montenegro by a team of inspectors representing Human Rights Watch. A U.S. Air Force analyst who was later briefed on the study commented that Human Rights Watch had "the best on-the-ground data of anyone in

After Allied Force ended, air power's detractors lost no time in seeking to deprecate NATO's achievement. In a representative case in point, retired U.S. Army Lieutenant General William Odom charged that "this war didn't do anything to vindicate air power. It didn't stop the ethnic cleansing, and it didn't remove Milosevic"—as though those were ever the expected goals of NATO's air power employment to begin with.[4] Yet because of the air war's ultimate success in forcing Milosevic to yield to NATO's demands, the predominant tendency among most outside observers was to characterize it as a watershed achievement for air power. One account called Operation Allied Force "one of history's most impressive air campaigns."[5] Another suggested that if the cease-fire held, the United States and its allies would have accomplished "what some military experts had predicted was impossible: a victory achieved with air power alone."[6] A *Wall Street Journal* article declared that Milosevic's capitulation had marked "one of the biggest victories ever for air power," finally vindicating the long-proclaimed belief of airmen that "air power alone can win some kind of victory."[7] And the *New York*

---

the West." "A New Bomb Damage Report," *Newsweek*, December 20, 1999, p. 4. A later report, however, indicated that Human Rights Watch had identified 90 separate collateral damage incidents, in contrast to the acknowledgment by NATO and the U.S. government of only 20 to 30. Bradley Graham, "Report Says NATO Bombing Killed 500 Civilians in Yugoslavia," *Washington Post*, February 7, 2000.

[4]Mark Thompson, "Warfighting 101," *Time*, June 14, 1999, p. 50. Regarding Odom's first charge, General Jumper categorically declared after the bombing effort successfully ended that "no airman ever promised that air power would stop the genocide that was already ongoing by the time we were allowed to start this campaign." Quoted in *The Air War Over Serbia: Aerospace Power in Operation Allied Force*, Washington, D.C., Hq United States Air Force, April 1, 2000, p. 19. One of the few detractors of air power who was later moved to offer an apologia for having been wrong was military historian John Keegan, who acknowledged a week before Milosevic finally capitulated that he felt "rather as a creationist Christian . . . being shown his first dinosaur bone." John Keegan, "Modern Weapons Hit War Wisdom," *Sydney Morning Herald*, June 5, 1999. Keegan, long a skeptic of air power's avowed promise, wrote on the eve of Milosevic's capitulation that the looming settlement represented "a victory for air power and air power alone." Quoted in Elliott Abrams, "Just War. Just Means?" *National Review*, June 28, 1999, p. 16.

[5]William Drozdiak and Anne Swardson, "Military, Diplomatic Offensives Bring About Accord," *Washington Post*, June 4, 1999.

[6]Paul Richter, "Air-Only Campaign Offers a False Sense of Security, Some Say," *Los Angeles Times*, June 4, 1999.

[7]Thomas E. Ricks and Anne Marie Squeo, "Kosovo Campaign Showcased the Effectiveness of Air Power," *Wall Street Journal*, June 4, 1999.

Times called the operation's outcome "a success and more—a refutation of the common wisdom that air power alone could never make a despot back down."[8] These and similar views were aired by many of the same American newspapers that, for the preceding 11 weeks, had doubted whether NATO's strategy would *ever* succeed without an accompanying ground invasion.

Similarly, defense analyst Andrew Krepinevich, a frequent critic of claims made by air power proponents, conceded that "almost alone, American air power broke the back of the Yugoslav military and forced Slobodan Milosevic to yield to NATO's demands. What air power accomplished in Operation Allied Force would have been inconceivable to most military experts 15 years ago." Krepinevich further acknowledged that unlike earlier times when air power was considered by other services to be merely a support element for land and maritime operations, that was no longer the case today, since air power had clearly demonstrated its ability in Allied Force to "move beyond the supporting role to become an equal (and sometimes dominant) partner with the land and maritime forces."[9]

It was not just outside observers, moreover, who gave such ready voice to that upbeat assessment. Shortly after the cease-fire, President Clinton himself declared that the outcome of Allied Force "proved that a sustained air campaign, under the right conditions, can stop an army on the ground."[10] Other administration leaders were equally quick to congratulate air power for what it had done to salvage a situation that looked, almost until the last moment, as though it was headed nowhere but to a NATO ground involvement of some sort. In their joint statement to the Senate Armed Services Committee after the air war ended, Secretary Cohen and General

---

[8]Serge Schmemann, "Now, Onward to the Next Kosovo. If There Is One," *New York Times,* June 16, 1999.

[9]Andrew Krepinevich, "Two Cheers for Air Power," *Wall Street Journal,* June 11, 1999.

[10]Pat Towell, "Lawmakers Urge Armed Forces to Focus on High-Tech Future," *Congressional Quarterly Weekly,* June 26, 1999, p. 1564. Actually, the air effort proved no such thing with respect to VJ forces operating in Kosovo.

Henry Shelton, the chairman of the JCS, described it as "an overwhelming success."[11]

With all due respect for the unmatched professionalism of those allied aircrews who, against difficult odds, actually carried out the air effort and made it succeed in the end, it is hard to accept such glowing characterizations as the proper conclusions to be drawn from Allied Force. In fact, many of them are at marked odds with the views of those senior professionals who, one would think, would be most familiar with air power and its limitations. Shortly before the bombing effort began, the four U.S. service chiefs uniformly doubted, in testimony before the Senate Armed Services Committee, whether air strikes by themselves would succeed in compelling Milosevic to yield.[12] Indeed, the Air Force chief of staff, General Michael Ryan, admitted less than a week later: "I don't know if we can do it without ground troops."[13] After Allied Force was over, the former commander of NATO forces during Operation Deliberate Force, Admiral Leighton Smith, remarked that the Kosovo experience should go down as "possibly the worst way we employed our military forces in history." Smith added that telling the enemy beforehand what you are *not* going to do is "the absolutely dumbest thing you can do."[14] Former Air Force chief of staff General Ronald Fogleman likewise observed that "just because it comes out reasonably well, at least in the eyes of the administration, doesn't mean it was conducted properly. The application of air power was flawed." Finally, the air component commander, USAF Lieutenant General Michael Short, declared that "as an airman, I'd have done this a whole lot differently than I was allowed to do. We could have done this differently. We should have done this differently."[15]

---

[11]Secretary of Defense William S. Cohen and General Henry H. Shelton, "Joint Statement on the Kosovo After-Action Review," testimony before the Senate Armed Services Committee, Washington, D.C., October 14, 1999.

[12]Bradley Graham, "Joint Chiefs Doubted Air Strategy," *Washington Post*, April 5, 1999.

[13]Quoted in "Verbatim Special: The Balkan War," *Air Force Magazine*, June 1999, p. 47.

[14]"Reporters' Notebook," *Defense Week*, July 19, 1999, p. 4.

[15]William Drozdiak, "Allies Need Upgrade, General Says," *Washington Post*, June 20, 1999.

Indeed, few Allied Force participants were more surprised by the sudden capitulation of Milosevic than the majority of the alliance's most senior airmen.[16] By the end of May, most USAF generals had concluded that NATO would be unable to find and destroy any more dispersed VJ troops and equipment without incurring more unintended civilian casualties.[17] General Short had reluctantly concluded that NATO's strategy, at its existing level of intensity, was unlikely to break Milosevic's will and that there was a clear need to ramp up the bombing effort if the alliance was to prevail.[18] True enough, on the eve of the cease-fire, General Ryan predicted that once the air effort began seeking strategic rather than merely battlefield effects, Milosevic would wake up to the realization that NATO was taking his country apart on the installment plan and that his ultimate defeat was "inevitable." The Air Force chief hastened to add, however, that Allied Force had not begun in "the way that America normally would apply air power," implying his belief that there was a more sensible way of going about it.[19] As a testament to widespread doubts that the air war was anywhere close to achieving its objectives, planning was under way for a continuation of offensive air operations against Yugoslavia through December or longer if necessary—although it remains doubtful whether popular support on either side of the Atlantic would have sustained operations for that long.

In sum, Operation Allied Force was a mixed experience for the United States and NATO. Although it represented a successful application of air power in the end, it also was a less-than-exemplary ex-

---

[16]Most others as well were caught off guard by the sudden ending of the Kosovo crisis. See Lieutenant General Bernard E. Trainor, USMC (Ret.), "The Council on Foreign Relations Report on the Kosovo Air Campaign: A Digest of the Roundtable on the Air Campaign in the Balkans," Council on Foreign Relations, New York, July 27, 2000. One notable exception was USAF Brigadier General Daniel J. Leaf, commander of the 31st Air Expeditionary Wing at Aviano Air Base, Italy, who confidently told his aircrews on the eve of Milosevic's capitulation that he could "smell an impending NATO victory in the air" (conversation with the author in Washington, D.C., November 16, 2000).

[17]John F. Harris and Bradley Graham, "Clinton Is Reassessing Sufficiency of Air War," *Washington Post*, June 3, 1999.

[18]William M. Arkin, "Limited Warfare in Kosovo Not Working," *Seattle Times*, May 22, 1999.

[19]General Michael E. Ryan, "Air Power Is Working in Kosovo," *Washington Post*, June 4, 1999.

ercise in strategy and an object lesson in the limitations of alliance warfare. Accordingly, any balanced appraisal of the operation must account not only for its signal accomplishments, but also for its shortcomings in both planning and execution, which came close to making it a disaster for the alliance.

THE ACHIEVEMENTS OF ALLIED FORCE

Admittedly, there is much to be said of a positive nature about NATO's air war for Kosovo. To begin with, it did indeed represent the first time in which air power coerced an enemy leader to yield with no friendly land combat action whatsoever.[20] In that respect, the air effort's conduct and results well bore out a subsequent observation by Australian air power historian Alan Stephens that "modern war is concerned more with acceptable political outcomes than with seizing and holding ground."[21]

It hardly follows from this, of course, that air power can now "win wars alone" or that the air-only strategy ultimately adopted by the Clinton administration and NATO's political leaders was the wisest choice available to them. Yet the fact that air power prevailed on its own despite the multiple drawbacks of a reluctant administration, a divided Congress, an indifferent public, a potentially fractious alliance, a determined enemy, and, not least, the absence of a credible NATO strategy surely testified that the air weapon has come a long way in recent years in its *relative* combat leverage compared to other, more traditional force elements. Thanks to the marked improvements in precision attack and battlespace awareness, unintended damage to civilian structures and noncombatant fatalities were kept to a minimum, even as air power plainly demonstrated its coercive potential.

---

[20]It bears noting here that the December 1972 bombing of Hanoi was also an example of successful coercive bombing, albeit with a very limited objective and in the context of a much larger war that ended in defeat for the United States. For more on this, see Wayne Thompson, *To Hanoi and Back: The U.S. Air Force and North Vietnam, 1966–1973*, Washington, D.C., Smithsonian Institute Press, 2000, pp. 255–280.

[21]Alan Stephens, *Kosovo, or the Future of War*, Paper Number 77, Air Power Studies Center, Royal Australian Air Force, Fairbairn, Australia, August 1999, p. 21.

In contrast to Desert Storm, the air war's attempts at denial did not bear much fruit in the end. Allied air attacks against dispersed and hidden enemy forces were largely ineffective, in considerable part because of the decision made by NATO's leaders at the outset to forgo even the threat of a ground invasion. Hence, Serb atrocities against the Kosovar Albanians increased even as NATO air operations intensified. Yet ironically, in contrast to the coalition's ultimately unsuccessful efforts to coerce Saddam Hussein into submission, punishment *did* seem to work against Milosevic, disconfirming the common adage that air power can beat up on an adversary indefinitely but rarely can induce him to change his mind.

Although these and other operational and tactical achievements were notable in and of themselves and offered ample grist for the Kosovo "lessons learned" mill, the most important accomplishments of Allied Force occurred at the strategic level and had to do with the performance of the alliance as a combat collective. First, notwithstanding the charges of some critics to the contrary, NATO clearly prevailed over Milosevic in the end. In the early aftermath of the air war, more than a few observers hastened to suggest that NATO's bombing had actually caused precisely what it had sought to prevent. Political scientist Michael Mandelbaum, for example, portrayed Allied Force as "a military success and political failure," charging that while it admittedly forced a Serb withdrawal from Kosovo, the broader consequences were the opposite of what NATO's chiefs had intended because the Kosovar Albanians "emerged from the war considerably worse off than they had been before."[22] Another charge voiced by some was that as Allied Force wore on, NATO watered down the demands it had initially levied on Milosevic at Rambouillet. As early as the air war's 12th day, this charge noted, NATO merely stipulated that Kosovo must be under the protection of an

---

[22]Michael Mandelbaum, "A Perfect Failure: NATO's War Against Yugoslavia," *Foreign Affairs*, September/October 1999, p. 2. That charge was based on the fact that prior to the air war's start on March 24, 1999, only some 2,500 civilian innocents had died in the Serb-Albanian civil war, whereas during the 11-week bombing effort, an estimated 10,000 civilians were killed by marauding bands of Serbs unleashed by Milosevic in direct response to Allied Force.

"international" security force, whereas at Rambouillet, it had insisted on that presence being a NATO force.[23]

There is no denying that the Serb ethnic cleansing push accelerated after Operation Allied Force began. It is even likely that the air effort was a major, if not determining, factor behind that acceleration. Yet it seems equally likely that some form of Operation Horseshoe, as the ethnic cleansing campaign was code-named, would have been unleashed by Milosevic in any event during the spring or summer of 1999. Indeed, what a Serb general was later said by SACEUR to have forecast as a "hot spring" in which "the problem of Kosovo . . . will definitely be solved" commenced more that a week *before* the start of Allied Force, when VJ and MUP strength in and around Kosovo was increased by 42,000 troops and some 1,000 heavy weapons—even as the Rambouillet talks were under way.[24] Administration defenders are on solid ground in insisting that the ethnic cleansing had already begun and that had NATO not finally acted when it did, upward of a million Kosovar refugees may well have been left stranded in Albania, Macedonia, and Montenegro, with no hope of returning home.[25]

Although NATO's air strikes were unable to halt Milosevic's ethnic cleansing campaign before it had been essentially completed, they did succeed in completely reversing its effects in the early aftermath of the cease-fire. Within two weeks of the air war's conclusion, more than 600,000 of the nearly 800,000 ethnic Albanian and other refugees had returned home. By the end of July, barely one month after the cease-fire, only some 50,000 displaced Kosovar Albanians still awaited repatriation (see Figure 8.1). By any reasonable measure, Milosevic's bowing to NATO reflected a defeat on his part, and his accession to the cease-fire left him worse off than he would have been had he accepted NATO's conditions at Rambouillet. Under the

---

[23]Robert Hewson, "Operation Allied Force: The First 30 Days," *World Air Power Journal*, Fall 1999, p. 24.

[24]"Briefing by SACEUR General Wesley Clark," Brussels, NATO Headquarters, April 13, 1999.

[25]See, for example, the riposte to Mandelbaum by the Clinton administration's deputy national security adviser, James B. Steinberg, "A Perfect Polemic: Blind to Reality on Kosovo," *Foreign Affairs*, November/December 1999, pp. 128–133.

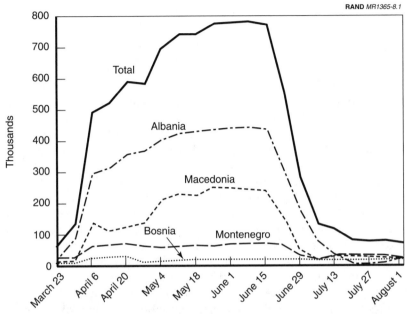

SOURCE: UN High Commissioner for Refugees, "Kosovo Crisis Update,"
March 31, 1999.

Figure 8.1—Refugee Flow

terms of Rambouillet, Serbia would have been permitted to keep
5,000 of its "security forces" in Kosovo. Thanks to the settlement ultimately reached before the cease-fire, however, there are now none.
Moreover, on the eve of Operation Allied Force, Milosevic had insisted as a point of principle that not a single foreign troop would be
allowed to set foot on Kosovo soil. Today, with some 42,000 KFOR
soldiers from 39 countries performing daily peacekeeping functions,
Kosovo is an international protectorate safeguarded both by the UN
and NATO, rendering any continued Serb claim to sovereignty over
the province a polite fiction. At bottom, as NATO's Secretary General, Javier Solana, declared in a retrospective commentary on the
experience, the alliance "achieved every one of its goals" in forcing a

Serb withdrawal from Kosovo.[26] Whether or not one chooses to call that outcome a "victory" entails what Karl Mueller has characterized as "a semantic exercise that should only really matter to social scientists seeking to code the event for data analysis."[27]

Second, NATO showed that it could operate successfully under pressure as an alliance, even in the face of constant hesitancy and reluctance on the part of many of the member-states' political leaders. For all the air war's fits and starts and the manifold frustrations they caused, the alliance earned justified credit for having done remarkably well in a uniquely challenging situation. In seeing Allied Force to a successful conclusion, NATO did something that it had been neither created nor configured to do. Indeed, it might well have been easier for Washington and SACEUR to elicit NAC approval to grant border-crossing authority at the brink of a NATO–Warsaw Pact showdown during the height of the cold war than to get 19 post–cold war players on board for an offensive operation conducted to address a problem that threatened no member's most vital security interests. As General Clark later recalled, the "ultimate proof" of the air war's success was that NATO realized its "ability to maintain alliance cohesion despite all the pressures of fighting a conflict, at the same time bringing in new members, and then going into Kosovo itself on an extended and uncertain campaign—uncertain in that there [was] no fixed exit date."[28]

Reflecting on the air war experience a year later, Admiral James Ellis, the commander of the U.S. contribution to Allied Force, observed that during the final days leading up to March 24, it was a question not of *how* the bombing effort would be conducted so much as *whether* it would take place at all. Before Rambouillet, the challenge had been to compel Milosevic to do something. Afterward, it became to compel him to *stop* doing something. Ellis speculated that had the allies known from the outset that they were signing up for a 78-day campaign, they might easily have declined the opportunity forth-

---

[26]Javier Solana, "NATO's Success in Kosovo," *Foreign Affairs*, November/December 1999, p. 114.

[27]Karl Mueller, "Deus ex Machina? Coercive Air Power in Bosnia and Kosovo," unpublished paper, School of Advanced Air Power Studies, Maxwell AFB, Alabama, November 7, 1999, p. 6.

[28]"Wesley Clark Looks Back," *National Journal,* February 26, 2000, p. 612.

with. Unlike the ad hoc group of nations that fought Desert Storm as a solidly united front, NATO was not a coalition of the willing but rather a loose defensive alliance of 19 democracies. They were all strongly inclined to march to different drummers, and all had varying commitments to grappling—at least militarily—with humanitarian crises in which they had no clear national security stake.[29]

As the bombing entered its third month without a clear end in sight, Ellis feared that allied cohesion might collapse within three weeks unless something of a game-changing nature occurred, such as a drastic move by Milosevic to alter the stakes or a firm U.S. decision to accede to a ground-invasion option. Offsetting that fear, however, was his belief that the allies were finally beginning to recognize and accept the need to come to terms with some thorny operational issues such as granting approval to attack electrical power and other key infrastructure targets. That took time, Ellis said, but the fact that it finally occurred constituted a signal that the alliance was slowly learning how to do what needed to be done.

Finally, for all the criticism that was directed against some of the less steadfast NATO members for their rear-guard resistance and questionable loyalty while the air war was under way, even the Greek government held firm to the very end, despite the fact that more than 90 percent of the Greek population supported the Serbs rather than the Kosovar Albanians—and held frequent large-scale street demonstrations to show that support.[30] True enough, there remain many unknowns about the outlook for NATO's steadfastness in any future confrontation along Europe's eastern periphery. Yet NATO was able to maintain the one quality that was essential for the success of Allied

---

[29]Interview with Admiral James O. Ellis, USN, commander in chief, Allied Forces, Southern Europe, Naples, Italy, May 30, 2000. This is not to say, however, that the allies had no intrinsic stake at all. Italy had a stake in preventing further depredations by Milosevic because of the refugee problem they created. Greece had a major stake in what happened to the Serbs because of a largely sympathetic population. Germany also found itself being inundated with refugees. Hungary had good reason to worry about the Hungarian population still inside Serbia. All of the NATO countries had an intrinsic interest in stability in Europe, and Milosevic was, if nothing else, a destabilizer of the first order. I am grateful to Alan Gropman of the Industrial College of the Armed Forces, Washington, D.C., for reminding me of these important facts.

[30]Air Commodore A. G. B. Vallance, RAF, chief of staff, NATO Reaction Forces (Air) Staff, Kalkar, Germany, "Did We Really Have a Good War? Myths in the Making," unpublished manuscript, no date, p. 2.

Force: its cohesion and integrity as a fighting collective. The lion's share of the credit for that, suggested Air Marshal Sir John Day, belongs to NATO Secretary General Solana, who, in what Day called a "brilliant" performance, showed both leadership and courage in the face of continuous U.S. pushing and an equally continuous reluctance on the part of many allies to go along.[31]

THE AIR WAR'S FAILINGS

Despite these accomplishments, enough discomfiting surprises emanated from the Allied Force experience to suggest that instead of basking in the glow of air power's largely single-handed successful performance, air warfare professionals should give careful thought to the hard work that still needs to be done to realize air power's fullest potential in joint warfare. As in the case of the various positive outcomes noted above, many of these surprises entailed shortfalls at the tactical and operational levels. As previous chapters have documented in detail, the targeting process was inefficient to a fault, command and control arrangements were excessively complicated, and enemy IADS challenges indicated much unfinished work for SEAD planners. In addition, elusive enemy ground forces belied the oft-cited claim of airmen that air power has arrived at the threshold of being able to find, fix, track, target, and engage any object on the surface of the earth.[32]

The biggest failures of Allied Force likewise occurred in the realm of strategy and execution. First, despite its successful outcome and through no fault of allied airmen, the bombing effort was clearly a suboptimal application of air power. The incremental plan chosen by NATO's leaders risked squandering much of the capital that had been built up in air power's account ever since its ringing success in

---

[31]Interview with Air Marshal Sir John Day, RAF, UK Ministry of Defense director of operations in Allied Force, RAF Innsworth, United Kingdom, July 25, 2000.

[32]These and other surprises should stand as a sobering reminder that the comparatively seamless and unfettered successes achieved by allied air power during Operation Desert Storm were most likely the exception rather than the rule for future joint and combined operations—both the operating area and the circumstances surrounding the 1991 Gulf War were unique. For more on this point, see Air Vice Marshal Tony Mason, RAF (Ret.), *Air Power: A Centennial Appraisal*, London, Brassey's, 1994, pp. 140–158.

Desert Storm nearly a decade before. General Clark's early comment that NATO would "grind away" at Milosevic rather than hammer him hard and with determination attested powerfully to the watered-down nature of the strikes.[33] By meting out those strikes with such hesitancy, NATO's leaders remained blind to the fact that air power's very strengths can become weaknesses if the air weapon is used in a way that undermines its credibility.[34] Almost without question, the first month of underachievement in the air war convinced Milosevic that he could ride out the NATO assault.

Indeed, the way Operation Allied Force commenced violated two of the most enduring axioms of military practice: the importance of achieving surprise and the criticality of keeping the enemy unclear as to one's intentions. The acceptance by NATO's leaders of a strategy that preemptively ruled out a ground threat and envisaged only gradually escalating air strikes to inflict pain was a guaranteed recipe for downstream trouble, even though it was the only strategy that, at the time, seemed politically workable. For U.S. defense leaders to have suggested afterward that NATO's attacks against fielded enemy ground troops "forced [those troops] to remain largely hidden from view . . . and made them ineffective as a tactical maneuver force" and that its SEAD operations forced Milosevic to "husband his antiaircraft missile defenses to sustain his challenge [to NATO air operations]" was to make a virtue of necessity on two counts.[35] First, it was the absence of a credible NATO ground threat that *enabled* Milosevic's troops to disperse and hide, making it that much more difficult for NATO's aircrews to find and attack them. The ineffectiveness of those troops as a tactical maneuver force was quite beside the point, considering that tactical maneuver was not required for the ethnic cleansing those troops managed to sustain quite handily throughout most of the air war's duration. Second, it would have been more honest to say that the Serb tactic of carefully conserving antiaircraft missile defenses throughout Allied Force made those

---

[33]Eric Schmitt, "Weak Serb Defense Puzzles NATO," *New York Times*, March 26, 1999.

[34]For a fuller development of this point, see Daniel L. Byman, Matthew C. Waxman, and Eric Larson, *Air Power as a Coercive Instrument*, Santa Monica, California, RAND, MR-1061-AF, 1999. See also Grant T. Hammond, "Myths of the Air War Over Serbia: Some 'Lessons' Not to Learn," *Aerospace Power Journal*, Winter 2000, pp. 78–86.

[35]Cohen and Shelton, "Joint Statement."

defenses a continuing threat to NATO's freedom to operate in Yugoslav airspace, undermining the effectiveness of many sorties as a
result.

In fairness to the U.S. and NATO officials most responsible for air operations planning, many of the differences between Allied Force and
the more satisfying Desert Storm experience were beyond the control
of the allies, and they should be duly noted in any critique of the way
the former was conducted. To begin with, as discussed earlier, bad
weather was the rule, not the exception. Second, variegated and
forested terrain limited the effectiveness of many sensors. Third,
Serb SAM operators were more proficient and tactically astute than
those of Iraq. Fourth, alliance complications were greater by far in
Allied Force than were the largely inconsequential intracoalition differences during the Gulf War. Finally, because the goal of Allied
Force was more to compel than to destroy, it was naturally more difficult for senior decisionmakers to measure and assess the air war's
daily progress, since there was no feedback mechanism to indicate
how well the bombing was advancing toward coercing Milosevic to
comply with NATO's demands. It was largely for that reason that
most Allied Force planners were surprised when he finally decided to
capitulate.

That said, the most important question with respect to Allied Force
has to do less with platform or systems performance than with the
more basic strategy choices that NATO's leaders made and what
those choices may suggest about earlier lessons forgotten—not only
from Desert Storm and Deliberate Force but also from Vietnam. Had
Milosevic been content to hunker down and wait out NATO's
bombing effort, he could easily have challenged the long-term cohesion and staying power of the alliance. Fortunately for the success of
Allied Force, by opting instead to accelerate his ethnic cleansing of
Kosovo, he not only united the West in revulsion but also left NATO
with no alternative but to dig in for the long haul, both to secure an
outcome that would enable the repatriation of nearly a million displaced Kosovars and to ensure its continued credibility as a military
alliance.

Because of the almost universal assumption among NATO's leaders
that the operation would last no more than two to four days, the first
30 days of the air war were badly underresourced. Among the results

of this erroneous assumption were erratic procedures for target nomination and review, too few combat aircraft on hand for conducting both night and day operations, and pressures from SACEUR for simultaneous attacks not only on fixed infrastructure targets but also on fielded VJ forces. Relatedly, there was an inadequate airspace management plan and no flexible targeting cell in the CAOC for servicing SACEUR's sudden demands to attack VJ forces in the KEZ. All of these problems, it bears stressing, were a reflection *not* on NATO's air power or its mechanisms for using air power per se, but rather on the strategy choices that were made (or, perhaps more correctly, forgone) by NATO's political leaders.

To be sure, allied capabilities for detecting and engaging fleeting enemy ground-force targets improved perceptibly as the weather grew more agreeable with approaching summer and as the KLA became more active. Nevertheless, persistent problems with the flexible targeting effort spotlighted further work that needs to be done. The CAOC went into the operation without an on-hand cadre of experienced target planners accustomed to working together harmoniously. Accordingly, General Short was forced to resort to a "pick-up team" during the first month of operations against VJ forces in Kosovo. The fusion cell also frequently lacked ready access to all-source reconnaissance information. At first, data from special operations forces and the Army's TPQ-36 and TPQ-37 firefinder radars in Albania were not provided to the CAOC. Indeed, there was an absence of allied ground-force representation in the CAOC until the air war's very end. Other needs that became apparent included regularized and centralized mensuration of target coordinates as new target candidates were detected and became available for prompt servicing.

Beyond that, the very nature of Operation Allied Force and the manner in which it was conducted from the highest levels both in Washington and in Brussels placed unique stresses on the JFACC's ability to command and control allied air operations. For example, General Short and his staff had to contend on an unrelenting basis with rapid shifts in political priorities and SACEUR guidance, as well as with the myriad pressures occasioned by a random and nonsystematic flow of assets to the theater, ranging from combat aircraft to staff augmentees in the CAOC. All of these problems emanated from a lack of consensus among the top decisionmakers on both sides of the Atlantic as to what the air effort's military goals were at any given moment and what it would take to "prevail." The de facto "no friendly loss" rule, stringent collateral damage constraints, and the absence of a NATO ground threat to force VJ troops to concentrate and thus make them easier targets further limited the rational employment of available in-theater assets and placed a premium on accurate information and the use of measures that took a disconcertingly long time to plan, carry out, and evaluate.[36] One realization driven home by these and other shortcomings was the need for planners in the targeting cell to train together routinely in peacetime *before* a contingency requires them to react at peak efficiency from the very start.

GRADUALISM AND ITS IMPLICATIONS

The greatest frustration of Operation Allied Force was its slow start and equally slow escalation. A close second entailed the uniquely stringent rules of engagement that limited the effectiveness of many combat sorties. Indeed, the dominance of political inhibitions was a signal feature of the air war from start to finish. Because it was an operation performed essentially for humanitarian purposes, neither the United States nor any of the European members of NATO saw their security interests threatened by ongoing events in Yugoslavia. Because the perceived stakes were not high, at least at the outset, any early commitment by NATO to a ground offensive was all but out of the question. Moreover, both the anticipated length of the bombing effort and the menu of targets attacked were bound to be matters of often heated contention.

On top of that, the avoidance of noncombatant fatalities among Yugoslavia's civilian population was rightly of paramount concern to NATO's leaders, further aggravating the complications caused by poor target-area weather throughout much of the air war. As USEUCOM's director of operations, USAF Major General Ronald Keys, later noted, while there was no single target whose elimination might have won the war, there was a profusion of targets that could potentially have *lost* the war had they been struck, either intentionally or inadvertently. In the presence of factors like these that could have split the alliance at any time, NATO's unity was a sine qua non

---

[36]I am indebted to my RAND colleagues James Schneider, Myron Hura, and Gary McLeod for these on-target summary observations.

for the success of Allied Force. Not surprisingly, the Serbs were aware of that fact and were frequently able to exploit it.[37]

Acceptance of these realities, however, hardly eased the discomfiture among air warfare professionals over the fact that NATO's self-imposed restraints were forcing them to fight with one hand tied behind their backs. One analyst, reporting the results of interviews conducted in late April with some two dozen senior active and retired Air Force generals, reported a collective sense of "disappointment that air power is being so poorly employed [and] frustration over the false promise of a perfect war and zero casualties." His interviews revealed a deep-seated concern that "with far too much political micromanagement but without a clear strategy and the aid of ground forces, the air war . . . is destined to fail." Worst of all, the generals complained, the United States and NATO did not take advantage of the shock effect of air power. Said retired General Charles Horner: "We are training [the Serbs] to live with air attacks." Said another Air Force general: "Air planners are not planning the air operation. They are being issued targets each day for the next day's operations, too late to do rational planning."[38]

There was no less disaffection among air warfare professionals at the working level. As one U.S. pilot flying combat sorties complained in an email message that made its way to public light: "This has been a farce from the start. We have violated every principle of campaign air power I can think of." The pilot hastened to add that "over-zealous air power advocates have, since Desert Storm, sold us as something we are not. Air power can do a lot of things, [but] it cannot change the mind of a dictator who has his people's tacit support." Nevertheless, he concluded, "it is not the USAF's fault that the air campaign is not going as well as Desert Storm. Hitting 5–8 targets a night, with sequential [as opposed to] parallel operations, is not the way to prosecute a campaign."[39]

---

[37]Cited in Colonel Steve Pitotti, USAF, "Global Environments, Threats, and Military Strategy (GETM) Update," Air Armament Summit 2000 briefing, 2000.

[38]William M. Arkin, "Inside the Air Force, Officers Are Frustrated About the Air War," *Washington Post*, April 25, 1999.

[39]Rowan Scarborough, "Officers Criticize Air War Strategy," *Washington Times*, May 10, 1999.

The UK Ministry of Defense's director of operations in Allied Force denied that there was ever a hard-and-fast rule that NATO *must* not lose an aircraft under any circumstances.[40] Yet NATO's leaders had powerful incentives to avoid any circumstances that might result in friendly aircrews being killed in action or taken prisoner of war, since the continued cohesion of the alliance was the latter's center of gravity and since any such losses would have been precisely the sorts of untoward events most likely to undermine it. Indeed, if there was any unwritten "prime directive" that guided NATO's strategy throughout the course of Allied Force, it was the preservation of its own solidity, especially during the air war's critical early weeks. In light of that concern, General Short admitted toward the end of May that zero losses was a primary goal in fact if not in name.[41] Not only would a split in the alliance have undermined the air war's effort against Belgrade, it would have raised fundamental questions about the future viability of NATO as a military alliance. It naturally followed that an incremental bombing effort and least-common-denominator targeting had to be accepted until it became clearer throughout the alliance that NATO was committed for the long haul.[42]

---

[40]Interview with Air Marshal Sir John Day, RAF, UK Ministry of Defense director of operations in Allied Force, RAF Innsworth, United Kingdom, July 25, 2000.

[41]William Drozdiak, "Air War Commander Says Kosovo Victory Near," *Washington Post*, May 24, 1999. Clark himself later indicated that his chief "measure of merit" in keeping Allied Force on track was "not to lose aircraft, minimize the loss of aircraft." He further stated that this exacting desideratum "drove our decisions on tactics, targets, and which airplanes could participate," but that it was motivated by a "larger political rationale: if we wanted to keep this campaign going indefinitely, we had to protect our air fleet. Nothing would hurt us more with public opinion than headlines that screamed, 'NATO LOSES TEN AIRPLANES IN TWO DAYS.'" General Wesley K. Clark, *Waging Modern War: Bosnia, Kosovo, and the Future of Combat*, New York, Public Affairs, 2001, p. 183.

[42]It bears noting that the zero-loss issue, however seriously it may have been regarded at the highest leadership levels, had little day-to-day impact on actual combat operations. As an F-15E instructor electronic warfare officer (EWO) who flew multiple combat missions with the 494th Fighter Squadron recalled from first-hand experience: "The issue of the 'no-losses rule' did not filter down to the aircrew level, since we always plan with that goal in mind. We were briefed that there were no 'high-priority' targets prior to the opening of hostilities, but that ended up having little effect on the risk level that we were willing to accept. The concrete effects of the 'no-loss rule' were the 15,000-ft floor and a number of unreasonable ROE restrictions. However, outside the immediate tactical constraints imposed by the ROE, the prevailing high-level attitude had no effect on tactical operations. We were aware of the priority placed on

Although the manner in which Allied Force was conducted fell short of the ideal use of air power, it suggests that gradualism may be here to stay if U.S. leaders ever again intend to fight wars for marginal or amorphous interests with as disparate a set of allies as NATO. As the vice chairman of the JCS at the time, USAF General Joseph Ralston, noted after the air effort ended, air warfare professionals will continue to insist, and rightly so, that a massive application of air power will be more effective than gradualism. Yet, Ralston added, "when the political and tactical constraints imposed on air use are extensive and pervasive—and that trend seems more rather than less likely—then gradualism may be perceived as the only option."[43] General Jumper likewise intimated that the United States may have little choice but to accept the burdens of an incremental approach as an unavoidable cost of working with shaky allies and domestic support in the future: "It is the politics of the moment that will dictate what we can do. . . . If the limits of that consensus mean gradualism, then we're going to have to find a way to deal with a phased air campaign. Efficiency may be second."[44]

Insofar as gradualism promises to be the wave of the future, it suggests that airmen will need to discipline their natural urge to bridle whenever politicians hamper the application of a doctrinally pure campaign strategy and to recognize and accept instead that political considerations, after all, determine—or should determine—the way in which campaigns and wars are fought. This does not mean that military leaders should surrender to political pressures without first making their best case for using force in the most effective and cost-minimizing way. It does, however, stand as an important reminder

---

minimizing losses, but the effect on the mission was overrated. There were no cases that I am aware of where the aircrew said, 'Well, this looks a little hairy, and the priority is not to lose an airplane, so I won't do it.' We were more likely to abort an attack for collateral damage concerns than we were to abort for survivability issues. As would be expected, aircrews pressed to the target in the face of serious opposition." Major Michael Pietrucha, USAF, personal communication to the author, July 9, 2001.

[43]"Ralston Sees Potential for More Wars of Gradual Escalation," *Inside the Pentagon*, September 16, 1999, p. 1.

[44]"Washington Outlook," *Aviation Week and Space Technology*, August 23, 1999, p. 27. It hardly follows, of course, that gradualism and coalitions must invariably be synonymous. They certainly were not in Desert Storm in 1991. Clearly, the extent to which gradualist strategies will prove unavoidable in the future will depend heavily on both the shared stakes for would-be coalition partners and the skill of their leaders in setting the direction and tone of coalition conduct.

that war is ultimately about politics and that civilian control of the military is an inherent part of the democratic tradition. It follows that although airmen and other warfighters are duty-bound to try to persuade their civilian superiors of the merits of their recommendations, they also have a duty to live with the hands they are dealt and to bend every effort to make the most of them in an imperfect world.[45] It also follows that civilian leaders at the highest levels have an equal obligation to try to stack the deck in such a manner that the military has the best possible hand to play and the fullest possible freedom to play it to the best of its ability. This means expending the energy and political capital needed to develop and enforce a strategy that maximizes the probability of military success. In Allied Force, that was not done by the vast majority of the top civilian leaders on either side of the Atlantic.[46]

On the plus side, the air war's successful outcome despite its many frustrations suggested that U.S. air power may now have become capable enough, at least in some circumstances, to underwrite a strategy of incremental escalation irrespective of the latter's inherent inefficiencies. What made the gradualism of Allied Force more bearable than that of the earlier war in Vietnam is that NATO's advantages in stealth, precision standoff attack, and electronic warfare meant that it could fight a one-sided war against Milosevic with near-impunity and achieve the desired result, even if not in the most ideal way.[47] That was not an option when U.S. air power was a less developed tool than it is today.

---

[45]On this point, Air Vice Marshal Mason remarked that he had not "spent the past 25 years trying to persuade unbelievers of the efficacy of air power only to finish up whining because political circumstances made operations difficult." Personal communication to the author, October 22, 1999. In a similar spirit, the leader of USAFE's post–Allied Force munitions effectiveness investigation in Kosovo later suggested that airmen should "consider a politically restricted target list like the weather: complain about it, but deal with it." Colonel Brian McDonald, USAF, briefing at RAND, Santa Monica, California, December 14, 1999.

[46]It further follows that airmen, for their part, need to learn not only how to conduct gradual campaigns more effectively, but also how better to explain convincingly to politicians the value of using mass and shock early and the greater strategic effectiveness of effects-based targeting.

[47]See Colonel Phillip S. Meilinger, USAF, "Gradual Escalation: NATO's Kosovo Air Campaign, Though Decried as a Strategy, May Be the Future of War," *Armed Forces Journal International*, October 1999, p. 18.

On this point, Admiral Ellis, a career fighter pilot himself, was no less disturbed by the air war's lethargic pace than was his air component commander, General Short, or any other airmen on down the line. However, mindful of the long-standing political and bureaucratic rule of thumb that "if a problem has no solution, it is no longer a problem but a fact," he recognized that ideal-world solutions were unworkable in the Allied Force setting and that flexibility was required in applying air doctrine in a difficult situation. As it turned out, NATO conducted its bombing effort in a way that was not maximally efficient, yet that worked in the end to foil Serb strategy, which was to wait out the alliance and strive mightily to fragment it. Because the escalation was gradual over time, the coalition succeeded in holding together. Because NATO used highly conservative tactics, it lost no aircrews and civilian casualties and collateral damage were kept to a minimum. In effect, a compromise was struck in which the air war was intense enough to maintain constant pressure on Milosevic yet measured enough to keep NATO from falling apart. Either the loss of friendly lives beyond token numbers or an especially gruesome spectacle of collateral damage could have been more than enough to incline at least some key allies to call it quits. Noting further that NATO fought in this case to establish conditions rather than to "win" in the classic sense, Ellis added that a campaign strategy that would have allowed Desert Storm–like intensity and scale of target attacks to be employed was simply never in the cards.

By the same token, RAF Air Commodore Andrew Vallance pointed out that because a key attraction of air power to civilian decision-makers is its adaptability for accommodating different situations in different ways as needed, "the purist 'one size fits all' approach to air doctrine needs to be moderated. Existing air doctrine is fine for high-intensity conflicts, but more subtle operational doctrines are needed in the complex world of peace support."[48] Echoing this point, Karl Mueller observed that "sometimes strategists will be called upon to execute gradually escalatory air campaigns whether they approve of the concept or not, and thus they should develop some expertise in the art form even if they abhor it."[49] With the air

---

[48]Air Commodore A. G. B. Vallance, RAF, "After Kosovo: Implications of Operation Allied Force for Air Power Development," unpublished paper, p. 4.

[49]Mueller, "Deus ex Machina?" p. 16.

weapon now largely perfected for such canonical situations as halting massed armored assaults, it needs to be further refined for handling messier, less predictable, and more challenging combat situations featuring elusive or hidden enemy ground forces, restrictive rules of engagement, disagreeable weather, the enemy use of human shields, lawyers in the targeting loop as a matter of standard practice, and diverse allies with their own political agendas, all of which were characteristic features of the Kosovo crisis. Moreover, although NATO's political leaders arguably set the bar too high with unrealistic expectations about collateral damage avoidance, it seems clear that the Western democracies have long since passed the point where they can contemplate using air power, or *any* force, for that matter, in as unrestrained a way as was characteristic of World War II bombing. Admiral Ellis noted that NATO barely averted legal consequences prompted by the collateral damage incidents that occurred in Allied Force. This implies that along with new precision-attack capability goes new responsibility, and air warfare professionals must now understand that they will be held accountable.[50]

On this point, one can fairly suggest that both SACEUR and his JFACC were equally prone throughout Allied Force to remain wedded to excessively parochial views of their preferred target priorities, based on implicit faith in the inherent correctness of their respective services' doctrinal teachings. They might more effectively have approached Milosevic instead as a unique rather than generic opponent, conducted a serious analysis of his distinctive vulnerabilities, and then tailored a campaign plan aimed at attacking those vulnerabilities directly, irrespective of canonical air or land warfare solutions for all seasons. A year after the air war, in a measured reflection on the recurrent tension that afflicted the interaction of Clark and Short, Admiral Ellis suggested that the failure of *all* the services to advance beyond their propensity to teach only pristine, service-oriented doctrines at their respective war colleges reflected a serious "cultures" problem and that the services badly need to plan for and

---

[50]This includes being held increasingly accountable for their own combat losses. The Allied Force SEAD experience showed that in crises where less-than-vital U.S. interests are at stake, near-zero attrition of friendly aircraft and their aircrews will be a high, and possibly determining, priority governing operational tactics.

accommodate the unexpected and the unconventional, both of which were daily facts of life during Operation Allied Force.[51]

Finally, the probability that coalition operations in the future will be the rule rather than the exception suggests a need, to the fullest extent practicable, to work out basic ground rules *before* a campaign begins, so that operators, once empowered, can implement the agreed-upon plan with a minimum of political friction. As it was, Allied Force attested not only to the strategy legitimation that comes from the force of numbers provided by working through a coalition, but also to the limitations of committee planning and least-common-denominator targeting. General Short commented that the need for 19 approvals of target nominations was "counterproductive" and that an appropriate conclusion was that "before you drop the first bomb or fire the first shot, we need to lock the political leaders up in a room and have them decide what the rules of engagement will be so they can provide the military with the proper guidance and latitude needed to prosecute the war."[52] As it was, Short later said in his PBS interview, the rules continuously ebbed and flowed in reaction to events over the air war's 78 days: "You can go to downtown Belgrade, oh my God, you've hit the Chinese embassy, now there's a five-mile circle going around downtown Belgrade into which you cannot go." As a result, he complained, strikers

---

[51]Conversation with Admiral James Ellis, USN, Headquarters Allied Forces Southern Europe, Naples, Italy, May 30, 2000.

[52]William Drozdiak, "Allies Need Upgrade, General Says." As sensible as this suggestion may have sounded after the fact, however, one must ask how workable it would have been in actual practice. Wars characteristically feature dynamics that push participants beyond anything imaginable at the outset. Setting clear going-in rules is easy and feasible enough for something short and relatively straightforward, like Operation Deliberate Force and Operation El Dorado Canyon, the joint USAF-Navy raid on Libya in 1986. Expecting them in larger and more open-ended operations, however, means counting on a predictability of events that does not exist in real life. The fact is that there *was* a consensus at the start of Allied Force about what was acceptable and what everyone was willing to do, and that was for 91 targets and two nights of bombing. NATO's cardinal error was not its failure to reach a consensus before firing the first shot; it was its refusal to be honest up front about what it would do if its assumptions about Milosevic's resolve proved false. I thank Dr. Daniel Harrington, Office of History, Hq USAFE, for having shared this insightful observation with me. I would add that had NATO's leaders done better at attending to that responsibility, they would have gone a long way toward satisfying General Short's expressed concern.

often ended up "bombing fire hydrants and stoplights because there just weren't targets of great value left that weren't in a sanctuary."[53]

THE COST OF THE MISSING GROUND THREAT

One of the most important realizations to emerge from Allied Force at the operational and strategic levels was that a ground component to joint campaign strategies may be essential, at least in some cases, for enabling air power to deliver to its fullest potential. The commander of Air Combat Command, General Richard Hawley, was one of many senior airmen who freely admitted that the a priori decision by the Clinton administration and NATO's political leaders not to employ ground forces had undercut the effectiveness of allied air operations: "When you don't have that synergy, things take longer and they're harder, and that's what you're seeing in this conflict."[54]

General Jumper later concluded similarly that the imperative of attacking fielded enemy forces without the shaping presence of a NATO ground threat had produced "major challenges," including creating a faster flexible targeting cycle; putting a laser designator on Predator; creating new target development processes within the CAOC; creating real-time communications links between finders, assessors, and shooters; and developing more rapid real-time retargeting procedures for the B-2s, the B-1s, the B-52s, and F-15Es carrying the AGM-130.[55]

Amplifying on the fallacy of having started the air effort without a credible ground threat, General Short noted that "this conflict was unlike others in that we did not have a ground element to fix the enemy, to make him predictable, and to give us information as to where the enemy might be."[56] Short went on to point out, however, that although NATO had not been formally allied with the KLA, the fact

---

[53]Interview with Lieutenant General Michael Short, USAF, PBS *Frontline*, "War in Europe," February 22, 2000.

[54]Bradley Graham, "General Says U.S. Readiness Is Ailing," *Washington Post*, April 30, 1999.

[55]General John Jumper, USAF, "Oral Histories Accomplished in Conjunction with Operation Allied Force/Noble Anvil."

[56]Drozdiak, "Allies Need Upgrade, General Says."

that the latter had begun to operate with some success in the end "made the Yugoslav army come out and fight and try to blunt their offensive. . . . And once they moved, or fired their artillery, our strikers learned where they were and could go in for the kill."[57] Had VJ forces in Kosovo faced an imminent NATO ground invasion, or even a credible threat of such an invasion later, they would have been obliged to move troops and supplies over bridges that NATO aircraft could have dropped. They also would have been compelled to concentrate and maneuver in ways that would have made it easier for NATO to find and attack them.

Earlier, White House national security adviser Samuel Berger maintained that taking ground forces off the table at the outset had been the right thing to do because anything else would have inevitably prompted an immediate public debate both in the United States and among the allies, which could have split the alliance and seriously impeded the overall air effort.[58] Yet there was a huge difference between acknowledging that a land offensive could be fraught with danger, on the one hand, and ruling out such an offensive categorically before the fact, on the other. The former would have been demanding enough even under the best of circumstances because of basing, airlift, and logistics problems. The latter, however, was a colossal strategic mistake, in that it gave Milosevic the freedom to act against the Kosovar Albanians and the power to determine when the war would be over. The opportunity costs incurred by NATO's anemic start of Allied Force without an accompanying ground threat included a failure to exploit air power's shock potential and to instill in Milosevic an early fear of worse consequences yet to come; the encouragement it gave VJ troops to disperse and hide while they had time; the virtual carte blanche it gave Milosevic for accelerated atrocities in Kosovo; and the relinquishment of the power of initiative to the enemy.

As for the oft-noted concern over the prospect of sustaining an unbearable level of friendly casualties had NATO opted to back up the air war with a ground element, there most likely would have been no

---

[57]Ibid.

[58]Doyle McManus, "Clinton's Massive Ground Invasion That Almost Was," *Los Angeles Times*, June 9, 2000.

need actually to *commit* NATO troops to battle in the end. The mere fact of a serious Desert Shield–like deployment of NATO ground troops along the Albanian and Macedonian borders would have made their VJ counterparts more easily targetable by allied air power. Had such a deployment commenced in earnest, it also might have helped to deter, or at least lessen, the ethnic cleansing of Kosovo by giving VJ troops a more serious concern to worry about. In both cases, it could have enabled a quicker end to the war.

Even had Milosevic remained unyielding to the point where an opposed NATO ground-force entry would have been unavoidable sooner or later, continued air preparation of the battlefield might have been sufficiently effective that the VJ's residual strength would not have presented a significant challenge to NATO land forces. The impending improvement of summer weather and the further establishment of NATO air dominance would have enabled more effective NATO air performance against VJ targets, especially had the KLA succeeded in maintaining enough pressure to force VJ units to bunch up and move.

Indeed, well before Allied Force ended, there was a gathering sense among some observers that Serbia's ground forces were being given more credit than they deserved as an excuse for ruling out a NATO land-invasion option. As one former U.S. Army officer pointed out, Milosevic's army was a small conscript-based force with an active component of only some 115,000 troops who relied on antiquated Soviet equipment, mainly the 1950s-vintage T-55 tank. Air strikes during the first few nights of Allied Force had already rendered Yugoslavia's small air force a non-factor in any potential NATO ground push. The VJ's petroleum and other stocks for sustainment had also been rapidly depleted by the bombing, leaving the Serbs with, at best, only a minimal capacity to wage conventional war against a serious ground opponent. In contrast, the modern and well-equipped NATO ground forces arguably possessed enough combat power "to make mincemeat of the Yugoslav army."[59]

Be that as it may, the problems created by NATO's having ruled out a ground option before the fact suggest an important corrective to the

---

[59]Andrew J. Bacevich, "Target Belgrade: Why a Ground War Would Be a Rout," *National Review*, May 3, 1999, p. 29.

seemingly unending argument between airmen and land combatants over the relative merits of air power versus "boots on the ground." Although Operation Allied Force reconfirmed that friendly ground forces no longer need to be inexorably committed to combat early, it also reconfirmed that air power in many cases cannot perform to its fullest potential without the presence of a credible ground component in the campaign strategy. The fact is that air power alone was not well suited to defeating VJ forces in the field. Once most of the combat returns were in, it became clear that few allied kills were accomplished against dispersed and hidden VJ units in the KEZ. Not only that, allied air power had been unable to protect the Kosovar Albanians from Serb terror tactics, a problem that was further exacerbated by the stringent rules of engagement aimed at minimizing collateral damage and avoiding any NATO loss of life. As former Air Force chief of staff General Merrill McPeak instructively elaborated on this point, "in a major blunder, the use of ground troops was ruled out from the beginning. I know of no airman—not a single one— who welcomed this development. Nobody said, 'Hey, finally, our own private war. Just what we've always wanted!' It certainly would have been smarter to retain all the options. . . . Signaling to Belgrade our extreme reluctance to fight on the ground made it much less likely that the bombing would succeed, exploring the limits of air power as a military and diplomatic instrument."[60]

TOWARD A "REPORT CARD" FOR ALLIED FORCE

As for what airmen and other observers should take away from Allied Force by way of lessons indicated and points worth pondering, the commander of the U.S. military contribution, Admiral Ellis, offered a good start when he declared in his after-action briefing to Pentagon and NATO officials that luck played the chief role in ensuring the air

---

[60]General Merrill A. McPeak, USAF (Ret.), "The Kosovo Result: The Facts Speak for Themselves," *Armed Forces Journal International,* September 1999, p. 64. In a similar vein, the chief of staff of the RAF later faulted NATO's decision to rule out a ground option from the start of the air war as "a strategic mistake" that enabled Serb forces to forgo preparing defensive positions, hide their tanks and artillery and make maximum use of deception against NATO attack efforts, and conduct their ethnic cleansing of Kosovo with impunity. Michael Evans, "Ground War 'Error,'" *London Times,* March 24, 2000.

war's success.[61] Ellis charged that NATO's leaders "called this one absolutely wrong" and that their failure to anticipate what might occur once their initial strategy of hope failed occasioned most of the untoward consequences that ensued thereafter.[62] These included the hasty activation of a joint task force, a race to find suitable targets, an absence of coherent campaign planning, and lost opportunities caused by the failure to think through unpleasant excursions from what had been expected. Ellis concluded that the imperatives of consensus politics within NATO made for an "incremental war" rather than for "decisive operations," that excessive concern over collateral damage created "sanctuaries and opportunities for the adversary—which were successfully exploited," and that the lack of a credible NATO ground threat "probably prolonged the air campaign."[63] It was only because Milosevic made a blunder no less towering than NATO's preclusion of a ground option that the war had the largely positive outcome that it did.

Indeed, that NATO prevailed in the end with only two aircraft lost and no combat fatalities sustained surely reflected good fortune at least as much as the professionalism of its aircrews and their commanders. General Jumper explained afterward that "we set the bar fairly high when we fly more than 30,000 combat sorties and we don't lose one pilot. It makes it look as if air power is indeed risk free and too easy a choice to make." Amplifying on the same point, retired RAF Air Vice Marshal Tony Mason observed that seeking to minimize one's losses is both admirable and proper up to a point, yet it can lead to self-deterrence when efforts to escape the costs of war are

---

[61]Amplifying on his suggestion that luck was the key player, Ellis pointed out how much worse matters would have been for the alliance had NATO experienced any one of a number of untoward developments: an enemy attack on its troops deployed in theater with ground forces or tactical ballistic missiles; the possibility of even a few NATO aircrews being killed in action or captured as POWs; the continuation of the fighting into the winter; the depletion of U.S. precision munitions stocks; the weakening or evaporation of public support; an allied ground invasion becoming the only option; or a decision by France or Italy to withdraw from further participation.

[62]Revealingly, barely a week into Allied Force, one senior Clinton administration official, when asked what NATO's strategy would be should Phase III of the air war fail to persuade Milosevic to admit defeat, replied: "There is no Phase IV." Quoted in John Broder, "In Grim Week, Pep Talk from the President," *New York Times*, April 1, 1999.

[63]Elaine M. Grossman, "For U.S. Commander in Kosovo, Luck Played Role in Wartime Success," *Inside the Pentagon*, September 9, 1999, p. 1.

pursued to a moral fault. Although force protection "must be a major concern for any force commander," Mason added, "my own view is that if Saint George's first priority with tackling dragons had been force protection, I don't think he would now be the patron saint of England."[64]

The Kosovo experience further suggested some needed changes in both investment strategy and campaign planning. The combination of marginal weather and the unprecedented stress placed on avoiding collateral damage made for numerous days between March 24 and mid-May when entire ATOs had to be canceled and when only cruise missiles and the B-2, with its through-the-weather JDAM capability, could be used. That spoke powerfully for broadening the ability of other aircraft to deliver accurate munitions irrespective of weather, as well as for ensuring that adequate stocks of such munitions are on hand to see the next campaign to completion. The extended stretch of bad weather underscored the limitations of LGBs and confirmed the value of GPS-guided weapons like JDAM that can bomb accurately through the weather.

Not surprisingly, the munitions used in Allied Force generally performed as advertised. The operation's results, however, confirmed the need for a larger U.S. inventory of precision-guided munitions (especially those capable of all-weather target attack), as well as greater accuracy and more standoff attack capability. At the same time, it indicated a continued operational utility for both unguided general-purpose bombs and cluster munitions for engaging soft military area targets deployed in the open. Other areas in which allied weapons performance showed a need for further improvement include interoperability across platforms, more multispectral sensors, higher-gain optical sensors for UAVs, more data-link interoperability, a wider range of bomb sizes, and weapons capable of conducting "auto-BDA."[65] Still other force capability needs highlighted by the

---

[64]Comments at an Air Force Association Eaker Institute colloquy, "Operation Allied Force: Strategy, Execution, Implications," held at the Ronald Reagan International Trade Center, Washington, D.C., August 16, 1999.

[65]These were among numerous other conclusions suggested by Major General Ronald Keys, USAF, director of operations (J-3), U.S. European Command, cited in Colonel Steve Pitotti, USAF, "Global Environments, Threats, and Military Strategy (GETM) Update," Air Armament Summit 2000 briefing, Eglin AFB, Florida, 2000.

Allied Force experience include better means for locating moving targets, better discrimination of real targets from decoys, and a way of engaging those targets with smart submunitions rather than with more-costly PGMs and cruise missiles.[66]   One airman later commented frankly that in being tasked by Clark to go after dispersed and hidden VJ forces, U.S. air power "was being asked to be a 21st century tactical air force . . . and the truth is, we're not very good at it," at least yet.[67]

As for the ultimate wisdom of the allied decision to proceed with the air war in the first place, the United States and NATO displayed an ability in this case to apply coercion successfully through air power from a poorly prepared battlefield at a remarkably low cost in noncombatant fatalities caused by direct collateral damage.[68]   Yet there is a danger that making a habit of such displays by accepting Allied Force as a model for future interventions could easily lead to an erosion of the U.S. claim to global leadership.[69] On the contrary, Allied Force should have underscored the fact that one of the most acute challenges facing U.S. policymakers in the age of a single superpower entails deciding when, and in what manner, to intervene in humanitarian crises that do not yet impinge directly on U.S. security interests.

ON THE USES AND ABUSES OF AIR POWER

Viewed in hindsight, the most remarkable thing about Operation Allied Force was not that it defeated Milosevic in the end, but rather

---

[66]Work on this is being performed by Alan Vick of RAND.

[67]Elaine M. Grossman, "U.S. Military Debates Link Between Kosovo Air War, Stated Objectives," *Inside the Pentagon*, April 20, 2000, p. 6.

[68]A heated argument arose after the war ended between defenders and critics of the Clinton administration's strategy for Kosovo over whether the approach taken, despite its low cost in noncombatant lives lost to *direct* collateral damage, nonetheless produced an unconscionably high loss of civilian innocents to the Serbian ethnic cleansing campaign which it allegedly accelerated. For a snapshot summary of the positions taken on both sides, see Christopher Layne and Benjamin Schwarz, "Kosovo II: For the Record," *The National Interest*, Fall 1999, pp. 9–15, and Ivo Daalder, "NATO and Kosovo," *The National Interest*, Winter 1999/2000, pp. 113–117.

[69]I am grateful to Lieutenant General Bradley Hosmer, USAF (Ret.), for bringing this point to my attention.

that air power prevailed despite a U.S. leadership that was unwilling to take major risks and an alliance that held together only with often paralyzing drag. Fortunately, the Clinton administration did a creditable job of keeping the allies together in the end, albeit at the cost of what Brent Scowcroft called "a bad strategy" that raised basic questions about the limits of alliance warfare and about whether the United States should, in the future, settle instead for coalitions of the willing, at least in less than the cataclysmic showdowns of the sort that NATO was initially created to handle.[70] One can only wonder what greater efficiencies might have been registered by a more assertive campaign approach had the U.S. government been willing to play a more proactive role in leading from the front and setting both the direction and pace for NATO's more hesitant allies.[71]

Lesson One from both Vietnam and Desert Storm should have been that one must not commit air power in "penny packets," as the British say, to play less-than-determined games with the risk calculus of the other side. Although it can be surgically precise when precision is called for, air power is, at bottom, a blunt instrument designed to break things and kill people in pursuit of clear and militarily achievable objectives. Not without reason have air warfare professionals repeatedly insisted since Vietnam that if all one wishes to do is to "send a message," call Western Union. On this point, Eliot Cohen summed it up well five years before the Kosovo crisis erupted when he compared air power's lately acquired seductiveness to modern teenage romance in its seeming propensity to offer political leaders a sense of "gratification without commitment."[72]

---

[70]John F. Harris, "Berger's Caution Has Shaped Role of U.S. in War," *Washington Post*, May 16, 1999.

[71]In a measured indictment of the Clinton administration's comportment in this regard, two Brookings Institution analysts wrote that "what was missing . . . was less allied will than a demonstrated American ability and willingness to lead a joint effort. NATO works best when Washington knows what it wants done and leads the effort to get the alliance there. In the runup to the Kosovo war, both elements were tragically lacking. . . . Although it is impossible to know whether the allies would have gone along with a more robust strategy, including early use of ground forces, the United States never made the case. U.S. policy presumed the allies' rejection, just as it presumed congressional opposition to the use of ground forces." Ivo H. Daalder and Michael E. O'Hanlon, *Winning Ugly: NATO's War to Save Kosovo*, Washington, D.C., Brookings Institution, 2000, pp. 98, 222.

[72]Eliot A. Cohen, "The Mystique of U.S. Air Power," *Foreign Affairs*, January/February 1994, p. 109.

To admit that gradualism of the sort applied in Allied Force may be the wave of the future for any U.S. involvement in coalition warfare in the years ahead is hardly to accept that it is any more justifiable from a military point of view for that reason alone. Quite to the contrary, the incrementalism of NATO's air war for Kosovo, right up to its very end, involved a potential price that went far beyond the loss of valuable aircraft, munitions, and other expendables for questionable gain. It risked frittering away the hard-earned reputation for effectiveness that U.S. air power had finally earned for itself in Desert Storm after more than three years of unqualified misuse over North Vietnam a generation earlier. For all his disagreement with so many other arguments put forward, to no avail, on the proper uses of air power by his air component commander, General Short, even General Clark emphasized after the air war ended that despite understandable pressures for a gradualist approach both from Washington and among the NATO allies, "once the threshold is crossed to employ force, then force should be employed as quickly and decisively as possible. The more rapidly it can be done, the greater the likelihood of success."[73]

As the Gulf War experience showed, and as both Deliberate Force and Allied Force ultimately reaffirmed, U.S. air power as it has evolved since the mid-1970s can do remarkable things when employed with determination in support of a campaign whose intent is not in doubt. Yet to conjure up the specter of "air strikes," NATO or otherwise, in an effort to project an appearance of "doing something" without a prior weighing of intended effects or likely consequences is to run the risk of getting bogged down in an operation with no plausible theory of success. After years of false promises by its most outspoken prophets, air power has become an unprecedentedly capable instrument of force employment in joint warfare. Even in the best of circumstances, however, it can never be more effective than the strategy it is intended to support.

---

[73]Joseph Fitchett, "Clark Recalls 'Lessons' of Kosovo," *International Herald Tribune,* May 3, 2000.

OFFICIAL PUBLICATIONS

Air Force Basic Doctrine, Maxwell AFB, Alabama, Headquarters Air Force Doctrine Center, AFDD-1, September 1997.

The Air War Over Serbia: Aerospace Power in Operation Allied Force, Washington, D.C., Headquarters United States Air Force, April 1, 2000.

Cohen, Secretary of Defense William S., and Chairman of the Joint Chiefs of Staff General Henry H. Shelton, *Kosovo/Operation Allied Force After-Action Report*, Washington, D.C., Department of Defense, Report to Congress, January 31, 2000.

Kosovo: Lessons from the Crisis, Report to Parliament by the Secretary of State for Defense, The Stationery Office, London, England, June 2000.

CONGRESSIONAL TESTIMONY

Clark, General Wesley, USA, testimony to the Senate Armed Services Committee, Washington, D.C., July 1, 1999.

Cohen, Secretary of Defense William S., and General Henry H. Shelton, "Joint Statement on the Kosovo After-Action Review," testimony before the Senate Armed Services Committee, Washington, D.C., October 14, 1999.

Esmond, Lieutenant General Marvin R., testimony to the Military Procurement Subcommittee, House Armed Services Committee, Washington, D.C., October 19, 1999.

Jumper, General John, USAF, testimony to the Military Readiness Subcommittee, House Armed Services Committee, Washington, D.C., October 26, 1999.

BOOKS

Andric, Ivo, *The Bridge on the Drina*, Chicago, University of Chicago Press, 1977.

Clark, General Wesley K., *Waging Modern War: Bosnia, Kosovo, and the Future of Combat*, New York, Public Affairs, 2001.

Daalder, Ivo H., and Michael E. O'Hanlon, *Winning Ugly: NATO's War to Save Kosovo*, Washington, D.C., Brookings Institution, 2000.

Dylewski, Major General Gary, "The USAF Space Warfare Center: Bringing Space to the Warfighter," in Peter L. Hays et al., eds., *Spacepower for a New Millennium: Space and U.S. National Security*, New York, McGraw-Hill, 2000.

Gentile, Gian P., *How Effective Is Strategic Bombing? Lessons Learned from World War II to Kosovo*, New York, New York University Press, 2001.

Glenny, Misha, *The Balkans: Nationalism, War and the Great Powers, 1809–1999*, New York: Penguin Books, 2000.

Ignatieff, Michael, *Virtual War: Kosovo and Beyond*, New York, Henry Holt and Company, Inc., 2000.

Judah, Tim, *Kosovo: War and Revenge*, New Haven, Connecticut, Yale University Press, 2000.

Lambeth, Benjamin S., *The Transformation of American Air Power*, Ithaca, New York, Cornell University Press, 2000.

Macgregor, Colonel Douglas A., USA, *Breaking the Phalanx: A New Design for Landpower in the 21st Century*, Westport, Connecticut, Praeger, 1997.

Mason, Air Vice Marshal Tony, RAF (Ret.), *Air Power: A Centennial Appraisal*, London, Brassey's, 1994.

Owen, Colonel Robert, USAF, ed., *Deliberate Force: A Case Study in Effective Air Campaigning*, Maxwell AFB, Alabama, Air University Press, January 2000.

Rackham, Peter, ed., *Jane's C4I Systems, 1994–95*, London, Jane's Information Group, 1994.

Short, Lieutenant General Michael C., USAF (Ret.), "An Airman's Lessons from Kosovo," in John Andreas Olsen, ed., *From Maneuver Warfare to Kosovo*, Trondheim, Norway, Royal Norwegian Air Force Academy, 2001, pp. 257–288.

Thompson, Wayne, *To Hanoi and Back: The U.S. Air Force and North Vietnam, 1966–1973*, Washington, D.C., Smithsonian Institute Press, 2000.

MONOGRAPHS AND REPORTS

Byman, Daniel L., Matthew C. Waxman, and Eric Larson, *Air Power as a Coercive Instrument*, Santa Monica, California, RAND, MR-1061-AF, 1999.

Hosmer, Stephen T., *The Conflict over Kosovo: Why Milosevic Decided to Settle When He Did*, Santa Monica, California, RAND, MR-1351-AF, 2001.

The Military Balance, 1998/99, London, International Institute for Strategic Studies, 1998.

Peters, John E., Stuart Johnson, Nora Bensahel, Timothy Liston, and Traci Williams, *European Contributions to Operation Allied Force: Implications for Transatlantic Cooperation*, Santa Monica, California, RAND, MR-1391-AF, 2001.

Stephens, Alan, *Kosovo, or the Future of War*, Paper Number 77, Air Power Studies Center, RAAF Fairbairn, Australia, August 1999.

Strategic Survey 1999/2000, London, England, The International Institute for Strategic Studies, 2000.

Watts, Barry D., *The Military Use of Space: A Diagnostic Assessment*, Washington, D.C., Center for Strategic and Budgetary Assessments, February 2001.

White, Lieutenant Colonel Paul K., USAF, *Crises After the Storm: An Appraisal of U.S. Air Operations in Iraq Since the Persian Gulf War*, Military Research Papers No. 2, Washington, D.C., Washington Institute for Near East Policy, 1999.

JOURNAL AND PERIODICAL ARTICLES

Abrams, Elliott, "Just War. Just Means?" *National Review*, June 28, 1999.

"Air Force Reluctant to Deploy All-Weather Predator UAVs to Balkans," *Inside the Air Force*, April 2, 1999.

Arkin, William M., "Fleet Praises JSOW, Lists Potential Improvements," *Defense Daily*, April 26, 2000.

_____, "In Praise of Heavy Bombers," *Bulletin of the Atomic Scientists*, July–August 1999.

_____, "Kosovo Report Short on Weapons Performance Details," *Defense Daily*, February 10, 2000.

_____, "Smart Bombs, Dumb Targeting?" *Bulletin of the Atomic Scientists*, May/June 2000.

_____, "Top Air Force Leaders to Get Briefed on Serbia Air War Report," *Defense Daily*, June 13, 2000.

Atkinson, David, "B-2s Demonstrated Combat Efficiency over Kosovo," *Defense Daily*, July 1, 1999.

_____, "Stealth Could Play Key Role in Kosovo, Despite Bad Weather," *Defense Daily*, March 23, 1999.

_____, and Hunter Keeter, "Apache Role in Kosovo Illustrates Cracks in Joint Doctrine," *Defense Daily*, May 26, 1999.

Aubin, Stephen P., *"Newsweek* and the 14 Tanks," *Air Force Magazine*, July 2000.

"B-2 Performed Better in Kosovo Than USAF Expected," *Inside the Pentagon*, July 8, 1999.

Bacevich, Andrew J., "Target Belgrade: Why a Ground War Would Be a Rout," *National Review*, May 3, 1999.

Barry, John, "The Kosovo Cover-Up," *Newsweek*, May 15, 2000.

Beaver, Paul, "Mystery Still Shrouds Downing of F-117A Fighter," *Jane's Defense Weekly*, September 1, 1999.

Ben-Eliahu, Major General Eitan, commander, Israeli Air Force, "Air Power in the 21st Century: The Impact of Precision Weapons," *Military Technology*, April 2000.

Bender, Roy, "Allies Still Lack Real-Time Retargeting," *Jane's Defense Weekly*, April 7, 1999.

Betts, Richard K., "Compromised Command: Inside NATO's First War," *Foreign Affairs*, July/August, 2001.

Bone, Margaret, "Kodak Moments in Kosovo," *The Hook*, Spring 2000.

Byman, Daniel L. and Matthew C. Waxman, "Kosovo and the Great Air Power Debate," *International Security*, Spring 2000.

Capaccio, Tony, "JSTARS Led Most Lethal Attacks on Serbs," *Defense Week*, July 6, 1999.

_____, "MiGs Tried to Shoot Down Air Force Tanker over Bosnia," *Defense Week*, May 17, 1999.

Cohen, Eliot A., "The Mystique of U.S. Air Power," *Foreign Affairs*, January/February 1994.

Colin, Benoit, and Rene J. Francillon, "L'OTAN en Guerre!" *Air Fan*, May 1999.

Corell, John T., "Assumptions Fall in Kosovo," *Air Force Magazine*, June 1999.

_____, "Lessons Drawn and Quartered," *Air Force Magazine*, December 1999.

Covault, Craig, "Military Space Dominates Air Strikes," *Aviation Week and Space Technology*, March 29, 1999.

Crawley, Vince, "Air Force Needs 90 Days Between Wars, Chief Says," *Defense Week*, August 9, 1999.

_____, "Air Force Secretary Advocates C-130, Predators," *Defense Week*, July 26, 1999.

_____, "B-2s See Combat over Yugoslavia," *Defense Week*, March 29, 1999.

Cviic, Christopher, "A Victory All the Same," *Survival*, Summer 2000.

Daalder, Ivo, "NATO and Kosovo," *The National Interest*, Winter 1999/2000.

"Despite Losses, Backers Say Unmanned Systems Excelling Over Kosovo," *Inside the Pentagon*, June 10, 1999.

Donnelly, John, "NRO Chief: Services Ill-Prepared to Work with Spy Satellites," *Defense Week*, July 12, 1999.

Foote, Sheila, "Shelton: Risk Was the Key in Decision Not to Use Apaches," *Defense Daily*, September 10, 1999.

Foreman, Jonathan, "The Casualty Myth," *National Review*, May 3, 1999.

Fulghum, David A., "Bomb Shortage Was No Mistake," *Aviation Week and Space Technology*, May 17, 1999.

_____, "Electronic Bombs Darken Belgrade," *Aviation Week and Space Technology*, May 10, 1999.

_____, "Joint STARS May Profit from Yugoslav Ops," *Aviation Week and Space Technology*, July 26, 1999.

_____, "Kosovo Conflict Spurred New Airborne Technology Use," *Aviation Week and Space Technology*, August 23, 1999.

_____, "Kosovo Report to Boost New JSF Jamming Role," *Aviation Week and Space Technology*, August 30, 1999.

_____, "Lessons Learned May Be Flawed," *Aviation Week and Space Technology*, June 14, 1999.

_____, "NATO Unprepared for Electronic Combat," *Aviation Week and Space Technology*, May 10, 1999.

_____, "Report Tallies Damage, Lists U.S. Weaknesses," *Aviation Week and Space Technology*, February 14, 2000.

_____, "Russians Analyze U.S. Blackout Bomb," *Aviation Week and Space Technology*, February 14, 2000.

_____, "Serb Threat Subsides, but U.S. Still Worries," *Aviation Week and Space Technology*, April 12, 1999.

_____, "Yugoslavia Successfully Attacked by Computers," *Aviation Week and Space Technology*, August 23, 1999.

_____, and William B. Scott, "Pentagon Gets Lock on F-117 Shootdown," *Aviation Week and Space Technology*, April 19, 1999.

_____, and Robert Wall, "Data Link, EW Problems Pinpointed by Pentagon," *Aviation Week and Space Technology*, September 6, 1999.

_____, and Robert Wall, "Intel Mistakes Trigger Chinese Embassy Bombing," *Aviation Week and Space Technology*, May 17, 1999.

Grant, Rebecca, "Air Power Made It Work," *Air Force Magazine*, November 1999.

Grier, Peter, "The Investment in Space," *Air Force Magazine*, February 2000.

Grossman, Elaine M., "Army Commander in Albania Resists Joint Control over Apache Missions," *Inside the Pentagon*, May 20, 1999.

_____, "Army's Cold War Orientation Slowed Apache Deployment to Balkans," *Inside the Pentagon*, May 6, 1999.

_____, "As Apaches Near Combat, White House Seeks Diplomatic Solution," *Inside the Pentagon*, May 6, 1999.

_____, "Clark's Firepower Request for Kosovo Prompts Anxiety Among Chiefs," *Inside the Pentagon*, April 15, 1999.

_____, "For U.S. Commander in Kosovo, Luck Played Role in Wartime Success," *Inside the Pentagon*, September 9, 1999.

_____, "U.S. Military Debates Link Between Kosovo Air War, Stated Objectives," *Inside the Pentagon*, April 20, 2000.

Hagen, William W., "The Balkans' Lethal Nationalisms," *Foreign Affairs*, July/August 1999.

Hammond, Grant T., "Myths of the Air War Over Serbia: Some 'Lessons' Not to Learn," *Aerospace Power Journal*, Winter 2000.

Harden, Blaine, "The Milosevic Generation," *New York Times Magazine*, August 29, 1999.

"'He Was Calm, Unyielding,'" *Newsweek*, April 5, 1999.

Hebert, Adam, "Air Force Follows Roadmap in Employment of Bombers Against Serbia," *Inside the Air Force*, April 2, 1999.

Hedges, Chris, "Kosovo's Next Masters?" *Foreign Affairs*, May/June 1999.

Hewson, Robert, "Allied Force, Part II: Overwhelming Air Power," *World Air Power Journal*, Winter 1999/2000.

_____, "Operation Allied Force: The First 30 Days," *World Air Power Journal*, Fall 1999.

"Hope for the Best, and a Spot of Golf," *The Economist*, April 3, 1999.

Hughes, David, "A Pilot's Best Friend," *Aviation Week and Space Technology*, May 31, 1999.

Ignatieff, Michael, "The Virtual Commander: How NATO Invented a New Kind of War," *The New Yorker*, August 2, 1999.

"Jumper on Air Power," *Air Force Magazine*, July 2000.

Kusovac, Zoran, "Russian S-300 SAMs 'In Serbia,'" *Jane's Defense Weekly*, August 4, 1999.

Layne, Christopher, and Benjamin Schwarz, "Kosovo II: For the Record," *The National Interest,* Fall 1999.

Levitin, Oleg, "Inside Moscow's Kosovo Muddle," *Survival,* Spring 2000.

Lorenzo, Ron, "Apache Deployment Has Cost Quarter Billion So Far," *Defense Week,* June 7, 1999.

Luttwak, Edward N., "Give War a Chance," *Foreign Affairs,* July/August 1999.

Mandelbaum, Michael, "A Perfect Failure: NATO's War Against Yugoslavia," *Foreign Affairs,* September/October 1999.

McGeary, Johanna, "The Road to Hell," *Time,* April 12, 1999.

McPeak, General Merrill A., USAF (Ret.), "The Kosovo Result: The Facts Speak for Themselves," *Armed Forces Journal International,* September 1999.

Meilinger, Colonel Phillip S., USAF, "Gradual Escalation: NATO's Kosovo Air Campaign, Though Decried as a Strategy, May Be the Future of War," *Armed Forces Journal International,* October 1999.

"Missouri-to-Kosovo Flights for B-2 Not a Concern to Wing Commander," *Inside the Air Force,* July 2, 1999.

Morrocco, John D., "Kosovo Reveals NATO Interoperability Woes," *Aviation Week and Space Technology,* August 9, 1999.

_____, and Robert Wall, "NATO Vows Air Strikes Will Go the Distance," *Aviation Week and Space Technology,* March 29, 1999.

_____, David Fulghum, and Robert Wall, "Weather, Weapons Dearth Slow NATO Strikes," *Aviation Week and Space Technology,* April 5, 1999.

Muradian, Vago, "Stealth Compromised by Not Destroying F-117 Wreckage," *Defense Daily,* April 2, 1999.

Muravchik, Joshua, "The Road to Kosovo, *Commentary,* June 1999.

Murphy, Vice Admiral Daniel J., USN, "The Navy in the Balkans," *Air Force Magazine,* December 1999.

"NATO Jets May Have Erred in Convoy Attack, General Says," *Aerospace Daily*, April 20, 1999.

"NATO's Game of Chicken," *Newsweek*, July 26, 1999.

Nelan, Bruce W., "Into the Fire," *Time*, April 5, 1999.

Newman, Richard J., "The Bombs That Failed in Kosovo," *U.S. News and World Report*, September 20, 1999.

————, "In the Skies over Serbia," *U.S. News and World Report*, May 24, 1999.

————, "U.S. Troops Edge Closer to Kosovo," *U.S. News and World Report*, June 7, 1999.

O'Beirne, Kate, "Defenseless: The Military's Hollow Ring," *National Review*, May 3, 1999.

Pocock, Chris, "Mirage IV Reconnaissance Missions," *World Air Power Journal*, Winter 1999/2000.

Posen, Barry R., "The War for Kosovo: Serbia's Political-Military Strategy," *International Security*, Spring 2000.

"Ralston Sees Potential for More Wars of Gradual Escalation," *Inside the Pentagon*, September 16, 1999.

"Reporters' Notebook," *Defense Week*, July 19, 1999.

Ripley, Tim, "Harriers over the Kosovo 'Kill Boxes,'" *World Air Power Journal*, Winter 1999/2000.

————, "'Serbs Running Out of SAMs,' Says USA," *Jane's Defense Weekly*, June 2, 1999.

————, "Tanker Operations," *World Air Power Journal*, Winter 1999/2000.

————, "Task Force Hunter," *World Air Power Journal*, Winter 1999/2000.

————, "Viper Weasels," *World Air Power Journal*, Winter 1999/2000.

Roberts, Adam, "NATO's 'Humanitarian War' over Kosovo," *Survival*, Autumn 1999.

Scott, William B., "JTIDS Provides F-15Cs 'God's Eye View,'" *Aviation Week and Space Technology*, April 29, 1996.

Seigle, Greg, "Prowler Jammers Used to Aid NATO Air Assault," *Jane's Defense Weekly*, March 31, 1999.

Sharer, Commander Wayne D., USN, "The Navy's War over Kosovo," *Proceedings*, U.S. Naval Institute, October 1999.

"Shinseki Hints at Restructuring, Aggressive Changes for the Army," *Inside the Army*, June 28, 1999.

Solana, Javier, "NATO's Success in Kosovo," *Foreign Affairs*, November/December 1999.

Steinberg, James B., "A Perfect Polemic: Blind to Reality on Kosovo," *Foreign Affairs*, November/December 1999.

Stroup, Lieutenant General Theodore G., Jr., USA (Ret.), "Task Force Hawk: Beyond Expectations," *Army Magazine*, August 1999.

"Stumbling into War," *The Economist*, March 27, 1999.

Sweetman, Bill, "B-2 Is Maturing into a Fine Spirit," *Jane's International Defense Review*, May 2000.

"Ten Years After," *Proceedings*, January 2001.

Thompson, Mark, "Warfighting 101," *Time*, June 14, 1999.

Tirpak, John A., "The First Six Weeks," *Air Force Magazine*, June 1999.

_____, "Kosovo Retrospective," *Air Force Magazine*, April 2000.

_____, "Lessons Learned and Re-Learned," *Air Force Magazine*, August 1999.

_____, "Short's View of the Air Campaign," *Air Force Magazine*, September 1999.

_____, "The State of Precision Engagement," *Air Force Magazine*, March 2000.

Tissue, Lieutenant Colonel Philip C., USMC, "21 Minutes to Belgrade," *Proceedings*, U.S. Naval Institute, September 1999.

Towell, Pat, "Lawmakers Urge Armed Forces to Focus on High-Tech Future," *Congressional Quarterly Weekly*, June 26, 1999.

"U.S. Mobilizes Guard, Reserve for Balkan Duty," *Air Force Magazine*, June 1999.

"Verbatim Special: The Balkan War," *Air Force Magazine*, June 1999.

Wall, Robert, "Airspace Control Challenges Allies," *Aviation Week and Space Technology*, April 26, 1999.

_____, "E-2Cs Become Battle Managers with Reduced AEW Role," *Aviation Week and Space Technology*, May 10, 1999.

_____, "Joint STARS Changes Operational Scheme," *Aviation Week and Space Technology*, May 3, 1999.

_____, "Maverick Fix Tested in Kosovo," *Aviation Week and Space Technology*, September 6, 1999.

_____, "NATO Shifts Tactics to Attack Ground Forces," *Aviation Week and Space Technology*, April 12, 1999.

_____, "SEAD Concerns Raised in Kosovo," *Aviation Week and Space Technology*, June 26, 1999.

_____, "Sustained Carrier Raids Demonstrate New Strike Tactics," *Aviation Week and Space Technology*, May 10, 1999.

"Washington Outlook," *Aviation Week and Space Technology*, May 3, 1999.

_____, *Aviation Week and Space Technology*, May 24, 1999.

_____, *Aviation Week and Space Technology*, June 7, 1999.

_____, *Aviation Week and Space Technology*, August 23, 1999.

_____, *Aviation Week and Space Technology*, September 20, 1999.

Wass de Czege, Brigadier General Huba, USA (Ret.), and Lieutenant Colonel Antulio J. Echevarria II, USA, "Precision Decisions: To

Build a Balanced Force, the QDR Might Consider These Four Propositions," *Armed Forces Journal International*, October 2000.

"Wesley Clark Looks Back," *National Journal*, February 26, 2000.

NEWSPAPER ARTICLES

Andrews, Edmund L., "Aboard Advanced Radar Flight, U.S. Watches Combat Zone," *New York Times*, June 14, 1999.

Apple, R. W., Jr., "With Decision to Attack, a New Set of U.S. Goals," *New York Times*, March 25, 1999.

Arkin, William M., "How Sausage Is Made," *Washington Post*, July 17, 2000.

_____, "Inside the Air Force, Officers Are Frustrated About the Air War," *Washington Post*, April 25, 1999.

_____, "Limited Warfare in Kosovo Not Working," *Seattle Times*, May 22, 1999.

Babington, Charles, "Clinton Sticks with Strikes as Poll Shows 51 Percent in U.S. Approve," *Washington Post*, March 30, 1999.

_____, and Helen Dewar, "President Pleads for Support," *Washington Post*, March 24, 1999.

_____, and William Drozdiak, "Belgrade Faces the 11th Hour, Again," *Washington Post*, March 22, 1999.

Balz, Dan, "U.S. Consensus Grows to Send in Ground Troops," *Washington Post*, April 6, 1999.

Barger, Julian, "Bloody Paper Chain May Link Torture to Milosevic," *The Guardian*, June 18, 1999.

Beaumont, Peter, and Patrick Wintour, "Leaks in NATO—and Plan Bravo Minus," *London Sunday Observer*, July 18, 1999.

Becker, Elizabeth, "Needed on Several Fronts, U.S. Jet Force Is Strained," *New York Times*, April 6, 1999.

_____, "They're Unmanned, They Fly Low, and They Get the Picture," *New York Times*, June 3, 1999.

Benedetto, Richard, "Support Not as High as for Other Strikes," *USA Today*, April 2, 1999.

Bennett, Philip, and Steve Coll, "NATO Warplanes Jolt Yugoslav Power Grid," *Washington Post*, May 25, 1999.

Black, Ian, and John Hooper, "Serb Savagery Exposed," *The Guardian*, June 18, 1999.

Block, Robert, "In Belgrade, Hardship Grows Under Sustained Air Assault," *Wall Street Journal*, May 12, 1999.

Broder, John M., "Clinton Says Milosevic Hurts Claim to Kosovo," *New York Times*, March 31, 1999.

_____, "How to Lay Doubt Aside and Put the Best Face on a Bad Week in the Balkans," *New York Times*, April 1, 1999.

_____, "In Grim Week, Pep Talk from the President," *New York Times*, April 1, 1999.

Brown, Justin, "Why U.S. Bombs Failed to Topple Milosevic," *Christian Science Monitor*, March 24, 2000.

Burkins, Glenn, "Serbs Intensify Effort to Down Allied Warplanes," *Wall Street Journal*, May 28, 1999.

Burns, Robert, "Use of Apache Copters Is Not Expected Soon," *Philadelphia Inquirer*, May 19, 1999.

Butcher, Tim, and Patrick Bishop, "NATO Admits Air Campaign Failed," *London Daily Telegraph*, July 22, 1999.

Carroll, James, "The Truth About NATO's Air War," *Boston Globe*, June 20, 2000.

Clines, Francis X., "NATO Opens Broad Barrage Against Serbs as Clinton Denounces 'Brutal Repression,'" *New York Times*, March 25, 1999.

Cohen, Secretary of Defense William S., interview, "Milosevic Is Far Weaker Now," *USA Today*, May 14, 1999.

Cox, James, "Poll: Mission Isn't Seen as U.S. Victory," *USA Today,* June 15, 1999.

Deans, Bob, "Pentagon Mum About Air Mission," *European Stars and Stripes,* April 27, 1999.

DeParle, Jason, "Allies' Progress Remains Unclear as Few Details Are Made Public," *New York Times,* April 5, 1999.

Diamond, John, "Yugoslavia, Iraq Talked Air Defense Strategy," *Philadelphia Inquirer,* March 30, 1999.

Dobbs, Michael, "'Europe's Last Dictator' Digs In," *Washington Post,* April 26, 1999.

_____, and Karl Vick, "Air Strikes Kill Scores of Refugees," *Washington Post,* April 15, 1999.

Drozdiak, William, "Air War Commander Says Kosovo Victory Near," *Washington Post,* May 24, 1999.

_____, "Allies Need Upgrade, General Says," *Washington Post,* June 20, 1999.

_____, "Allies Target Computer, Phone Links," *Washington Post,* May 27, 1999.

_____, "NATO Leaders Struggle to Find a Winning Strategy," *Washington Post,* April 1, 1999.

_____, "Politics Hampered Warfare, Clark Says," *Washington Post,* July 20, 1999.

_____, "Yugoslav Troops Devastated by Attack," *Washington Post,* June 9, 1999.

_____, and Bradley Graham, "NATO Frustration Grows as Mission Falls Short," *Washington Post,* April 8, 1999.

_____, and Steven Mufson, "NATO Sending Tough Terms to Belgrade," *Washington Post,* June 2, 1999.

_____, and Anne Swardson, "Military, Diplomatic Offensives Bring About Accord," *Washington Post,* June 4, 1999.

Eisman, Dale, "Kosovo Lesson: Navy Says It Needs More High-Tech Tools," *Norfolk Virginian-Pilot*, June 10, 1999.

_____, "Over Balkans, It's Beauty vs. the Beast," *Norfolk Virginian-Pilot*, April 26, 1999.

Erlanger, Steven, "Economists Find Bombing Cuts Yugoslavia's Production in Half," *New York Times*, April 30, 1999.

_____, "NATO Was Closer to Ground War in Kosovo Than Is Widely Realized," *New York Times*, November 7, 1999.

_____, "U.S. Issues Appeal to Serbs to Halt Attack in Kosovo," *New York Times*, March 23, 1999.

Evans, Michael, "Ground War 'Error,'" *London Times*, March 24, 2000.

_____, "Serb Army Talks of Peace as Armor Takes a Pounding," *London Times*, June 2, 1999.

Fitchett, Joseph, "Clark Recalls 'Lessons' of Kosovo," *International Herald Tribune*, May 3, 2000.

_____, "For NATO, Keeping Peak Air Traffic on the Go Was a Critical Goal," *International Herald Tribune*, March 31, 2000.

_____, "NATO Misjudged Bombing Damage," *International Herald Tribune*, June 23, 1999.

Gellman, Barton, "Key Sites Pounded for 2nd Day," *Washington Post*, March 26, 1999.

_____, and William Drozdiak, "Conflict Halts Momentum for Broader Agenda," *Washington Post*, June 6, 1999.

"General Admits NATO Exaggerated Bombing Success," *London Times*, May 11, 2000.

Gerstenzang, James, and Elizabeth Shogren, "Serb TV Airs Footage of 3 Captured U.S. Soldiers," *Los Angeles Times*, April 1, 1999.

Gertz, Bill, "Remote Radar Allows Serbs to Keep Firing at NATO Jets," *Washington Times*, April 13, 1999.

_____, and Rowan Scarborough, "Dangerous Drawdown," *Washington Times*, April 30, 1999.

_____, and Rowan Scarborough, "Inside the Ring," *Washington Times*, May 19, 2000.

_____, and Rowan Scarborough, "No War," *Washington Times*, April 16, 1999.

Gilligan, Andrew, "Russia, Not Bombs, Brought End to War in Kosovo, Says Jackson," *London Sunday Telegraph*, August 1, 1999.

Gordon, Michael R., "Allied Air Chief Stresses Hitting Belgrade Sites," *New York Times*, May 13, 1999.

_____, "NATO to Hit Serbs from 2 More Sides," *New York Times*, May 11, 1999.

_____, "NATO Says Serbs, Fearing Land War, Dig In on Border," *New York Times*, May 19, 1999.

_____, "A War out of the Night Sky: 10 Hours with a Battle Team," *New York Times*, June 3, 1999.

_____, and Eric Schmitt, "Shift in Targets Let NATO Jets Tip the Balance," *New York Times*, June 5, 1999.

Graham, Bradley, "Air Power 'Effective, Successful,' Cohen Says," *Washington Post*, June 11, 1999.

_____, "Bombing Spreads," *Washington Post*, March 29, 1999.

_____, "General Says U.S. Readiness Is Ailing," *Washington Post*, April 30, 1999.

_____, "Joint Chiefs Doubted Air Strategy," *Washington Post*, April 5, 1999.

_____, "Report Says NATO Bombing Killed 500 Civilians in Yugoslavia," *Washington Post*, February 7, 2000.

_____, "U.S. Analysts Misread, Relied on Outdated Maps," *Washington Post*, May 11, 1999.

_____, and William Drozdiak, "Allied Action Fails to Stop Serb Brutality," *Washington Post*, March 31, 1999.

_____, and John Lancaster, "Most NATO Bombing Raids Target Previously Hit Sites," *Washington Post*, April 21, 1999.

_____, and Dana Priest, "Allies to Begin Flying Refugees Abroad," *Washington Post*, April 5, 1999.

_____, and Dana Priest, "'No Way to Fight a War': Hard Lessons of Air Power, Coalitions," *Washington Post*, June 6, 1999.

"Ground Troops Lauded," *European Stars and Stripes*, August 6, 1999.

Gurdon, Hugo, "France Kept in Dark by Allies," *London Daily Telegraph*, April 9, 1999.

_____, "U.S. Admits Milosevic Spies Are Inside NATO," *London Daily Telegraph*, April 15, 1999.

Harris, John F., "Berger's Caution Has Shaped Role of U.S. in War," *Washington Post*, May 16, 1999.

_____, "Clinton Saw No Alternative to Airstrikes," *Washington Post*, April 1, 1999.

_____, "Clinton Says He Might Send Ground Troops," *Washington Post*, May 19, 1999.

_____, "Reassuring Rhetoric, Reality in Conflict," *Washington Post*, April 8, 1999.

_____, and Bradley Graham, "Clinton Is Reassessing Sufficiency of Air War," *Washington Post*, June 3, 1999.

Havemann, Joel, "Convoy Deaths May Undermine Moral Authority," *Los Angeles Times*, April 15, 1999.

Hedges, Chris, "Angry Serbs Hear a New Explanation: It's All Russia's Fault," *New York Times*, July 16, 1999.

Hoffman, Lisa, "U.S. Taxpayers Faced with Mounting Kosovo War Costs," *Washington Times*, June 10, 1999.

Kaminski, Matthew, and John Reed, "NATO Link to KLA Rebels May Have Helped Seal Victory," *Wall Street Journal*, July 6, 1999.

Keegan, John, "Modern Weapons Hit War Wisdom," *Sydney Morning Herald*, June 5, 1999.

King, Neil, Jr., "War Against Yugoslavia Lapses into Routine, but Clock Is Ticking," *Wall Street Journal*, May 6, 1999.

Krepinevich, Andrew, "Two Cheers for Air Power," *Wall Street Journal*, June 11, 1999.

Lippman, Thomas W., and Bradley Graham, "NATO Chief Asks Review of Invasion Planning," *Washington Post*, April 22, 1999.

Lippman, Thomas W., and Bradley Graham, "Yugoslavs Fire on U.S. Troops; 3 Missing," *Washington Post*, April 1, 1999.

Lippman, Thomas W., and Dana Priest, "NATO Builds Firepower for 24-Hour Attacks," *Washington Post*, March 30, 1999.

Loeb, Vernon, and Steven Mufson, "CIA Analyst Raised Alert on China's Embassy," *Washington Post*, June 24, 1999.

Marshall, Tyler, and Richard Boudreaux, "Crisis in Yugoslavia: How an Uneasy Alliance Prevailed," *Los Angeles Times*, June 6, 1999.

McManus, Doyle, "Clinton's Massive Ground Invasion That Almost Was," *Los Angeles Times*, June 9, 2000.

Miller, Marjorie, "KLA Vows to Disarm If NATO Occupies Kosovo," *Los Angeles Times*, June 7, 1999.

Moniz, Dave, "Eye-to-Eye with a New Kind of War," *Christian Science Monitor*, March 23, 2000.

Moore, Molly, and Bradley Graham, "NATO Plans for Peace, Not Ground Invasion," *Washington Post*, May 17, 1999.

Morin, Richard, "Poll Shows Most Americans Want Negotiations on Kosovo," *Washington Post*, May 18, 1999.

Myers, Steven Lee, "Chinese Embassy Bombing: A Wide Net of Blame," *New York Times*, April 17, 2000.

_____, "Damage to Serb Military Less Than Expected," *New York Times*, June 28, 1999.

_____, "Early Attacks Focus on Web of Air Defense," *New York Times*, March 25, 1999.

_____, "Pentagon Said to Be Adding 300 Planes to Fight Serbs," *New York Times*, April 13, 1999.

"NATO Chief: Targeting Goals Leaked to Yugoslavia," *Pacific Stars and Stripes*, August 13, 1999.

"A New Bomb Damage Report," *Newsweek*, December 20, 1999, p. 4.

Pearlstein, Steven, "NATO Bomb Said to Hit Belgrade Hospital," *Washington Post*, May 21, 1999.

Peltz, James, and Jeff Leeds, "Stealth Fighter's Crash Reveals a Design's Limits," *Los Angeles Times*, March 30, 1999.

Perlez, Jane, "Clinton and the Joint Chiefs to Discuss Ground Invasion," *New York Times*, June 2, 1999.

_____, "For Albright's Mission, More Problems and Risk," *New York Times*, June 7, 1999.

_____, "Holbrooke to Meet Milosevic in Final Peace Effort," *New York Times*, March 22, 1999.

_____, "Serbs Try to Empty Disputed Province, NATO Aides Assert," *New York Times*, March 29, 1999.

_____, "U.S. Option: Air Attacks May Prove Unpalatable," *New York Times*, March 23, 1999.

Pfaff, William, "After NATO's Lies About Kosovo, It's Time to Come Clean," *International Herald Tribune*, May 11, 2000.

Priest, Dana, "A Decisive Battle That Never Was," *Washington Post*, September 19, 1999.

_____, "France Acted as Group Skeptic," *Washington Post*, September 20, 1999.

_____, "NATO Pilots Set to Confront Potent Foe," *Washington Post*, March 24, 1999.

_____, "NATO Unlikely to Alter Strategy," *Washington Post*, March 26, 1999.

_____, "Target Selection Was Long Process," *Washington Post*, September 20, 1999.

_____, "Tension Grew with Divide in Strategy," *Washington Post*, September 21, 1999.

_____, and Peter Finn, "NATO Gives Air Support to Kosovo Guerrillas," *Washington Post*, June 2, 1999.

Raum, Tom, "Cohen: NATO Process Prolonged Air Strikes," *Philadelphia Inquirer*, July 21, 1999.

Rice, Donald B., "No Stealth to Pentagon's Bias Against the B-2," *Los Angeles Times*, May 9, 1999.

Richter, Paul, "Air-Only Campaign Offers a False Sense of Security, Some Say," *Los Angeles Times*, June 4, 1999.

_____, "B-2 Drops Its Bad PR in Air War," *Los Angeles Times*, July 8, 1999.

_____, "Bunker-Busters Aim at Heart of Leadership," *Los Angeles Times*, May 5, 1999.

_____, "Milosevic War Machine Has a Lot of Fight Left," *Los Angeles Times*, April 29, 1999.

_____, "Officials Say NATO Pounded Milosevic into Submission," *Los Angeles Times*, June 5, 1999.

_____, "Time Is Not on the Side of U.S., Allies," *Los Angeles Times*, March 25, 1999.

_____, "U.S. Pilots Face Perilous Task, Pentagon Says," *Los Angeles Times*, March 20, 1999.

_____, "U.S. Study of War on Yugoslavia Aimed at Boosting Performance," *Los Angeles Times*, July 10, 1999.

_____, "Use of Ground Troops Not Fully Ruled Out," *Los Angeles Times*, March 29, 1999.

_____, and John-Thor Dahlburg, "NATO Broadens Its Battle Strategy," *Los Angeles Times*, March 24, 1999.

_____, and Lisa Getter, "Mechanical Error, Pilot Error Led to Apache Crashes," *Los Angeles Times*, May 13, 1999.

_____, and Doyle McManus, "Pentagon to Tighten Targeting Procedures," *Los Angeles Times*, May 11, 1999.

Ricks, Thomas E., "Why the U.S. Army Is Ill-Equipped to Move Troops Quickly into Kosovo," *Wall Street Journal*, April 16, 1999.

_____, and Anne Marie Squeo, "Kosovo Campaign Showcased the Effectiveness of Air Power," *Wall Street Journal*, June 4, 1999.

Robbins, Carla Anne, and Thomas E. Ricks, "Time Is Running Out If Invasion Is to Remain Option Before Winter," *Wall Street Journal*, May 21, 1999.

Robbins, Carla Anne, Thomas E. Ricks, and Neil King, Jr., "Milosevic's Resolve Spawned Unity, Wider Bombing List in NATO Alliance," *Wall Street Journal*, April 27, 1999.

Ryan, General Michael E., USAF, "Air Power Is Working in Kosovo," *Washington Post*, June 4, 1999.

"Sacked Yugoslav Air Chief Killed," *London Times*, June 2, 1999.

Scarborough, Rowan, "Air Force Search and Rescue Operations Called 'Broken,'" *Washington Times*, September 13, 1999.

_____, "Apaches Were Sent to Scare Serbs," *Washington Times*, May 21, 1999.

_____, "As Strikes Mount, So Do Errors," *Washington Times*, May 11, 1999.

_____, "Kosovo Target Data Stalled in Transit," *Washington Times*, July 28, 1999.

_____, "Military Experts See a Need for Ground Troops," *Washington Times*, March 30, 1999.

_____, "Momentum for Troops Growing," *Washington Times*, April 5, 1999.

_____, "Officers Criticize Air War Strategy," *Washington Times*, May 10, 1999.

_____, "Pentagon Intends to Issue Final Count of Serbian Losses," *Washington Times*, July 9, 1999.

_____, "Record Deployments Take Toll on Military," *Washington Times*, March 28, 2000.

_____, "Smaller U.S. Military Is Spread Thin," *Washington Times*, March 31, 1999.

_____, "U.S. Pilots Call NATO Targeting a 'Disgrace,'" *Washington Times*, April 1, 1999.

Schmemann, Serge, "Now, Onward to the Next Kosovo. If There Is One," *New York Times*, June 16, 1999.

Schmitt, Eric, "Aim, Not Arms, at the Root of Mistaken Strike on Embassy," *New York Times*, May 10, 1999.

_____, "New Army Chief Seeks More Agility and Power," *New York Times*, June 24, 1999.

_____, "Pentagon Admits Its Maps of Belgrade Are Out of Date," *New York Times*, May 11, 1999.

_____, "Shrewd Serb Tactics Downed Stealth Jet, U.S. Inquiry Shows," *New York Times*, April 11, 1999.

_____, "Weak Serb Defense Puzzles NATO," *New York Times*, March 26, 1999.

_____, and Michael R. Gordon, "British Pressing Partners to Deploy Ground Troops," *New York Times*, May 18, 1999.

_____, and Steven Lee Myers, "NATO Said to Focus Raids on Serb Elite's Property," *New York Times*, April 19, 1999.

Sciolino, Elaine and Ethan Bronner, "How a President, Distracted by Scandal, Entered Balkan War," *New York Times*, April 18, 1999.

Smith, R. Jeffrey, "Belgrade Rebuffs Final U.S. Warning," *Washington Post*, March 23, 1999.

_____, and Molly Moore, "Plan for Kosovo Pullout Signed," *Washington Post*, June 10, 1999.

_____, and Dana Priest, "Yugoslavia Near Goals in Kosovo," *Washington Post*, May 11, 1999.

Stanley, Alessandra, "Albanian Fighters Say They Aid NATO in Spotting Serb Targets," *New York Times*, April 2, 1999.

Suro, Roberto, and Thomas E. Ricks, "Pentagon: Kosovo Air War Data Leaked," *Washington Post*, March 10, 2000.

Taylor, Humphrey, "Win in Kosovo and the Public Will Approve," *Wall Street Journal*, June 3, 1999.

Walker, Tom, "Bomb Video Took Fight out of Milosevic," *London Sunday Times*, January 30, 2000.

Weiner, Tim, "From President, Victory Speech and a Warning," *New York Times*, June 11, 1999.

Whitney, Craig R., "NATO Chief Admits Bombs Fail to Stem Serb Operations," *New York Times*, April 28, 1999.

_____, "NATO Had Signs Its Strategy Would Fail Kosovars," *New York Times*, April 1, 1999.

_____, "On 7th Day, Serb Resilience Gives NATO Leaders Pause," *New York Times*, March 31, 1999.

Williams, Daniel, "Yugoslavs Yield to NATO Terms," *Washington Post*, June 4, 1999.

_____, and Bradley Graham, "Milosevic Admits to Losses of Personnel," *Washington Post*, May 13, 1999.

Wilson, George C., "Memo Says Apaches, Pilots Were Not Ready," *European Stars and Stripes*, June 20, 1999.

Wintour, Patrick, and Peter Beaumont, "Revealed: The Secret Plan to Invade Kosovo," *London Sunday Observer*, July 18, 1999.

"Yugoslav Army Lost 524 Soldiers, Top General Says," *International Herald Tribune*, July 22, 1999.

BRIEFINGS

Baldazzi, Colonel E., Italian Air Force, "Host Nation Support for the Kosovo Air Campaign," briefing at a conference on "The NATO Joint Force Air Component Commander Concept in Light of the Kosovo Air Campaign," Headquarters NATO Reaction Force Air Staff, Kalkar, Germany, December 1–3, 1999.

Bivins, Colonel Robert, USAF, Director of Operations, U.S. Air Force Space Warfare Center, "Space Support to Operation Allied Force: Preliminary Lessons Learned," Schriever AFB, Colorado, February 25, 2000.

Clark, General Wesley, SACEUR, Brussels, NATO Headquarters, April 13, 1999.

Corley, Brigadier General John, USAF, news briefing, Office of the Assistant Secretary of Defense (Public Affairs), the Pentagon, Washington, D.C., May 8, 2000.

Crawford, Natalie, and others, "USAF EW Management Process Study," October 1, 1999.

Dallager, Major General John, USAF, "NATO JFACC Doctrine," briefing at a conference on "The NATO Joint Force Air Component Commander Concept in Light of the Kosovo Air Campaign," Headquarters NATO Reaction Force Air Staff, Kalkar, Germany, December 1–3, 1999.

Ellis, Admiral James O., USN, commander in chief, U.S. Naval Forces, Europe, and commander, Allied Forces Southern Europe and Joint Task Force Noble Anvil, "The View from the Top," 1999.

Hinson, Major General Robert, USAF, commander, 14th Air Force, "Space Doctrine Lessons from Operation Allied Force," command briefing, Vandenberg AFB, California, December 16, 1999.

Leaf, Brigadier General Daniel, USAF, videotaped press statement, Brussels, Belgium, NATO Office of Information and Press, April 19, 1999.

Pitotti, Colonel Steve, USAF, "Global Environments, Threats, and Military Strategy (GETM) Update," Air Armament Summit 2000 briefing, 2000.

Robertson, General Charles T., Jr., USAF, commander in chief, U.S. Transportation Command, and commander, Air Mobility Command, "Air War Over Serbia: A Mobility Perspective," 2000.

Watts, Barry D., "The EA-6B, E-8C, and B-2 in Operation Allied Force," Northrop Grumman Analysis Center, Rosslyn, Virginia, May 8, 2000.